MOTHERPEACE

MOTHERPEACE

A Way to the Goddess through Myth, Art, and Tarot

VICKI NOBLE

1817

HARPER & ROW, PUBLISHERS, SAN FRANCISCO
CAMBRIDGE HAGERSTOWN NEW YORK PHILADELPHIA
LONDON MEXICO CITY SÃO PAULO SYDNEY

PHOTO CREDITS:
Horned Goddess from Tassili in the Sahara: photo by
Gerard Franceschi, copyright © 1958 by Les Éditions
Arthaud, Paris, and reproduced by permission.
Goddess figures from Peche-Merle: reproduced from S.
Giedion, *The Eternal Present* (1962) by permission of
Princeton University Press.
Artist in Mithila, India: photo by Edouard Boubat,
reproduced by permission of Agence de Presse Rapho-TOP,
Paris.
High Priestess card from Waite-Rider Tarot deck:
copyright © 1971 by, and reproduced by permission of, U.S.
Games Systems, Inc., New York 10016.
Snake Quilt: in collection of the author, and reproduced
by permission of the artist, Barbara Comstock.

Designed by Nancy Benedict

Library of Congress Cataloging in Publication Data

Noble, Vicki.
   Motherpeace: a way to the goddess through myth, art, and
   tarot.

   Bibliography: p. 257
   Includes index.
   1. Women and religion.   2. Spiritual life.   3. Tarot.
4. Tarot in art.   5. Goddesses.   I. Title.
BL458.N63 1982   291.2'11   82-47752
ISBN 0-06-066300-6

86 87 10 9 8 7 6 5

Contents

		Preface vii
Prologue		Into the Labyrinth 1

One   Major Arcana

Introduction	1	Secrets and Elixirs 17
Fool	2	Trusting One's Elf 23
Magician	3	Dancing the Fire 29
High Priestess	4	Paying Attention 35
Empress	5	Giving Forth 41
Emperor	6	Separating Off 47
Hierophant	7	Repressing Others 53
Lovers	8	Joining Together 60
Chariot	9	Winning One's Own Way 66
Justice	10	Setting Things Right 71
Crone	11	Turning Within 76
Wheel of Fortune	12	Going the Great Round 81
Strength	13	Finding Magical Helpers 89
Hanged One	14	Accepting Initiation 94
Death	15	Letting Go 100
Temperance	16	Grounding Cosmic Energy 107
Devil	17	Denying the Spirit 113
Tower	18	Shattering the Structure 118
Star	19	Opening to the Goddess 123
Moon	20	Experiencing the Mystery 129
Sun	21	Raising Consciousness 134
Judgement	22	Healing the Earth 139
World	23	Casting the Circle 144

Two		Minor Arcana
Introduction	24	Dramas of Everyday Life 151
Aces, Twos, and Threes	25	Cardinal Signs 158
Fours, Fives, and Sixes	26	Fixity 168
Sevens, Eights, and Nines	27	Mutability 178
Tens	28	Transformation 190
Daughters	29	Youthfulness 194
Sons	30	Male Polarity 201
Priestesses	31	Sacredness 209
Shamans	32	Experience 217

Three		The Spirit of Motherpeace
	33	Reading the Cards 227
	34	Group Work 237
	35	Creating a New Mythology 241
		Notes 250
		Bibliography 257
		Motherpeace Images 264
		Index 267

Preface

Motherpeace was written as if I were talking with four particular friends. In this diverse group, the first friend is a feminist sister who, in addition to the struggles to improve the quality of our everyday lives, wants to recover a vision of the Goddess and the kind of society that would honor her.

My second friend uses a traditional Tarot deck, as millions do, but is excited to hear about a wholly new set of Tarot images that, while drawing upon tradition, recast it to embody more fully the lives and aspirations of women.

While working on the book, I also kept in mind a third friend. Strongly visual, she records and meditates on her dreams and, like others influenced by Jung, seeks to deepen her knowledge of myth as a way of understanding her own psyche and the dramas being acted out around her.

This brings us to the fourth member of my imaginary audience—a friend who is deeply concerned about the lack of peace in the world and, in particular, about the numbing prospect of a "nuclear exchange." No longer believing that the system will cure itself, he wants to explore visions of society other than the patriarchal one now dominant.

In response to the concerns of these friends—who, of course, are also parts of myself—I have addressed the issue of personal and global peace in a positive spirit, through pictorial images, against a background of myth and art that date from an age when the Goddess was still the joy of humankind's desiring.

The pictures are a set of seventy-eight original Tarot images that I created with Karen Vogel. All of them appear in this book, many in color, and they are also available separately in the form of the Mother-peace Tarot Cards.*

Through these images, and through feminist scholarship, I share a vision of hope and transformation—a vision based upon our expanding knowledge of ancient Goddess-worship, and also upon my own experience as an artist, activist, healer, and teacher of yoga.

Acknowledgments

My thanks first of all to Karen Vogel for six years of co-creativity, full of love and dynamic struggle, in which we mirrored each other, transforming from the inside out as we collaborated in creating the Motherpeace Tarot images. In the spirit of the Six of Wands (my first Motherpeace image), it was I who started the Tarot card project; in the spirit of Athene's Chariot (Karen's first drawing), it was she who finished the cards, painting the completed drawings (with the help of artist Lily Hillwomyn) and becoming the publisher of the Motherpeace Tarot deck.

I am grateful to Betsy Ferber for introducing me to the Tarot and for giving me Sally Gearhart's *Feminist Tarot*. It was Cassandra Light who opened me to the magic of art, originated the name "Motherpeace," and, when the drawings were done, painted the circular Tantric design for the backs of the cards. Thanks to Carol Murray for her early belief in my writing, and to writers Jana Harris and Mary Mackey for their sisterly support. Special thanks to Hillary Hurst, whose laughter goes with Motherpeace into the world every time she reads the cards.

This book is largely about healing—ourselves and the planet. In this work, we always have to ask: who heals the healers? I am grateful to Maudelle Shirek for starting me on the path to physical healing and transformation; to Susie Christian for introducing me to psychic healing techniques; to Alta Kelly for her fierce, unwavering clarity; to Iris Crider for her loving use of acupuncture needles; to chiropractor Surya Lieberman for her warm hands and open heart; and to my Hearth Fire ritual sisters —Charlene Tschirhart, Caroline Verheyen, Nan Crawford, Katie Janney,

---

*To obtain a deck of Motherpeace cards, ask at your bookstore or at a shop that sells Tarot decks. If they are unable to help you, write directly to the manufacturer, Motherpeace Tarot Cards, P.O. Box 1511, Cave Creek, Arizona, 85331. The author regrets that she is seldom able to respond to individual questions; but if you would like to receive information about her intensive workshops, tape cassettes, or subsequent writings, send a stamped, self-addressed envelope to Motherpeace, P.O. Box 5544, Berkeley, California 94705.

and crystal-healing friend Bonnie MacGregor—for their living faith in the Goddess. Without a supportive and active healing community, it would have been much harder to keep the energies flowing during the all too mental work of writing.

I appreciate the opportunities offered by friends such as Davidka Cantanzarite, who invited me to present the Motherpeace slides at a War Resisters' League Benefit in Berkeley; and Mara Keller, who asked me to speak at San Francisco State University on Motherpeace and the art of healing. Thanks to Angie Arien and Jane English for inviting Karen and me to present the Motherpeace project to the Tarot symposium they organized in San Francisco; to Hearth Fire for including the Motherpeace slides within our ritual at a Stanford conference on the arms race; and to the Judy Chicago Birth Project, where I led a workshop including the slides.

I appreciate Richard Toumey and David Quigley of the Tarot community for their recognition and support of my work, and Suzanne Judith for her ongoing Tarot wisdom; Jean Robertson for her interviews on KPFA radio; and Barbara Kossy, host of "Art Waves," for the Motherpeace television debut. Students in my Tarot classes have been wonderfully illuminating and supportive, from teenagers at the Berkeley Alternative Public School to adults from all over the Bay Area. Thanks especially to Laura de Baun for proofreading and typing during final manuscript preparation, and to Jonathan Tenney for insights on Kabalistic numerology and the Tarot.

I am grateful to my mother in Iowa for her goodhumored acceptance of me, and my grandmother for the name Noble—her "maiden" name— which I adopted at the start of the Motherpeace project. Blessings to my precious daughters, Robyn and Brooke Ziegler, for putting up with an absentee Mom, and to Sandra Whitney for holding the fort during completion of this manuscript. I appreciate all the meals at Cathleen Roundtree's restaurant during the early stages of the book, and the healing massages from Mara Keller.

At Harper & Row, I have had the good fortune to work with John Loudon who, from the first moment, has treated me and my work with respect and integrity. Thanks also to the quick eye of Bob San Souci, who saw a poster for the Motherpeace cards and brought me to John's attention.

Heartfelt gratitude flows out to my editing partner Craig Comstock who, in the most matri-archetypal sense, "fathered" this book. That is, he fertilized it with his ideas and energy, then shared with me the labor and delivery of it into the world. Like an ancient son of the Goddess, he does not seek to own what he helped to create, but his love shines like a light through every page.

Finally, I thank the Goddess, whose presence in my life makes everything possible.

Vicki Noble
Berkeley, May Eve, 1982

*I who am the beauty of the green earth and the white moon among the stars
and the mysteries of the waters,*

I call upon your soul to arise and come unto me.

For I am the soul of nature that gives life to the universe.

From Me all things proceed and unto Me they must return.

*Let My worship be in the heart that rejoices, for behold—all acts of love
and pleasure are My rituals.*

*Let there be beauty and strength, power and compassion, honor and
humility, mirth and reverence within you.*

*And you who seek to know Me, know that your seeking and yearning will
avail you not, unless you know the Mystery:*

*for if that which you seek, you find not within yourself, you will never find
it without.*

*For behold, I have been with you from the beginning, and I am that which
is attained at the end of desire.*

Traditional "charge of the Star Goddess," in version by Starhawk, with photograph of the
horned Goddess from Tassili in the Sahara.

PROLOGUE

Into the Labyrinth

Patriarchy has brought us no peace. Instead, its leaders try to reassure us by arguing, as Winston Churchill did, that "safety will be the sturdy child of terror and survival the twin brother of annihilation." What Churchill apparently meant, in his apologia for the nuclear age, was that we could assure survival not by actually annihilating people but by threatening to do so, perpetually, and hoping that no accident or folly would lead to war. Today leaders warn us about terrorists, while themselves commanding the terrible power to wreck, within half an hour, whole continents. And the ideologists of Patriarchy tell us that "man" has always been a killer, his first tools a club to break an arm, a stone to smash a skull. In this view, all that changes is the sophistication of the weapons and the "causes" over which to fight.

Is there another way to live? A growing number of feminists think so, along with men who share a vision of peace. In listening to Churchill's language, we ask whether "safety" doesn't need a parent other than "terror." In this book, the name I give to this lost parent of humankind is Motherpeace. In ancient times, this figure was the Goddess, source of matriarchal consciousness. Centered in the heart, rather than the head, matriarchal consciousness requires a "nonrational" means of approach. It is a creative, intuitive mode of consciousness in contrast to the logical mode in which we usually function. It requires a surrender of our daily waking consciousness and an opening to what Jose and Miriam Arguelles call "the Feminine—spacious as the sky."

Especially for Westerners not accustomed to meditation or to stilling the active mind, this surrender and transformation process is facilitated by techniques of visualization such as Tarot. Through looking medita-

1

tively at the pictures in a Tarot deck, one's mind is not only quieted, but stimulated on a deep level by ancient symbols of life and spirit, symbols that enter the heart and heal it. The wisdom available to the sturdy children of Motherpeace has reached us mainly in the form of esoteric teachings.

Although frequently couched in patriarchal language and terminology, the inner meaning of the "secret teachings" will always reveal itself as the wisdom of the Mother. As more and more people today become interested in Tarot, a door opens to seekers of the Great Mother, allowing us to journey to the center of the Self as well as to our collective source. The Goddess is buried in the depths of the collective and personal unconscious—any system of thought or practice that aims at unlocking the unconscious will eventually cause her to be seen.

Most of us these days find ourselves less than fully well, physically or mentally—somehow out of balance. We can feel our dis-ease, but don't ordinarily know the solutions to it. If we knew how to make ourselves well, we would almost certainly do so. The great gift of the Goddess is such a healing. To the individual, she brings personal well-being and an experience of fully living. To humanity, she could bring the harmony that comes with a recognition that we are all connected in spirit to this planet. We depend upon it for survival and we owe it the gift of life.

The Motherpeace images that appear throughout this book embody a large number of early pictures and sculptures of the Goddess. From the small "Venus" figures found in Old Stone Age Europe to the pre-Columbian statues discovered in Mexico and the Americas, the Goddess has been a mythic presence respected and revered by women and men around the world. In Paleolithic caverns—sometimes as much as twenty thousand years ago—priestesses danced her dance; today in isolated pockets of the world, they still do. Modern western women are calling her back through ritual and magical evocation of her names and her multiple aspects.

In ancient times, "worship" of the Goddess was accompanied by a mother-centered culture. Nancy Tanner, comparing human development with that of chimpanzees, posits that the key innovation in human development from our ape ancestors was "gathering plants (and small animals such as insects) by mothers for sharing with their offspring." In this view, culture emerged, in part, from the act of caring for others and gathering the earth's bounty, not from killing. Its Goddess offered nurturance and compassion.

She also, of course, represented "fertility." From his thorough scholarship on various aspects of early Middle Eastern forms of the Goddess,

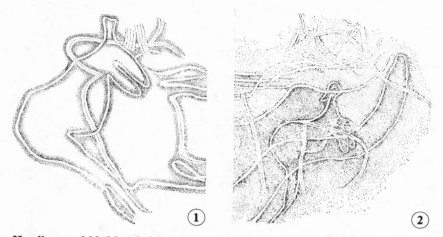

Headless and bird-headed females drawn with finger in wet clay on ceiling of "hall of hieroglyphs," Pech-Merle cavern, ca. 30,000 B.C.

Lawrence Durdin-Robertson states that "the fundamental premise" of ancient religion was that "creative power is the exclusive possession of the female sex." It is sexual-creative power that makes the Goddess so disturbing to the modern world, with its conceptions of the female as secondary and inferior to the dominant male. Merlin Stone makes a fine exposition of women's power in her chapter on the "sacred sexual customs" and the priestesses known as "holy women" who performed the rites of Inanna, Ishtar, Astarte, Ashtoreth, Aphrodite, and Isis (to name but a few). These "sacred women of the Goddess" (*qadishtu*) lived within the temple complex, which was the center of the community; they owned property, transacted business, and carried on their own affairs freely.

A woman's ability to give birth stood not as her exclusive form of "fulfillment," but as a symbol for her other forms of creativity; and her children were heirs to the female line of descent. There were no "illegitimate" children. In this extended sense, "fertility" must refer not only to the mystery of procreation and birth, but to the development of culture itself. In the case of Motherpeace, this culture included such elements as fire, precise observations of the heavens, art that awes us still, and a worldview that we are now rediscovering under the name of ecology.

Scholars are coming to acknowledge that the Goddess was alive in the prehistoric imagination and that her images represented a human commitment to "fertility" and "nature." Early religion revolved around "fertility cults" in which the Great Mother was worshiped and women acted as her priestesses. Found in many parts of the ancient world, these fertili-

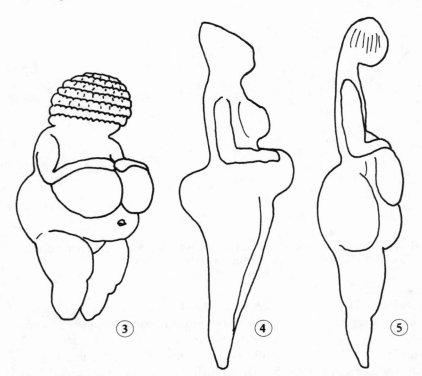

"Venus of Willendorf," of limestone, Austria, ca. 20,000 B.C.; "Venus of Menton," of vitreous rock, France; "Venus of Lespugne," of ivory, France, ca. 15,000 B.C.

ty religions extended far back into the prehistoric Ice Age, reflecting the abundance of the Earth Mother and the biological mysteries of the female group. The characteristic features of a "fertility figure" are pendulous breasts, a fat, generally pregnant belly, and well-marked yoni (female genitalia). Probably the best-known example is the "Venus of Willendorf" (Figure 3).

In contrast to fertility cults is another form of ancient religion, known as shamanism, generally regarded as a predominantly male religious calling. Shamanism is a religion of ecstasy, associated most often with the ability of the spirit-body to detach from the physical body and fly like a bird to the spirit realms. The object of shaman "journeys" is usually a healing of the physical body or the human spirit, of the individual or the community at large.

A shaman's ability to leave the physical body is often represented in art by a bird, a human with the head of a bird, or a figure without a head

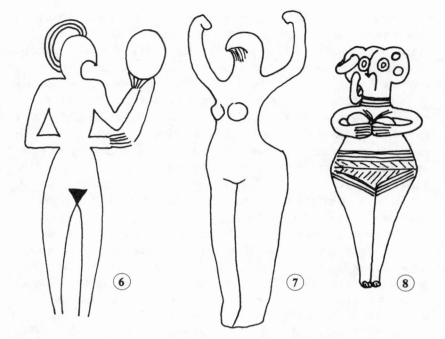

Geometric bird-headed female holding mirror, painted on pottery, Mesopotamia, 3,100 B.C.; terra cotta bird-headed priestess figure with arms raised, pre-dynastic Egypt, before 3,000 B.C.; clay bird-headed female figure holding her breasts, Cyprus, 2,500 B.C.

(suggesting death of the ego). Similarly, a potential shaman may dream of losing his head or, in many cases, of total dismemberment and rebirth as a new being. Through trance journeys into the cosmos, the shaman learns to live in both worlds—material and spiritual—saving lost souls and dealing directly with the supernatural. During such journeys, the shaman experiences ecstasy and learns things about the universe hidden from other mortals. Having passed from "this side" to the "other side," he or she no longer fears death, or anything else, and thus becomes a powerful religious figure.

Another universal feature of shamanism is a very lively connection to the animal world, both material and spiritual. Shamans always have animal "helpers" or "allies," just as witches have their "familiars." The shaman journeys to the other side and communes with the animals in order to take on some of their power and to learn things out of reach of ordinary human consciousness.

Among shamans in recent times, probably the best known have been Siberian and Eskimo shamans, along with Native American "medicine men." But archeological finds point more and more to their ancient roots, through links between modern shamanic motifs and Ice Age cave art. In this way the shaman artist is frequently traced back as far as the later Ice Age (the Magdalenian period ending around 10,000 B.C.), when the earliest male figures, wearing animal skins and dancing, are thought to have appeared on cave walls. Found in the cave called Les Trois Frères, these earliest figures exhibit the shamanic vocation: part human and part animal, they dance in ecstasy. One of the figures is known today as "the Sorceror of Les Trois Frères," as a "god" or "lord." In sharp contrast, scholars often treat the female fertility figures merely as "cult" objects, symbols of messy biological destiny.

Yet we should be given pause by the fact that, for thousands of years prior to that period, the only human forms traced on cave walls were female. According to cultural historian Siegfried Giedion, male representations began much later. The earliest images of humans that we know of are in the innermost sanctuary of the cavern of Pech-Merle. Both are female. One is the headless female illustrated in Figure 1; the other, the bird-headed female in Figure 2. Both embody shamanic qualities: they dance, they are headless (ecstatic) or bird-headed (able to fly to spirit realms). They are not alone, but drawn in wet clay among animals, the lines merging and blending as if there were little distinction between the human and animal worlds, another mark of the shamanic consciousness.

Many other versions of the same motif—headless and bird-headed female figures—follow throughout the millennia, down to the time when the first male figures appear. Giedion points out that whereas the female figures never appear alone but always dance together, the male figures are isolated and individual.

Furthermore, the female images from Pech-Merle and their many successors present a powerful conjunction that I have never seen mentioned anywhere. Not only do these early images embody all the known and accepted qualities of shamanism; they are also pregnant. Their bellies are huge, their breasts pendulous. Thus, the iconography of fertility worship was conjoined thirty thousand years ago with shamanic attributes of bird-headedness and magical dance. At that time, preparation to give birth did not imply confinement; on the contrary, it led to a joyous abandonment, a dance of life, a rapturous journey into the spirit world on the occasion of an intensely physical experience. What is so striking in these early images is the conjunction of what later cultures would separate into shamanism and fertility cults. In the early world, the Goddess represented the miraculous blending of spirit and matter, the divine incarnation of the spirit in the body—the joy of life on earth.

By dating the first worship of divine figures in the very late Ice Age, at the close of the great era of cave art, we miss a great deal of our evolutionary history. Rather than ignoring the earlier female representations or regarding them as insignificant, we should be asking, What do they mean? Later sculptural works, such as various "Venus" figures (illustrated in Figures 3, 4, and 5), reflect the same world view as the first drawings, made at least thirty thousand years ago. Scholars have found them "peculiar" or "bizarre," yet as we have seen, the bird heads and lack of heads suggest not an artistic whim or a lack of ability to draw faces, but the mark of the shamanic spirit. If one assumes that spiritual authority must be masculine, this evidence seems mysterious; but if one looks at the art without sexual bias, its meaning jumps off the cave walls.

Not only did these ancient people make pictures on the walls and ceilings of sacred caves, they carved on bones the first calendars, based upon menstrual cycles and the phases of the moon. Religion, science, and measurement of time were not separate from the body and the biological or fertility mysteries of sexuality and reproduction; they were one body of knowledge. It is from this ancient holistic framework that we have fallen away, and which we are just beginning culturally to rediscover. The return to the Goddess implied by contemporary interest in astrology, Tarot, and other "right brain" activities—along with the re-awakening of human sexuality as a mystery, a magical activity—is the start of healing. And behind all of these activities is the wisdom that comes to us from our ancient cave-dancing foremothers.

In giving a historical, mythological, and artistic context for the Motherpeace images, I hope to unfold a vision of culture as it once existed, to sketch the transition during which that culture was deliberately suppressed, and to show a variety of ways through which we can recover the energy and wisdom needed to heal our civilization.

Before setting out on the path, however, we are faced with some questions. If such a powerful form of consciousness existed so widely, and for such a long time, and if it provided such a harmonious environment, why did it "die out"? Why is it so difficult to find examples of this "matriarchal consciousness" anywhere in the world today? If humankind once enjoyed a sort of peace, why has it seemed, for at least five thousand years, that our condition is one of "incessant suffering" and our only hope is to escape?

To all of these questions there is a single answer: the subjugation of the Mother by the rule of the father who "owns" his family and household and who, as Emperor, owns the state. In a word, Patriarchy. As we will discover throughout this book, the problem with patriarchs is not that they are men, but that, in place of egalitarian relationships, they impose a society of dominance and submission.

In order to suppress the resentment of their "inferiors," patriarchs justify their role through a pervasive ideology; and when that fails to mystify their subjects, they resort to violence, often under color of their law. In an atmosphere of trickery and greed, the patriarchs never feel satisfied because their own methods bar them from the deepest satisfactions of life. They find it hard to "feel."

They also worry that someone just like them is planning to conquer them, as a pathetic substitute for building a world together. Merlin Stone explains that in the mythology of the newly installed patriarchal gods, castration frequently appears as the means used to "depose" the ruling male and replace him with a usurper. The severing of the male genitals was apparently synonymous with the wresting of power away from the current King-of-the-Hill. Naturally, then, the new ruler would eventually fear the same outcome for himself and would live in a state of justifiable paranoia.

Patriarchs are not happy. And they are utterly bewildered about how to attain peace, which they usually regard as the temporary absence of battle. After five thousand years, the patriarchs have created a world that fully justifies their fears. And they have taught us to assume that human life has always included violence and war; that violence is, in fact, an unhappy but "natural" part of the human condition; and that we just have to accept the possibility of mass destruction.

In contrast, matriarchal consciousness regarded all males as sons of the Mother, all females as daughters. The group was built around mothers, but not around one individual woman. The power of matriarchal consciousness is the power of the female group as a civilizing and governing force. This power kept the individual ego aware of its connection to the group and its responsibility as a member, rather than as an individual in isolation. Instead of worshiping the destructive exploits of "heroes," matriarchal consciousness more properly worshiped the earth itself, as the body of the Great Mother.

In two beautiful, courageous books, Michael Dames shows how the adjacent English prehistoric sites of Silbury, Avebury, and Stonehenge together depict the form of the Great Mother, her distinctive shape covering a thirty-three mile course over the landscape. Around this outline of the Mother's body our ancient ancestors walked in sacred processions, year after year, in celebration of the seasonal cycles of life, death, and renewal.

Images of Motherpeace also appear in caves in the form of figurines, paintings in red ochre, and of abstract feminine symbols such as circles, spirals, dots, and discs. Today, in a largely patriarchal world, these prehistoric and "primitive" Goddess images of dignity and quiet religious power challenge existing paradigms of our culture and open the way for spiritual transformation. Yet even in the case of these Goddess images, some contemporary scholars blandly assume that the artists were men. Until recently, scholars could get away with asking, "When were there ever great women artists?" Their next step is the assumption that prehistoric man painted what "turned him on," and the conclusion that he must have liked his women fat—such as the broad-hipped, fullbreasted, pregnant "Venus" figurines. Perhaps, as in the age of Rubens, cave men did appreciate a full figure—how will we ever know? But to reduce the Goddess images to Paleolithic pin-ups is wholly to miss their numinous power, as well as the likelihood that they were created by the female "in her own image."

Fortunately, the tradition of ancient women painters has not everywhere died out. The Mithila women of India have been painting sacred images for at least three thousand years. In their simple, unassuming approach, they squat on the ground amidst the sounds of children playing and, in trance, create some of the most beautiful contemporary art to come out of India. In one lovely photograph of this modern matriarchal culture, a woman completes a painting with her right hand while holding a child to her breast for feeding with her left. Her calm concentration and the peaceful eyes of the nursing infant convey the essence of the matriarchal consciousness, in which many forms of generativity coexist.

Among contemporary Western women artists, perhaps the best-known group effort to embody matriarchal consciousness has been *The Dinner Party,* a triangular table set for a feast attended by goddesses, heroines, and other female leaders, artists, and writers. Created under the leadership of Judy Chicago, the piece includes embroidered place settings and ceramic plates that celebrate women's sexuality. One of the things I like best about the show, as well as the subsequent book, is the well-researched time-line that traces Goddess culture from its prehistoric roots to the present. Walking around the table, I felt what the artists doubtless intended—that all these women had come together for a moment, our sisters and foremothers, their energies combined.

Other artists have focused on ritual enactment of their creative visions. Women such as Mary Beth Edelson do workshops and performances, invoking Goddess energies to enter their bodies and minds during live "envisionings" that take place within installations created by the artist as a backdrop for the spiritual drama. One of the finest feminist

painters of our time is certainly Monica Sjöö, author of *The Ancient Religion of the Great Cosmic Mother of All*, a wonderfully comprehensive Goddess-book illustrated with Sjöö's original paintings. What these modern artists share is a power to heal. Since Patriarchy is at the root of our dis-ease, to imagine a world without it is to heal ourselves and the world.

My own effort to discover and express matriarchal consciousness began in the women's health movement. While helping to establish a feminist gynecological clinic and working as a paramedic and counselor, I fell into the usual activist lifestyle of rushing around, working too much and resting too little, drinking coffee and eating sugar without understanding any of the basic elements of what has come to be called holistic health. At the same time, I was a scholarship student at college, developing a women's studies program, a women's center, and an interdisciplinary major program; and I was also the divorced mother of two small daughters. Not surprisingly, I developed "burn out," which in my case consisted of a stomach ulcer on top of daily tension-headaches, culminating in dependence on prescription drugs. By the time I made my "change of location" to Berkeley, I was a physical wreck.

With Mildred Jackson's *Alternatives to Chemical Medicine* in hand, I started using herbs to relax and herbs to heal, both with fairly quick results. I quit smoking, and changed my diet, cutting out white flour, meat and sugar, adding brown rice and beans. I started taking lessons in beginning psychic skills from a local teacher. I learned simple visualization techniques and began to practice imagining my stomach healing, my head relaxing. Finally, I began to take an herb bath every night and to touch my stomach in small repeated circles, because it seemed to feel good. One night I felt it being healed. I felt my stomach tickle, as if my hand had gone inside my abdomen. Pleasure replaced the pain I had felt there.

Everyone who begins to open psychically has experiences that resemble this one in some way. Healing is a natural process that the body already knows how to do. All we have to do, basically, is get out of the way, mentally speaking, and let the body work. But we have not been taught to trust the body, so this simple process takes time and patience. While healing myself, I was doing a lot of research into the ancient religion of the Goddess, mostly by browsing through old art books, looking at statues, paintings, and figurines of the Great Mother, and responding very strongly to this heritage.

One day a friend came over and showed me a Tarot deck—my first. As she demonstrated how to use it, I asked questions about my life and she interpreted the cards I chose. I was smitten—clearly, I had found my psychic path. The cards my friend gave me were the "Waite-Rider" Tarot cards, designed by Edward Waite and painted by Pamela Smith in 1910. Even in this medieval, male-oriented set of images, I could see that the Goddess was remarkably present. I understood that my research on the ancient Goddess religion was somehow contained in the esoteric wisdom of the Tarot.

There she was in her various aspects—the High Priestess representing the moon and the power of female periodicity; the Empress, ruled by Venus, symbolizing love and active female sexuality; the Strength card, representing strength of mind and heart—matriarchal consciousness. I entered into a six-month love affair with the Tarot—using the cards everyday, reading every Tarot book I could get my hands on, including obscure and esoteric texts. The more I studied, the more I understood that traditional approaches to Tarot reflected exclusively male views of the world. I got the "Thoth" deck, designed by Aleister Crowley and painted by Frieda Harris in 1943. While the images in this deck are magically potent and in some ways beautiful, they are tainted by Crowley's "satanic" approach to the magical arts and embody a disturbing negativity.

I started to draw pictures to improve my eyesight. They were light, playful pictures of how I imagined the ancient cultures must have been, mostly showing women and children in groups, interacting and sharing food and ritual together. I thought I might make a coloring book with a text on matriarchal history. Under the guidance of artist friend Cassandra Light, I began to model images in clay and to create dolls and masks. On my own, in addition to more realistic artwork, I made over a hundred line drawings with my left, "intuitive" hand.

In July 1978, my two daughters were preparing to live with their father for a year—our longest separation. I bought them a deck of Tarot cards, but two were missing. I decided to draw the missing cards for them, just for fun, without any pressure about perfection. In the simplest way, it pleased me. I sent my daughters off, and a week later I drew the first image in what would become the Motherpeace Tarot deck.

The first card was the Six of Wands, a Shakti image reflecting my deepening practice of yoga. The Six of Wands expresses creativity and self-confidence, a burst of ability (Shakti means "to be able to"). The image itself is round, a six-spoked wheel radiating fire and a magical dark woman in the center radiating heat and light herself. It became clear from this image that the cards would be circular, rather than rectangular like traditional decks.

My friend Karen Vogel, with whom I had collaborated in Goddess

Six of Wands

research, asked to enter the project with me. She too had begun to work with Tarot. She drew the Chariot card as a sample, and we agreed to be partners in creating the Motherpeace images.

In retrospect, it all seems orderly and has a chronological form. But at the time, things were moving very fast and seemed to lack conscious control. The distinctive quality of the journey back to the Mother is that you don't always know where the path will take you. As in the Moon card described in Chapter 20, you walk through a maze as if it were night and your eyes were closed. You find your way through an unknown wilderness with only the Moon to guide you, a process dramatic in its intensity, without much precedent for a westerner. In the labyrinth you must surrender to the inner feeling that you are going somewhere, perhaps that you are being led or called, or at least that there will have been purpose in your journey.

As my psychic and healing experiences increased in intensity, sometimes seeming "over my head," I found books to explain and ground my process in rational understanding. I would wander into local used bookstores and browse until the right volume would practically fall off the shelf into my hands. I would open it to a page and read, frequently finding precisely the information I needed.

What I began to realize in studying the books and working on the Motherpeace images was that visionary (or shaman) art lies at the root of human culture and functions as a base for any leap into the future. If we would heal the body, we must first imagine it well. If we would heal the planet, we must first envision peace, not as an abstract wish but as a practical reality, a subject to which I return in Part Three. I found that art is prayer—sacred, powerful, communicative. Every time another image took shape, I felt another part of me being healed.

Likewise, I hope this book will be a healing journey for you—a journey to the age before Patriarchy, through the medium of words as well as visual images. Once you go into this labyrinth of spiritual development, you move along in a fog, sometimes not knowing how you would explain, even to your own mother, what you are doing in your life; and suddenly, in a timeless moment, everything is clear. You glimpse the purpose and wholeness of the thing. You feel lighter, more alive, as you go on your way around the next bend in the road.

In recent years, feminist writers have given some brilliant, desperately needed critiques of our society, especially of the many ways in which it oppresses women. I am particularly grateful to Merlin Stone for *When God Was a Woman,* as well as her more recent Goddess books; to Susan Griffin for *Woman and Nature: The Roaring Inside Her;* and to Mary Daly for *Gyn/Ecology* (as well as her earlier work). While drawing on this material, my own book mainly joins them in the task of envisioning an alternative. I think of the characters in Louis Malle's film *My Dinner with Andre.* Theatrical director Andre asks his companion, "How do you think it affects an audience to put on one of those plays in which you show that people are totally isolated now, and they can't reach each other, and their lives are obsessive and driven and desperate?" With the goal of empowering people, he asks, "Does that help to wake up a sleeping audience? You see, I don't think so. . . ."

Like Andre, I believe that what makes us want to get out of bed is not fear or despair, but hope. If our present way of life is making us feel desperate and isolated, it is reasonable to ask, "How can we envision something better?"

Visionary art takes many forms. In depicting the present, it shows possibilities not generally recognized, aspects of the world we neglect. In imaging the future, it keeps pressing us to say, in some detail, what we most deeply want (or fear). And in peering back into the past—in the case of Motherpeace, into prehistory—visionary art may allow us to reclaim what has been systematically pilfered, buried, and burned, but which, nonetheless, still has life and power in it and demands to be revealed. As more of us allow the Goddess to awaken in us and to help us "re-member our Selves," we may be able collectively to change the course of planetary destruction now awaiting us, and actively to create a future dedicated to life.

ONE

Major Arcana

CHAPTER 1

INTRODUCTION

Secrets and Elixirs

Arcana are profound secrets. At its Latin root, the word means "chest." One kind of chest is a storage box where, as in the Ark of the Covenant, a sacred text might safely be kept. "Arca" also refers to Noah's remedy against the Flood, a boat inside the ribs of which a remnant of terrestrial life could survive. In alchemical thought, "arcana" refers to another kind of remedy, a marvelous elixir for the prolongation of life. Linking these senses of the word, we find the themes of containers (and more broadly of vessels) that save from disaster. In the case of alchemy, the vessel is an alembic, in which a remedy is produced.

What has all this to do with Tarot, or with the Goddess? Madame Blavatsky, the late-nineteenth-century theosophist, links arcane wisdom to "Arka, the Divine Virgin—Mother of the Heavens." Likewise, Robert Graves mentions that Arka was the home of the "Arkites"—ancient Canaanites who worshipped the Moon Goddess Astarte or Ishtar. Just as Noah's Ark was a craft for preserving life, so the Arcana in Tarot are a vessel for salvaging spiritual wisdom from the period when the Goddess was worshiped. According to Lawrence Durdin-Robertson, the predecessor of Noah was Nuah, a Chaldean Mother Goddess.

Not only are the Arcana an Ark: in Erich Neumann's view, the Ark is a woman. In his massive study *The Great Mother*, Neumann compares the female body at length to boats, ships, and arks, as well as to cups, chalices, and cauldrons. Likewise, Gareth Knight intuitively links "the Womb of the Great Mother" with cauldrons, arks, and the shape of the crescent moon. Like the moon, the cauldron is a preeminent symbol of the Goddess, and returns us to alchemy's elixirs. On the physical plane, alchemy did involve attempts to change base metals to gold, but as psychologist C. G. Jung has shown, the esoteric quest of the alchemists was a transformation of the self.

What the Major Arcana promise is just such a transformation, which is based, in the Motherpeace images, upon a rediscovery of the Goddess. In the dominant culture of Patriarchy, the Goddess survives mainly in esoteric forms. As we have seen, Arcana both safeguard secret wisdom and, if properly used, produce a cure. The cure, however, requires work. Unlike passive experiences such as watching television, Arcana demand active involvement. The remedy they offer takes the form not of an easily swallowed pill, but of a process of self-discovery.

In order to grasp the value of the secrets, we need to suspend disbelief and open our imaginations to dreamlike images from another realm. If these matriarchal images strike us as strange, it is not because they lack relevance for our lives today, but because, on the contrary, they directly challenge the premises of the dominant, patriarchal culture.

The Major Arcana are the twenty-two Roman-numeraled Tarot cards that represent cosmic cycles of creation and return—what occult science calls "involution" and "evolution," the larger-than-life journey that the soul may undergo. In esoteric terms, everything in the world comes into manifestation and goes out again. According to "natural law," this process just keeps happening on every level of the universe. The most interesting of these cycles for most human beings is that of the human soul, which comes into a physical body, presumably learns some valuable truths during each lifetime, and "distills" the essences of those experiences when it "passes once more to the other side." Back and forth, in and out, the soul lives and learns, moving in a progressive direction toward "liberation" or "cosmic consciousness," which releases the spirit from what has been called the "captivity" of the body. What is the nature of this captivity? Not that a soul must pass into a human body. As Buddhists tell us, this passage is a great and holy gift. A soul is captive as long as the person in whose body it resides is unconscious of its holy presence. The goal of spiritual development is to become conscious of the soul and reunite with it. In this sense, the Major Arcana offer a spiritual discipline, at least when they are used properly as an object of meditation.

A similar lesson was taught in the initiation schools of every early civilization. From Druid to Egyptian priesthoods, from Mayan to Arctic shamanism, this "teaching" was provided for certain members of the community to help them understand the purpose of human life on the planet and live harmoniously as they took part in individual and collective evolution. We do not know how far back this teaching went. An oral tradition does not leave traces as easily found or interpreted as a hieroglyph. However, it would seem probable that around the end of the "paradisiacal" era of human history, the Wise Ones understood that a Dark Age was coming. Seeking to preserve their teachings for posterity, these prehistoric "sages" expressed their wisdom in pictorial form, some of which has survived through the millennia as "secret doctrine." Tarot traditionally draws upon this source; and thus the Major Arcana contain seeds of ancient and sophisticated knowledge of cosmic law and of Goddess-worship. During the past few thousand years, Patriarchy has suppressed this knowledge, sometimes with terrible violence.

In America today, Tibetan Buddhists are preparing for a similar Dark Age. Because of their oracular understanding that things will get worse before they get better, these Buddhists are gathering the sacred teaching in what they hope will be "safe space" where it might survive in the years ahead.

In Tarot, the Arcana have taken various graphic forms. In the popular Waite deck, for example, the figures are given medieval costumes and settings. The High Priestess, for instance, is shown as a kind of prioress or Mother Superior. In contrast, Aleister Crowley set his Tarot deck mainly in ancient Egypt, which he believed to be the source of the Arcana. In his deck, the High Priestess is portrayed as the Goddess Isis. Robed and veiled, she raises her arms, praying or channeling energy. This is a much more rooted portrayal. It shows that the Arcana contain the seeds of a sacred mystery tradition that had been enacted for thousands of years, and to which modern people might again find access through various esoteric schools active today.

The Initiation Mysteries of Isis are particularly appropriate as an entry into Tarot, since they reach into remote Egyptian pre-Dynastic history, but underwent a tremendous revival in the Hellenistic period three thousand years later. Durdin-Robertson says the worship of Isis at that time spread all over the Mediterranean as both a "city-state cult" (with popular or "mass" ceremonies) and a private "mystery cult." Isis became the leading Goddess, synthesizing the characteristics of various older Goddesses in a "purified" or refined form—a model for the later Virgin Mary. The Mysteries of Isis were the prototype of the later Eleusinian Mysteries, as well as of initiation rites at Corinth, Pompeii, Rome, and even Ireland.

In the Motherpeace images, we press back even further, into the prepatriarchal era and the more "primitive" or root meanings of the teachings. When the mother-centered group was alive, the entire community was able to experience the mysteries of initiation. Regular seasonal festivals and ritual celebrations allowed for the release of tension and a

THE HIGH PRIESTESS

The Priestess

healing reunion with cosmic energies experienced as the divine presence of the Great Mother of All.

In this context, the Motherpeace High Priestess no longer signifies an individual woman, but represents instead the power of the "cosmic feminine" as incarnate in the female group. The Zulu woman in the Motherpeace image is literally the "chest" or "womb" in which the secrets are contained. Her body itself holds the latent power of the "sleeping *kundalini*." When the women of the tribe allowed this force to awaken through dance or some other form of worship, the entire community was healed.

The Major Arcana attempt to illustrate basic universal laws that structure the natural world. Metaphysical or cosmic in their meanings, they are sometimes interpreted as phases of life or evolution, other times as stages on a spiritual path. Numbered in sequence from 0 (the Fool) to XXI (the World), they form a cycle representing the creation of life, its growth and development on earth, and the human soul's coming into conscious knowledge of itself, followed by a return to an original connection with its source.

Like a creation myth, they function to develop a coherent picture of the beginnings of life and what historian of religion Mircea Eliade calls "the cycle of return." Jungian therapist Marie Louise von Franz believes

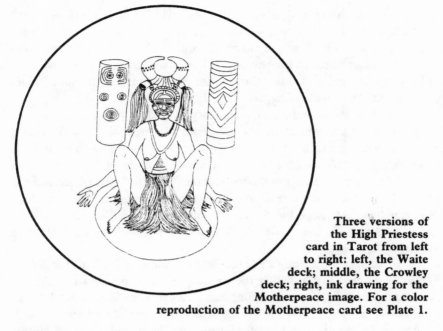

Three versions of
the High Priestess
card in Tarot from left
to right: left, the Waite
deck; middle, the Crowley
deck; right, ink drawing for the
Motherpeace image. For a color
reproduction of the Motherpeace card see Plate 1.

that "creation is an awakening toward consciousness" and that when a human being has become unrooted and split apart, the first step toward healing is the emergence from within the psyche of some sort of creation dream or metaphor. She reports that whenever the Fiji Islanders are "threatened by dissociation, panic and social disorder, they try to restore the Creation and the whole cosmos by re-telling the creation myth." In light of the world situation today, the current revival of the Tarot, especially the Major Arcana, does not seem accidental. Are we taking part in the collective emergence of a much-needed metaphor of creation and the future possibility of life?

According to Donald Sandler, Navaho healing follows four principles, which I believe also apply to the natural cycle of the Major Arcana: the first is return to the origins; the second, confrontation and manipulation of evil; the third, death and rebirth; and the fourth, restoration of the universe." Since we created the Motherpeace Major Arcana before ever knowing about Navaho healing, I am led to wonder whether both systems might draw in part on the same basic sources of wisdom.

In the cycle of Motherpeace images, the first few represent the "return to the origins." They look at prehistoric culture and speculate, from archeological evidence and mythology, about the nature of early humanity. Beginning with the Emperor (Chapter 6), the next few cards deal with the "confrontation and manipulation of evil," which continues until Strength and the Hanged One (Chapters 13 and 14) lead us into "Death and rebirth." The Star and Moon (Chapters 19 and 20) point the way toward the eventual and inevitable "restoration of the universe," which is fully represented by the last three Major Arcana images, the Sun, Judgement, and the World (Chapters 21, 22, and 23).

Both symbolic and actual, this story of healing pertains to the individual going through a therapeutic process as well as the culture as a whole going through a similar cycle of restoration. The first chapters speak of a history we have lost almost wholly, but are beginning to recover; the middle chapters tell the story of our "historic" experience and our world as it exists at the culmination of the patriarchal era; and the final Arcana speak of hope for the future, offering suggestions for active involvement in the restoration of our personal as well as our collective world.

In Chapters 2 through 23, the first portion of each will discuss the mythology and art in which the particular Tarot image is rooted. For example, the chapter on the Empress includes a discussion of "Venus" figurines and other early prehistoric sculpted images of Goddess as Earth Mother. It also includes her later forms from the period of the agricultural revolution, during which matriarchal civilization peaked. The final portion of each Major Arcana chapter is a more personal "reading," for those who would like to know how to apply the image to their personal lives.

Thus the bulk of each chapter speaks mainly to the abstract "mind-soul" of the reader, providing background and the "stuff of initiation." The latter part speaks more to the personality, grounding the material in the "real world." Taken together, the two illuminate one another; but it is possible to consult either part separately if the reader chooses. For instance, the first parts of the chapters on the Major Arcana can be read in sequence as a long essay—a story of cultural evolution, based upon Goddess symbols in myth, art, and Tarot. Likewise, the second, shorter section of each chapter can be used separately to provide a basic Tarot interpretation of each Major Arcanum for use in counseling, divination, and character reading. Naturally the fullest interpretation will arise out of attention paid to both parts, just as each person will want to attend to both soul and body, the spiritual and material planes.

CHAPTER 2

FOOL

Trusting One's Elf

Represented by the "number" Zero, the Fool in Tarot has been a symbol of the void, the precreation state containing all possibilities but not yet manifesting any particular things. In many creation myths, this state is called Chaos and considered to be female. The Goddess of All Things rose naked from Chaos and found nowhere to place her foot. Separating the sea from the sky, she brooded over the waters until she gave birth to life: Herself. Consciousness hovering over the face of the waters is a biblical idea as well, describing the Holy Spirit in its original feminine form—the breath of life.

In words borrowed from Jungian analyst Marie Louise von Franz, the Fool is a glyph of "psychic wholeness . . . before the rise of ego consciousness, or any kind of dividing consciousness." Hence the traditional appearance of the Fool in Tarot decks as a happy-go-lucky mortal about to step off a cliff into the abyss. There is in the Fool an element of the divine Trickster. I think of "Roadrunner" cartoons I saw as a child. No matter how wily the coyote was, the Roadrunner could always outtrick him, because the Roadrunner was really the Fool who had the ability to walk off cliffs into space and not be killed. The Fool doesn't know what she is doing, in the sense of logical thought, but moves from an impulse that arises out of the infinite possibilities alive in the embryonic state represented by zero.

Containing all possibilities, the Fool represents the phenomenon of "synchronicity" or "coincidences" between happenings. The Fool is the part of us that unconsciously connects to the greater universal whole, so

See color illustration on back cover.

23

Fool (0)

things are constantly "just happening" that involve the unspoken and usually unacknowledged links between thoughts and events. If one is open to magical phenomena, then one accepts these little correlations between the worlds. Once we accept this synchronicity on the intellectual level, we notice such events more frequently and learn to appreciate them more fully.

The Motherpeace Fool is a child walking on its hands, completely unaware of the dangers all around it, and unself-consciously happy to be alive. The child is a symbol of the human soul that does not yet reflect upon itself, the spark of life that reincarnates again and again until it awakens to itself. Reincarnation is the secret key to the Fool, and the Fool is the secret key to the entire Tarot. Alone among the Major Arcana, the Fool has come down to modern times as part of traditional playing cards, where it appears as the Jester or Joker.

In the Motherpeace image, the child balances a bag with her left toes—the traditional Fool's bag, which contains what Jungians call the "collective unconscious." This bag represents the archetypes and symbols that evoke cosmic awareness in the soul and that go into the creation of a Tarot deck. In this way, the Fool contains all the Tarot cards within itself in embryonic form. The open eye on the bag represents the awakening of the soul that is presently taking place for humanity. (Earlier decks have pictured the eye closed, representing secret or esoteric knowledge). Initiation, which used to be an individual, secret matter, has now become a collective process taking place in the open minds and lives of many modern people. This marks the beginning of a cycle leading back to the wholeness that characterized early humanity.

When we open the Fool's bag, we may begin to remember "past lives" and understand a larger reality of the soul's experience of life. Like a child, whose awareness is limited to the present moment, the Fool moves from moment to moment, or life to life, without intellectual analysis of what has gone before or what might come in the future. In this way, the Fool is perpetually young, always starting fresh, like the sunrise. It represents innocence, without ideas of sin or transgression.

Still basically "unformed" and open to the "now," the child approaches the future—the crossing of the water—without fear or doubt or even thought. It believes in itself and automatically trusts its body and the general flow of its life. Impulsively, the child turns a handspring, seeing the world upside-down. For the Hanged One, later in the series, this decision to turn upside-down is made consciously and probably with apprehension. For the Fool, it is a completely spontaneous act.

Watching over the child is the sacred griffon-vulture of the Egyptian Goddess Maat. Goddess of wisdom and inner truth, Maat protects each soul through the long journey of spiritual evolution. The peacock feather on the Fool's wand is a sign of this ancient intelligence that urges a person on toward truth.

The Fool enjoys the pure spontaneity that yoga and other meditation forms strive to recover, and whose purpose is to reunite the soul with the spirit while it is incarnated in the body. Mircea Eliade suggests that a "nostalgia" exists in human beings for the "primordial completeness and bliss" we knew in "paradise," a bliss embodied in Tarot by the Fool. In personal terms, this nostalgia is often seen as a wish for a return to the amniotic bliss of the womb. In feminist terms, this yearning points to the early life of our species, marked by homage to and worship of a Great Mother figure who represented life and love for all.

In the Motherpeace image, the crocodile represents dangers and the instinctual unconscious; yet clearly this dwarf crocodile poses no threat to the child. Reptilian wisdom is a primitive form of psychic receptivity. The pineal brain of a snake or reptile is the evolutionary precursor of the human potential for higher wisdom symbolized by the "third eye" of psychic or inner sight. Because the Fool is psychically connected to the crocodile by virtue of sharing the same primordial consciousness, there is nothing to fear.

The cat that accompanies the Fool is a friend and psychic companion —what a witch would call her "familiar"—who has chosen to share its life with the Fool. Because the Fool is not limited by ordinary social conventions, she can relate fully to her animal friends, including telepathic communication and other forms of magical relationship. Witches say that their familiar animals are able to "go out on the astral" and do favors for them. In the words of a newspaper for psychics, "animals communicate in the primal, right-brain 'language' of images and emotions. They empathize and support their human friends in time of grief, pain, loneliness, joy. They understand directions and communication if couched in their language."

The Fool is not afraid to believe in something divine or greater than ego. She invites a return of the Mysteries and a leap of faith into cosmic experience. In the foreground of the Motherpeace image, are *amanita muscaria*, the "magic" mushroom known in ancient times for its qualities of trance-induction, prophecy, and ecstatic visions, but poisonous unless used with exact knowledge.

The lotus flower or water lily grows out of the bottom of the streambed, reminding the Fool that high and low are connected and that beauty grows from roots as common as mud. The blossom symbolizes the crown *chakra*—the highest of the seven focal points or "energy centers" of the human body. The crown or "seventh chakra" relates the human being to the one universal spirit, seen in the Fool's openness to cosmic light and divine guidance. An example of this kind of natural and spontaneous "channeling" occurs when children read the Tarot cards. Without any study or preparation (and with very little thought about what they "should" know), they interpret the pictures as accurately as any expert, and they do it in the spirit of play. All forms of "sacred play" are direct routes to the Goddess and the pure wisdom of the lotus blossom.

The mountains in the Fool card are pink, representing a ground of affection and spiritual love. The snowy caps signify a cool purity at the top of the climb, which melts into the flowing river of life that the Fool prepares to cross. This stream represents the constant flow of thoughts through the mind. The morning sun peeking over the tops of the mountains suggests a freshness and early spring, putting the Fool on the astrological cusp between Pisces (endings) and Aries (beginnings).

It is the Fool in us who urges the personality away from lethargy, toward enlightenment, and transformation—without fear of the future. Whenever change happens, the Fool in us is reborn and released into activity. As von Franz reminds us, "every time a human being makes real progress in consciousness, the whole world for him has changed; relationships change and the outlook on the outer world and on his own situation changes. There is complete rebirth of the world."

Like the jester in the court of a medieval king, the childlike Fool is free to speak the truth without punishment or censorship, because we trust in the absolute innocence of her motivation. She can function for us as an agent of awakening, like the child of the famous fairy tale who announces to the entire community of people trapped in illusion: "the Emperor is not wearing any clothes!" The equivalent of this perspective today is any Fool who risks speaking the truth about our civilization, perhaps about the value of "security" based upon a nuclear arms race, of prosperity for which we risk radioactive melt-downs, or of culture sustained by watching six hours of television per day.

When you get the Fool in a Tarot reading, it is probably best to let go of any desire to be sophisticated in your approach, because the time is right for your kid to emerge. If you try to hang onto logic or rationality, you are likely to get stuck in a hard place. Since the Fool is about pure spontaneity, better get in touch with your unacknowledged impulses and unprepared responses to the world. The Fool is generally very light and joyful, reaching back in time to a "paradise" of simple freedom where all energy is good energy. Has any of us wholly and finally discarded the belief in such a "golden age," in a realm where "sin" or guilt have no sway?

The Fool is the part of you who, paradoxically, does not worry about being "foolish" and, at the same time, is probably more open to the accusation. Fools pick up feathers or special rocks at the beach and know they contain magic; read the future in cards; feel touched by the Goddess personally and individually when something "special" happens. "Why do Fools fall in love?" And why do they walk off cliffs of hard truth into open space? The Fool is truly the part of you who just doesn't care what other people think or how things look.

The Fool moves from within you. It is not the clear, calm voice of the inner sage that moves you, but the carefree, irrational impulse—the irrepressible surge of energy that propels you into something. Maybe you know better, maybe there are logical reasons to exercise caution, make plans, "be careful." But the Fool enjoys a charming, playful sense of life, a willingness to experience things. When the Fool is acting through your life, you throw caution to the wind, or rather to the life breath that the Fool represents; you let it carry you where it will.

The universe seems to "like" those people who are open and willing to be moved. It blesses them with experiences of growth and delight; it helps them learn; it keeps them young in spirit, regardless of biological age. A person who identifies with the Fool is about to be impractical and possibly silly—to take a chance and risk something. She is trusting the love that flows through the universe and letting her desires emerge into reality. To know the Fool, it is necessary to trust "one's elf"—the eternal trickster that lives within the composed external reality we think of as the "self."

CHAPTER 3

MAGICIAN

Dancing the Fire

The alchemy of fire is the Magician's great secret. Her activating power changes one thing into another. She represents the toolmaker and the shaman. Of all early techniques, fire was the most powerful and versatile: it allowed people to turn grain into bread, clay into stone, inflammable matter to ashes. As people congregated around the central hearth fire, its warmth and light could protect them from wild animals and the cold, as well as ensuring a magical sense of sacred power embodied in the flames. Recent archeological evidence suggests that fire has been intelligently used for as many as four or five million years. The original power of the female group to harness and use fire is acknowledged in mythology all over the world and pertains to the sexual fire as well as the use of physical fire for cooking and transformation mysteries.

Shamanism is the oldest religion in the world and goes back to the early matriarchal roots of human culture. Geoffrey Ashe suggests that shamanism was "formerly a women's cult, which was united when the people themselves were. It passed into male hands . . . after the tribes were separated and drifted out of touch with each other."

The shaman channels healing heat—the fire of the universe coming through the human being. Like any modern shaman, the Magician is a mediator between two worlds—the inner, spiritual heaven and the outer, physical earth. Faced with the task of discriminating and making choices, she must be responsible to herself as well as the larger organism of which she—and we—are a part. As toolmaker, the Magician symbolizes differentiation—that great moment of mental awakening when the human ego

See color illustration on Plate 1.

recognized itself, felt its power to discriminate, and began to reason. (The earliest evidence of human tool-making comes from the continent of Africa and dates back to one and one-half million years ago.) In every human being, this evolutionary moment is recapitulated when the infant child, merged with its mother, begins to realize itself as a separate entity and has to deal with the shock of this discovery. In a state of wonder, she understands: I am. The bright yellow light radiating from the solar plexus reflects this magical mind power.

Traditionally the Magician represents Aries, cardinal fire sign ruled by the fertilizing fire of Mars and the life-giving rays of the sun coming to power in the springtime. Aries is the first zodiacal sign, and the Magician is number One in the Tarot sequence. She represents the ego, sitting like the sun at the center of the personality, with the fire of will manifesting her desires into reality through the power of thought. The Magician represents the breaking apart of the universal egg of the Fool, and the release of the energies contained in it. "What comes from the egg is a shining being: the sun." As the One she represents an individual unit, a microcosm. Symbolized by a dot or a point, something definite that has come out of nothing, she bodies forth the *yang* quality of outward activity.

Our earliest recognized evidence of shamanism exists on cave walls from the Paleolithic (Old Stone Age) period of human "prehistory." Early shaman artists made knives ("bladelets") and "hand-axes" from stone to be used, in part, for the carving and engraving that they did on cave walls. The earliest pictures were abstract symbols, mainly "cupules" or round holes carved in rock. Some archeologists say the symbols refer to breasts; others, that they suggest stars.

The earliest and most numerous human representations on the walls are pictures of shaman-women without heads—early precursors of the Goddess Kali in her headless aspect. Figures without heads are found alongside other female figures with bird heads, both of them clearly representing magical "shaman flight," the process of the spirit leaving the body and becoming, for a time, formless and free of limitation.

The human-animal hybrid figure appears early in prehistoric art. According to Siegfried Giedion, "the female is the fundamental type; the male type came later." The interaction between the human and animal realms suggested by hybrid forms is characteristically shamanistic. In the Motherpeace image, the Magician wears an animal skin in order to identify magically with it and take on its power. This image recalls the bird-headed woman on the ceiling of the Hall of Hieroglyphs at Pech-Merle, a cavern in Spain. Giedion calls her "the earliest known representation of the fusion of a human being with an animal." And what is she doing on that ancient ceiling? She is dancing.

Most famous of the hybrid forms is probably the "Sorceror of Les Trois Frères" in France. Almost everyone has seen sketches of this highly praised male figure dressed in animal skin and horns or mask. He is assumed to be the first masked dancer, considered to be at least a shaman, but more likely a god—the spirit of the animals or the Lord of the Beasts, like the later Hindu Shiva who is Kali's partner in sexual union. Two other male hybrid figures have been discovered in the same cave—men wearing bison skins.

The later male figures at Les Trois Frères differ from the earlier female bird-headed figures at Pech-Merle. All of these figures are surrounded by animals, but whereas each male figure stands apart from other people, the female figures are crowded together, dancing in a group, covering the ceiling of the cave. The earliest bird-headed female is "inseparably bound up with earthly existence," with "rudimentary arms, heavy breasts, pregnant belly, strongly emphasized hips, and human feet." (See ink drawings in Prologue.)

In the Motherpeace image, the Magician continues the ancient tradition of dancing the fire of magic and sexuality. The knife in her right hand, like a witch's "athalme," draws energy to earth like a lightning rod. The wand in her left hand directs the energy toward manifestation—she breathes in power and magically wills it toward what she wants to have happen. Similar to a Native American prayer stick or a royal scepter, the magic wand is frequently considered by western culture to represent a "phallus," but the Magician directs her will with the left hand, the female one.

In the Hindu tradition, these same elements are employed by Kali, Goddess of Fire. She holds a sword or knife aloft and dances the world into creation, having the power to destroy it as well. Like the Magician, the red Kali represents active female force—Shakti, the power to act—the shamanic power to make heat. The fiery Kali destroys falseness and conquers egotism.

The Magician's dance celebrates not a superiority to animals, but her connection with their world, her ability to project herself into animal forms or take them into herself, at will. She is Neith, described by Mary Daly as "the skin-clad Triple Goddess of Libya who belonged to an epoch in which fatherhood was not recognized." What this means is that although people knew that mating was required for women to get pregnant, "fatherhood" as an institution was not even dreamt of: children were not owned and there was no such thing as illegitimacy. The Magi-

cian is a "divine *yogini*" of Indian heritage like Bhairavi, the prepatriarchal Indian Goddess who wore a lion's skin around her waist and thighs
and an elephant skin across her shoulders. Her hairstyle includes a snake
as her tiara; she stands with her hip out in the traditional *yogini* posture.
Both Bhairavi and Neith are Goddess archetypes that predate the religious institutionalizing of fatherhood and the invention of father gods.

Egyptian culture, particularly the pre-Dynastic (earlier than 3000
B.C.), portrays women with upraised arms, bird heads, and legs tapering
to a point, descendents of the Paleolithic figures from ten millennia earlier. Throughout the Dynastic period (after the agricultural Goddess-
worshiping period) the mysteries celebrate the ability of the human being
to take flight from the body and return to the human form at will, to rise
like flame from a wick.

In the Motherpeace image, the Magician's eye is on the Sphinx behind her, which embodies the mystical merging of human and animal
forms and retains ancestral secrets otherwise lost. The Magician, as human ego, studies the mysteries of the Sphinx in order to stay in touch
with what is sacred. Without this connection to magic and the sacred rites
of fire, the ego becomes egocentric and thinks of itself as the center of the
universe. The Magician's stance allows for eye-to-eye contact with divinity, while at the same time touching the more physical elements of water
and earth—the cups and coins at her feet. She knows that the ego must
mediate between Nature and the Divine and finally come to understand
that the two are one.

Because of this understanding that a human is different from the
other animals by virtue of having an intellect and the facility for toolmaking, humanity has become cut off from the equally important realization
that all animals are sacred and we are only a part of the whole of Nature
—not its "boss." The Magician represents a time when human beings
understood that they shared a common fate with animals and, in what has
come to be called totemism, identified with animals. Hunters thought
that the animal they stalked would willingly offer its life, and that, as
Giedion says, "everything should therefore be done to ease its death. . . .
Above all, the animal must be given an opportunity of re-entry into life."
Modern feminist Monica Sjöö takes this anthropological view a step further:

*Totem means "related through the mother." . . . Masked dances were a
deliberate means of approach to this bio-mystical animal nature, and therefore to the Divine Mother within and beyond all natural forms. The totemic*

animal is eaten as a sacrament by the group; or it is totally avoided as a group taboo. . . . Dancing to—and with—the spirits of the animals is the most ancient human ceremony that we know: Pantomime dance is the essence of each and every mystery . . . the group becomes emotionally one— wearing animal masks and disguises, dancing to a common rhythm, common excitement. . . .

The Magician dances on behalf of all life, a dance of the universal fire inherent in all beings.

When you get this card in a reading, it means you have the gift of energy; you are motivated to do, to act, to go forth. The Magician stands for solar consciousness (the bright yellow light of day) and Mars energy (the red of action). Now is the time for beginning projects, taking a stand, affirming some idea you believe in. You may feel goal-directed now, with a sense of purpose and self-motivation. There is warmth to your personality, a radiant self-confidence that shows to others and spurs them on to action. You have a strong desire to do something creative or active, to get what you want.

The fire of your passion to succeed gives you power. What you want may be personal and self-centered, or it may be directed by a "higher" will or purpose that you are channeling. You may take up a cause of some kind or pioneer in some way, helping others at the same time that you help yourself. The witches' creed for working successful and positive magic is: "Do what you will and harm none."

Creative achievement demands a certain diligence or self-discipline that is hard to come by. If you want to manifest something worthwhile, you will have to visualize your goal and then work toward it without getting distracted. In the arts of healing and magic, intention is everything. What you see is what you get, so hold the goal in view and get to work. All good ideas need a channel to bring them down to earth, to make them real on the physical plane. Otherwise, they simply fade away into the ethers, unmanifested. With the Magician on your side, you should be able to accomplish whatever you set out to do.

As Master of the Fire, you are able at this time to initiate sexually. You may reach out and touch someone else, awakening their life force energies with the intensity of your own. Eros is on your side; the power of Shakti is strong. Dance yourself into ecstasy, like your ancient foremothers, the shamans and witches of old. Feel the regenerative power of the fire of rebirth and new growth, like the returning sun of spring-time.

CHAPTER 4

HIGH PRIESTESS
Paying Attention

The High Priestess represents the Moon and the element of water. She is the archetypal feminine receptive mode of consciousness—the inner knowing of the heart. She signifies moisture and rainmaking, the night, womb, breast, vulva, heart, and the inner eye of wisdom. What the Magician needs daylight to understand, the High Priestess knows in the dark. Bound up with the eternally recycling moon, her mysteries were the original sacred rites enacted by the female group during their menstrual cycle as they ovulated, bled, and meditated together.

The Magician's transformations, ruled by the sun and fiery Mars, occur in the outer world for all to see, where one thing visibly becomes another: food cooks, the serpent sheds its skin. The transformations of the High Priestess are interior: an egg becomes embryo, fetus becomes child. The female body alternates between receptive and active during each monthly cycle, like the ebb and flow of the tides. The Magician and High Priestess symbolize the alternating modes of perception and activity represented by the shamanistic lunar cycle.

The waxing moon signifies birth and growth, the full moon illumination and light, the waning moon death and healing power. These three— Daughter, Mother and Crone—represent the archetypal stages in a woman's life and the alternating flux of everything in the cosmos. The High Priestess is Artemis the Daughter, youthful and free, nymph or maiden; she is Selene the Mother, Pasiphae the full moon ("She Who Shines For All"); and she is Hekate, the old wise woman whose powers

See color illustration on Plate 1.

35

include divination and healing, midwifery, and the secrets of death and renewal.

The High Priestess is the "guardian at the gate," what Nor Hall calls the "medial feminine" who sits between the pillars of opposites providing equilibrium and guidance on our journeys through the unconscious. She sees through the darkness of the underworld; through her right-brain consciousness, we encounter the deep electric blue of creative space. The High Priestess is the Seer who tunes into everything happening anywhere, anytime. She represents dreaming consciousness, the Australian aboriginal dream-time, and latent psychic abilities. As Monica Sjöö explains, "dream-body language is the deepest type of thinking—it is right-brain thinking activated by the left hand—and it is a mode of perception that Western culture has scorned, to its own harm."

Nowadays, an authentic Goddess-worshiper would not want anything to do with what are called "black" rites—such as black sabbaths or black magic—since they have come to signify the truly demonic element of harmful magic. But in ancient times, before patriarchal ideas of light-over-dark and male-over-female, the Black Rite of Isis was the central mystery celebration. Black Isis initiated one into the secrets of death and resurrection. She was certainly not an evil figure, but a very sacred one; and her Mexican counterpart, the Black Madonna, was no doubt the same.

In the Motherpeace image, the black African woman pictured as the High Priestess embodies the highest spiritual values, representing an open door to the sacred realms of mysticism and magic. The pillars between which she sits are covered with aboriginal engravings like the earliest carvings on stone, which represented lunar calendars and abstract geometric symbology. Traditionally, the High Priestess is seen as the archetypal feminine, and is represented by the earliest female symbols: circles, discs, rings, dots, breasts—and, most often, the vulva. The High Priestess, since at least Aurignacian times, represents the entrance to the womb-cave of the Mother.

The Greek word *delphi* is linked to "uterus" and connects the High Priestess (and women) with prophecy and oracles. In the words of Sjöö, "women were everywhere the original Mantics—the shamans, the prophets, the visionary poets. . . . Mantism is the natural art of prophesying, divining, receiving and channeling psychic-biological energy from the moon." The High Priestess is the original Sybil, whose ability to enter the trance state and divine the future made her the mouthpiece of the Goddess. Madame Blavatsky suggests that mantism and prophecy derive from the same root and concern the "soma" of the ancient *manti* cup, which was drunk in order to "stir up" the spirit—"the highest divine essence itself"—which would then enter the body and take possession of the initiate. "Hence, ecstatic vision, clairvoyance, and the gift of prophecy."

The High Priestess represents the astrological sign Cancer, cardinal water sign, which rules the breasts. Breasts are the symbol par excellence of Mother-love and the transformation mystery of changing body-fluid into milk. In the cavern of Pech-Merle (mentioned in Chapter 3), a "natural protuberance" occurs in the shape of a female breast "which has been encircled by twenty red dots." In the innermost sanctuary of the same cave, adjacent to the headless female figures carved on the ceiling, natural stalactites form a wreath of female breasts with the nipples painted black. In Dynastic Egyptian art, a stone inscription reads: "I have breasts, therefore I am."

The High Priestess symbolizes the female body as vessel for the holiest of mysteries and divine experiences available to the human being. Later mystery and Eastern religions use the female body and its functions as metaphors for male initiation rites. A remnant of the early female power exists in present-day Tantrism, in which the highest teacher is recognized as female, and the most powerful initiation experience possible for a male is to have intercourse with her during her "red" or menstrual period.

In our modern-day culture, because of diet and dissociation from the natural processes, most women experience tension or trauma around the menstrual period, making it hard to grasp the power inherent in the female "period." Professor Durdin-Robertson tells us that the earliest offering on the "sacrificial altar" was the menstrual blood of the priestess. The High Priestess had no need for human or animal sacrifice; her blood offering came naturally once a month and was freely given to the Mother. The word Eucharist comes from the blood of the Goddess "Charis" (grace) and represents this early female rite of purification and monthly cleansing, then quite removed from today's connotations of "unclean" and "cursed."

The blood given at the altar partly symbolized life unborn—the ovum unfertilized or sloughed off, returned to the Mother Earth. A woman paying attention to her monthly cycle and her bodily processes knows when she ovulates and when she will bleed. A tribe of women cycling together (as women do, even modern women who live in the same dwelling) could accurately limit the number of births without interference from outside chemicals or authorities. "Lunaception" is no joke—it is undoubtedly the oldest form of birth control known to the human race and was practiced with a wise understanding missing from the birth control of today.

Our intelligent High Priestess ancestors not only kept track of their own lunar phases thirty thousand years ago by marking on bone, but also invented the first lunar calendars as they watched the moon go through her cycles. They made tiny notations that anthropologists, until recently, considered accidental markings. Monica Sjöö argues that "women invented abstract notation, observational science and early mathematics." Their observances and chartings of lunar cycles revealed to them a knowledge of plants and lunar tides, migrations of animals, birds, and fish, and eventually agriculture. Astronomy is only now catching up with some of the ancient materials inscribed on cave walls and artifacts around the world.

Most of this "Stone Age" wisdom was so sophisticated and esoteric that it has been mistaken, until now, for gibberish and meaningless marks. It even seems that some of the early markings were the beginnings of writing and alphabets. In the late phase of prehistoric Spanish art, for instance, people painted pebbles with magical signs. The pebbles were found around the caves of "earlier artistic splendor," but have been considered less wonderful by archeology. One writer reports that these "Azilian" pebbles from Spanish art look a lot like the "sacred pebbles" of the Australians (called *Churinga*). Among these haunting designs we find "M's and E's and crosses, dots, lines and vague schematizations in imitation of the age-old fertility symbol of the cowrie shell."

The crescent horns of fertility that the High Priestess wears as headdress connect her to the moon cycle—the waxing moon forms one horn, the waning its opposite—and also, like the Magician, to the animal world. The Egyptian Mother Goddess Hathor was symbolized by the horns of a cow. In Asia and Africa, the Moon Goddess wore cows' horns; and breasts and cows' horns adorn the walls of sacred rooms in the ancient ruins of Catal Hüyük in what is now Turkey. All animals belong to the Lady of the Beasts. The horned animals in particular belong to Virgin Artemis, who is thought by Geoffrey Ashe to be connected with the earliest formulations of shamanism rooted in Asia Minor. The horns symbolize the transformation inherent in the shedding and yearly growth of horns for goats, stags, reindeer, and others.

The Horned Priestess, like the priestess with upraised arms, is a worldwide, age-old motif of woman as sacred channel. "Drawing down the moon" is the ancient rite of the priestesses of western witchcraft and eastern Tantra. Artemis the Virgin has survived in her aspect as "Archer" in rock carvings and stone engravings all over the world. One extremely vivid and beautiful example is a Black Artemis (or Diana) in the Sahara with a crescent moon on her head for horns. She is portrayed running, as in the photograph on page xi just before the Prologue. Robert Temple associates the bow with the star Sirius, sometimes called the "Bow Star," and Michael Dames links the arrows and the running with rainmaking, women's ancient art of influencing the weather and seasonal cycles. "The flight of arrows symbolizes the rain shower." Similar running women are found in Australian rock carvings and the Hopi signs for rain always include arrows (like lightning).

When the High Priestess comes up in a reading for you, it means your intuition is functioning more strongly than your intellect. A wisdom is activated in you that is older and deeper than your ordinary mode of thinking. Stay open to your body and your emotions in order to come into contact with what you already know.

By paying close attention to your own body and its natural rhythms, you will come into harmony with your inner wisdom. A woman paying close attention to her menstrual cycle will be able to know when she ovulates and thereby be able to help prevent conception. A pregnant woman may be able to tell the sex and temperament of the child by tuning into it psychically. In India, for example, it is widely assumed that by the third month of pregnancy a woman will know whether it is a girl or a boy.

If you are in the process of trying to answer an important question about your life, the High Priestess invites you to relax and listen to your intuition. Take a deep breath, and imagine an open space in the center of your chest where all wisdom resides, and let the answer come to you.

Maybe this is a time to get to know your feminine self better. A way of getting in touch with your lunar cycles might be to chart your menstrual periods and, if you can feel it, your ovulation. In addition to this, you can record feelings and thoughts, highs and lows, throughout your monthly cycle and see what patterns show up. You might do yoga or take up meditation of some kind, perhaps reading the Tarot cards regularly enough to learn to recognize your inner messages and to divine the future. Another way to ask questions and help to understand yourself better is the *I Ching*, a Chinese divinatory method wherein the oracle is obtained by interpreting "hexagrams" chosen by a throw of special coins or yarrow sticks. You might likewise keep track of your dreams and see when your deepest dreaming takes place—new moon, full moon, ovulation, or bleeding? Take your time waking up in the morning—allow that extra few moments it takes to remember a dream fragment or image. Writing it down may stimulate the memory.

CHAPTER 5

EMPRESS

Giving Forth

The Empress represents the Great Mother, pure and simple. She promises abundance, birth, growth, harmony, community, and relationship. She was the earliest provider, the socializer, the mother-lover-teacher embodied in the archetypes of Ishtar and Aphrodite, Babylonian and Greek Goddesses of love. She is Demeter, the Greek grain Goddess worshiped in the Eleusinian mysteries and later reflected in the Roman Goddess Ceres. The Empress signifies, chronologically, the development of agriculture and the first civilizations that grew up during the Neolithic period.

In the Motherpeace image, the Empress as Great Mother represents the earth from which all life is born, and to which it returns at the end of its natural cycle. The first Empress-type statues were the small pregnant "Venus" figurines from the Ice Age in Europe and Russia (at least 30,000 B.C.). These tiny Goddess figures are pregnant to the bursting point and generally without distinctive features of face or hands or feet. Their importance clearly lay in their full breasts and bellies.

The fertility of the Mother and the fertility of the Earth were always connected in these early cultures, from Paleolithic times when people hunted and gathered food, into agricultural times when they cultivated grains and domesticated animals. The bull represents the early domestication of animal helpers, as well as the astrological sign and constellation of Taurus the Bull. Taurus—"the sign of the Mothers"—is linked with the Pleiades and the Empress's ruling planet, Venus.

The earliest known city was Catal Hüyük (in what is now Turkey),

See color illustration on Plate 2.

where the first temple-building started around 7000 B.C. Along with cow's horns and female breasts, the central religious imagery was women grinding grain and baking bread within the temple, a conjunction between the mystery of food transformation and the mystery of sexual-initiatory transformation by fire. Both were celebrated as holy, a gift from the Mother.

How long ago was bread first eaten? It is hard to know, in part because the gathering of grains leaves no traces as obvious as the heaps of animal bones left by meat-eaters. We do know, however, that thousands of tiny flint "bladelets" have been found in the Pyrenees from around 9500 B.C. What was so exciting was the discovery that the bladelets were coated with vegetable "glue," which led archeologists to the understanding that they had been used not as weapons, but as sickles to harvest wild grasses that grew in the valleys. They subsequently identified stone mortars and grinders, "which would have been essential for turning the grasses into palatable flour," and they assumed from this evidence that bread or porridge of some kind was created to accompany the "reindeer feasts" held in the shelter of the cliff.

Another piece of evidence comes from the "New World" where the Aztecs grew amaranth, a high-yield grain crop that supported their huge population. Amaranth has been cultivated in Central and South America for at least eight thousand years. Botanists are now regarding such Indian agricultural knowledge as a lost potential that we need to recover.

The Ice Age sculpture portrayed on the right in the Motherpeace Empress image is the famous "Venus of Laussel," frequently called "The Woman with the Horn." The cornucopia she holds is a "horn of plenty" and also a crescent moon. Dating from the Paleolithic, at least thirty thousand years ago, and originally painted with red ochre, she was found at the center of a prehistoric cave sanctuary assumed to be a "fertility shrine." It is interesting to note that a modern African tribe considers a horn filled with blood to be a most powerful symbol, suggesting a possible connection with this earlier horn and menstrual blood.

More than twenty thousand years later than the "Venus of Laussel," the statue shown on the left in the Motherpeace image was carved by a sculptor living in the early city of Catal Hüyük. As Marija Gimbutas observes, "the earliest agriculture must have grown up around the shrines of the Mother Goddess, which, thus, became social and economic centers, as well as holy places and were the germs of future cities." This enthroned Goddess who sits between two leopards—Aphrodite's beasts—extends the pregnant image to one of administrative power. She holds the human race on her very abundant lap and is squatting, ready to give birth. Even later, the Egyptian name Isis means "throne" or "seat." As Erich Neumann says, "the Great Mother is the throne, pure and simple." The image of the Great Mother changed in some ways between the Paleolithic and later Neolithic periods, but as she had done so much earlier, she appears before us ready to give forth.

The Empress represents the blending of spirit and matter, the Goddess within the body. In these early civilizations, ritual was integrated into the cycle of planting and the harvest, birth and death, and homage paid to the Great Mother for her gift of fertility. As in the case of Catal Hüyük, cities were built without fortresses, suggesting that people found ways to share space without war. Property was owned in common and passed through the female line, which meant the priestesses and the temple, just as matrilineal descent is still recognized among some African and Native American cultures today.

In the Motherpeace image, the Empress herself reclines in the wild grasses and seems to await a lover or "celebrant" of the mysteries, recalling figures found at the entrance to La Magdaleine, an Ice Age cavern in France. On either side, the entrance depicts a reclining female figure carved on the rock. "What seems so strange about these figures is their unusual pose, which is very unlike an idol's. Both figures lie stretched out in positions of utter repose, one arm bent and supporting the head. They arise from the rock as 'foam-born' Aphrodite arose from the sea." Giedion further suggests that these relief sculptures "anticipate" the later reclining Artemis figures, "which expressed that deity's manifold attributes: Mother Goddess, Moon Goddess, ruler of the animal world, Goddess of love." He also mentions similar small nudes from Babylon (earlier Sumer) from the third and second centuries B.C. which, like the figures at La Magdaleine, strongly accentuate the pubic triangle.

In the lower front portion of the Motherpeace image, the Demeter plaque is borrowed from a relief sculpture done in classical Greece depicting the Eleusinian Mysteries toward the end of the Goddess-worshiping times. Marija Gimbutas points out that from Paleolithic times down to classical antiquity, the image of the Goddess began to split off into fragments of her earlier full self. The mysteries, overseen in the end by a Hierophant or male priest, could not retain much of what had been in the beginning strictly female mysteries. Still, these late initiation rites celebrated the reunion of mother and daughter, as well as the harvest of sacred grains, which probably included some ancient knowledge and oral tradition that is lost to us now.

In her hand, the Greek Demeter (or later Roman Ceres) holds the snake of regeneration and the sheaths of grain that symbolize abundance.

These images, although esoteric and removed from the social organization that surrounds them, still must have carried some power for the initiates, even if only on the symbolic level. Today, of course, the female mysteries once expressed in a way of life, and later in the weakened form of an esoteric ritual, are known to us mainly through the even paler version offered by scholarship. But the basis for these mysteries remains to us in our bodies. Our modern initiations take place on the unconscious level, during our dreams and visions. The Empress in her contemporary "seductive" pose symbolizes the unconscious knowledge modern women share of the ancient mysteries of healing and transformation that live on in our much-diminished sexuality and our ever-present desire for life.

The Empress feels her connection to the Earth. She smells the rose—red, like passion or menstrual blood—and she knows the mystery of procreation, the potential of growing and nurturing life within her womb, followed by the sacred act of birthing. She represents communal life close to the soil—a time when people did not make war, but spent their leisure making art and love, a contrast that should not be made trite for us by slogans of the 1960s.

When agriculture became agribusiness, the life-giving qualities of the Empress were lost, and work became the tedium it is for most people today—cut off from any ultimate meaning. The disconnection of humanity from the green healing energy of the Empress and her fertile earth was the fall from grace. The day we stopped loving the Earth as our Mother, and the woman as her holy representative, was the day we left the Garden. The Mother beckons to us to return to her before we destroy ourselves. Like the energy of the sleeping Goddess Kundalini, she asks to be re-awakened in us, so that we might once more know the joy and purpose of life on the planet.

The hand-mirror beside the Empress is modeled after the many mirrors found in archeological sites of Goddess-worshiping peoples. Archeologists often interpret the prevalence of hand-mirrors in early culture as evidence of "women's vanity." But there is a much older, more sacred sense of the mirror still understood by cultures such as Native Americans or the Japanese Shinto worshipers who keep a mirror in every shrine and believe it to be a representation of the human heart. According to G. H. Mees, the "mirror of consciousness" and the pictures in the mirror reflect "the dynamism of consciousness." In the *Book of Signs*, Mees says the mirror of Mother Earth is material nature, and the mirror of Venus represents the emotional plane. "The ancestors of the human race looked in 'the mirror of Venus,' and beheld in it the waters, the wind, heaven and earth, mountains and meadows, trees and animals, and a whole world of animate and inanimate objects." The mirror connects the Empress with the central initiation mysteries, in which the main objective is to "Know Thyself."

When you get the Empress in a reading, you are probably coming into touch with your ancient sensual nature. The Empress rules through love, so let your heart lead the way, relax into your senses, let your sexuality flow. The Empress is the part of you who engages a partner or mothers a child—she is fundamentally "in relation" to others. When you get in touch with the Empress, your gentleness may come to the fore, bringing spiritual nourishment and sensitivity to the daily pattern of your life. Whether you are cooking, parenting, making love, or cleaning house, you will feel the presence of the Mother with you.

The Empress brings out your artistic side, opens your love of beauty, and heightens your asthetic appreciation. This might be a good time to redecorate a room or arrange a bouquet of flowers. Maybe your urge to make art will be stimulated—you may get out the clay and sculpt something, or paint a picture, or make that new design you've been planning. You may want to get closer to the earth by gardening or hiking or just sitting somewhere in the sunshine listening to birds sing and smelling the flowers.

On a deeper level, the Empress may activate ancient feelings you have toward life. You may realize how desperately you want the world to be different—more humane—and think of something to do toward that. The ancient cultures of the Goddess may awaken a desire in you for communal life where material things are shared, or life without war. Maybe you desire a world where all children are wanted children, or the freedom to express your sexuality the way you wish you could underneath all the patterns and cultural ideas about love. If you feel these feelings growing in you, it would be good to express them in some way—through art, speech, or as I have here, through writing.

Since the Empress is the Great Mother, you may get this card when you are considering whether to have a child. She represents the part of you who is fully committed to the idea and who wants to experience the miracle of conception, pregnancy, and birth. If you have doubts or fears, you might meditate on her other quality of "great provider." She is the one who gives all—and one who has all to give. She is the part of you who knows how to manifest what you need in order to survive on the physical plane, as well as the part of you whose "mother instinct" gives you the energy and compassion and enjoyment you need for dealing with children.

The Empress represents "prosperity thinking" and the very real power of positive imagination. "What's out there comes around" is a magical saying about manifestation. You just have to envision it and think you deserve it—not always an easy task. It is a nurturing time for you, a time to nourish yourself as well as others. Let your open, sympathetic heart be touched by faith in love. Let your desire for harmony influence your thoughtforms and your wishes. Ask the Great Mother for what you need. Remember, Venus (Ishtar-Aphrodite) is the wishing star.

CHAPTER 6

EMPEROR

Separating Off

The Tarot Emperor is traditionally a symbol of Patriarchy in its active form, representing the King, the patriarch, the boss. Sometimes a glyph of fatherhood, he is always an authority figure seeking to establish control and dominance. Chronologically, he represents the Indo-Aryan invaders of the astrological Age of Aries (second and first millennia B.C.) who swept into the ancient world and destroyed the religion and culture of the Mother. Erich Neumann hints at the brutal, aggressive changeover from one culture to another: "Although the beginnings of the psychological matriarchal age are lost in the haze of pre-history, its end at the dawn of our historical era unfolds magnificently before our eyes." What had been the sphere of the Goddess is "replaced by the patriarchal world, and the archetype of the Great Father or the Masculine, with its different symbolism, its different values, and its different tendencies, becomes dominant."

In place of the sacred rites of the Goddess, these invaders and others established the worship of warring sky-gods such as the angry, jealous Yahweh or Jehovah of the Old Testament and the thundering Zeus whose main form of interaction with the female was rape. Whereas once the Great Mother had ruled magnanimously over all her children, now the Father God came on the scene to oppress women and Nature with the doctrine of male supremacy. Where the male archetype had earlier been formulated as the "Son" and, when he grew up, the "Consort" of the Mother, what becomes central after the patriarchal transition is "fatherhood." And if biological fatherhood is to have meaning, then "promiscuous" or untamed female sexuality must be eliminated and the institution of monogamous marriage enforced by law. The overriding characteristic

47

Emperor (IV)

of patriarchal culture is that female control over birth and sexuality is brought to an end, the woman belongs to the patriarch, and the children bear their father's name.

With the influx of patriarchal gods and their laws, the philosophy that "sex is bad" and "sexual intercourse is dangerous" became widespread, at the same time that rape became institutionalized as a form of social control over the female group. In the religious literature of East and West, one can still see this ambiguity at work. The theme is certainly not limited, however, to mythology and literature, as contemporary rape statistics so disturbingly suggest. Recently, our society has begun to confront the phenomenon of fathers who rape or molest their own daughters or uncles who molest their nieces, an aberration that would shock most "primitives." At the same time we are hearing more about wife-battering, as well as the deliberate maiming and killing of infants and small children —either the father's own or children of the woman he lives with.

Whereas the fire of the female was shamanistic, healing, and sexual, the fire of the Emperor is warlike, ascetic, and domineering. In astrological terms, the Magician's fire was Aries—"I am." The Emperor's fire is Leo—"I will."

Since imperialism marks the patriarchal style, the Motherpeace Emperor portrays Alexander "the Great." During his twelve years of conquest, his goal was to take over the world. It was during Alexander's reign that the great matriarchal libraries were burned to the ground, most thoroughly destroying the ancient wisdom. The Emperor represents the

"craftsman" archetype of a god "who fashions the world as a dead object" and represents a stage in which "consciousness has already to a
certain extent developed as an independent power apart from the unconscious." Patriarchy is proud of this separation from the unconscious and
the world of natural instinct. In the Emperor's world, God is no longer
immanent in the material world, like the Mother, but "exists outside of,
and treats the world as his object, as a craftsman uses his material."

During the transitional times, the element of fire became a symbol of
the masculine force—the "Logos" or "word"—and this wordy God
became the creator of the universe. Fire became "the intelligent substance . . . which contains and brings intelligent order to all things." The
power of writing became the right to have power over. "Logos is ordering, conscious thought that can be expressed in words." Writing, which
had been a sacred expression of religious power, became a deadly tool of
the separated intellect, used by the ego to dominate anyone close to Nature. Hymns to the Goddess were displaced by stories describing the
Hero's exploits, which mainly consisted of killing other men who were
slightly less heroic, raping women, and slaying monstrous representations
of the Goddess.

Von Franz equates the King with the "integrated ego structure,"
saying: "He sits on his throne above the world, making a plan like an
architect for building a house, and in that way he fashions, or creates, the
world." The throne of the Emperor—cold, detached, disconnected from
life—represents authority usurped from the natural world of women. As
Erich Neumann explains, "The seated Great Mother is the original form
of the 'enthroned Goddess' and also of the throne itself. . . . The King
comes to power by 'mounting the throne' and so takes his place on the lap
of the Great Goddess, the earth."

Rape as social control, the forcible "mounting" of the female by the
male, as Susan Brownmiller makes clear, keeps all women in a state of
fear and bolsters the institution of monogamy. Each woman needs a single man to protect her from all the others who might potentially rape her.
Women had no need for male protection before the establishment of a
culture in which it is men themselves whom women have need to fear.

The Emperor's ego emerges against a red backdrop of fire as life,
passion, and vision. Unfortunately, the Emperor rarely sees into another
soul or touches a living thing with real feeling. He crosses his legs, cutting off his sexual feelings, and his arms protect the power center in his
solar plexus from interaction with anyone else. I believe he longs to be
touched himself, yet is impervious to feelings and the song of the heart.
Like every hero since Gilgamesh, he wanders alone, a victim of his own

sex-role system, yearning in vain for that unnameable something that will wake him up to his senses and allow him the freedom to feel love. A study in blocked emotions, he periodically erupts into aggression, war, anger, and oppression of those "beneath" him. He is the epitome of a four-year-old child whose temper tantrums abound with the affirmations: "I, me, mine."

In the Motherpeace image, a table holds the spoils of his victories—the wine, women, and song so lauded by patriarchal poetry. Occult tradition teaches that "the slaying of the Animal begins on the Path of the Fall." If we feed our livestock artificial hormones, fatten them in a feedlot, slaughter them factory-style on a sort of disassembly line, and then overindulge on the meat, can we be surprised when a variety of diseases are linked to this set of practices? One does not have to be a vegetarian to regard this relationship to animals as brutal, another result of separating off.

In comparing historical art with its predecessors from prehistoric times, Giedion sees a tremendous revolution about five thousand years ago, when the brilliance of the earlier art, its "complete freedom and independence of vision," were replaced by what I would call the ordering ego of the Emperor. In terms of composition, says Giedion, "Paleolithic man's indifferent relationship to an unlimited number of directions became replaced by one overriding relationship: to the vertical . . . the rectangular." This change occurred not only in painting, but in everyday habits of life. Our rectangular way of looking at things leads to all straight lines and boxes, categories, and definitions. None of this is natural, but all of it is logical, and patriarchy says: "If it isn't logical, it isn't right." The frame or square is stable, boxing things in and thereby exerting control over them.

Traditionally equated with Jupiter, the Emperor represents "the thunderer," holding the power of Mars (the thunderbolt) in his hand. (This is the destructive or punitive aspect of thunder, which also has a transformative aspect, the "flash of illumination" of the Tower, discussed in Chapter 18.) As Jupiter, according to Hinduism, the Emperor is "Ruler of the Senses," having control of the four elements. The number four and the geometric square both represent the physical world and the order of conscious structure. As von Franz explains in a different context, "The number four . . . always points to a totality and to a total conscious orientation, while the number three points to a dynamic flow of action. You could also say that three is a creative flow and four is the clear result of the flow when it becomes still, visible and ordered." In the person of the

Emperor, the creative flow of the Empress is brought to a standstill, crystallized for posterity.

The Emperor symbolizes the intellect—powerful, creative building-tool of the human mind—having detached itself from the rest of Nature; it is functioning now like the "dissociated" or "autonomous complex" of a neurotic personality. The separation of the human mind from the rest of Nature is the major cause of the alienation found in the world today. Giedion speaks of the initial severance "of man from animal" and the revolutions that followed it: hierarchy and patriarchal cities, kingdoms, and empires. "But," he says, "none of these upheavals penetrated so deeply into the very marrow of man's relation to the world and into his environment as the gulf which opened up at the end of the zoomorphic age between creature and creature." With what consequences? "This process of separation . . . opened the way to man's alienation from those natural laws which govern every living being." This separation is the triumph of the Emperor.

When you get the Emperor in a reading, look out—you are up against an angry, patriarchal structure of some kind, and probably have to deal with rigidity, or even with nastiness. Probably the card implies some confrontation with authority, maybe your boss or your father. The personality implied by the Emperor is not an easy one to get along with— egotistical, self-centered, and not in touch with feelings. It will be up to you to stay with whatever emotional current is present in this encounter, and to realize that this person has extremely fixed ideas about reality. He believes, for one thing, that his way is right and he should be the boss.

Now, if this image represents you, then you might wish to look deeper into yourself and try to figure out why you are feeling so rigid and afraid. What is it in your situation that would make you tighten up and have to protect yourself at all costs? Try to relax and let another reality come into potential focus. Maybe you don't have to pout or feel defeated and bossy. Maybe you can open your heart a little and try to see the other person's point of view. There is a lot of life force in the red border of this card—why not try to tap it, rather than cutting yourself off from it in self-defense?

And speaking of being cut off, you might be feeling defensive right now, which will make it hard to relate to others with anything other than fear. If so, you might do well to take a hot bath or sauna, or jog a mile, or do something really nurturing for yourself or someone else. Loosen up your tension, otherwise it will become pockets of pain in your body. And when that happens, sooner or later you'll become ill or else unleash all that pain and tension on somebody nearby—probably the person you're closest to and would rather not hurt.

It is important when dealing with the Emperor to realize that he represents the intellect gone rigid—your creativity is probably anxious and nervously expressed and just needs the right outlet. If you could tune into your inner feelings and express them, things would immediately improve. If you feel angry at someone, just say so; it works much better than holding on to the angry feelings until they erupt inappropriately. If it's love you want, then why not soften enough to receive it?

Most of all, what's needed here is a return to the consciousness represented by the Empress card—the Mother Goddess of archaic wisdom and compassionate understanding. Maybe it's time to take a walk and experience Mother Earth—touch a tree or sit on a rock, and feel its ancient energy. You need to do something physical to unlock your senses and free up your body. Then you will be able to yield a little to the world around you and not feel you have to be completely in control. Remember, too, the childlike wisdom of the Fool.

CHAPTER 7

HIEROPHANT

Repressing Others

At its root, the word "hierophant" means a bringer to light of sacred things. In the tradition of Tarot, the Hierophant represents a priest or Pope, the paternal religious authority. "Twin and counterpart" to the Emperor, he provides spiritual authority for the martial law imposed over the empire. Sometimes both offices are claimed by a single man. Jocelyn Godwin says every emperor from Julius Caesar onwards was "Pontifex Maximus of the State religion, high priest or 'bridge-builder' between man and gods." Primarily a ritual-maker, the Hierophant may be a minister or other religious leader, or even a psychiatrist—any officer of an orthodoxy who transmits its prevailing beliefs and attempts to adjust people to them.

Representing a hierarchical view of religion, the Hierophant stands on a pedestal, raised up from the earth, above the common person. In the Motherpeace image, he has taken over the robes and skirt of the High Priestess, along with the breasts which symbolize her sacred power, but he has forsaken her "Sophia" or wisdom. He represents the newly installed male clergy who dispossessed the priestesses of the Great Mother —a male priest of the mystery cults of Serapis, Mithras, Orpheus, Pythagoras, or Christ. The forms of his rites are familiar in tone, borrowed from the religion of the Mother, yet corrupted almost beyond recognition.

The authority of the Hierophant is based, in large part, on repression of women and the natural instincts that women symbolize. The sacred rituals of the Goddess were considered criminal by the new patriarchal leaders, who subsequently suppressed them. "It is chastity above all that distinguishes the monk's life from that of lay people," says Godwin, and

Hierophant (V)

anything less than chastity, at least in the case of women, became punishable by death. Female rites of Ishtar, Astarte, Ashtoreth, Hathor, Isis, and Aphrodite were outlawed in favor of the puritanical repression that has played such a dominant role in Judaism, Buddhism, Christianity, Islam, and other religions so familiar to us today.

Patriarchal religion runs on the belief that physical incarnation—bodily life—is a "veritable crucifixion: a nailing of their divinity to the fourfold cross of the elements." This repudiation of the body is a far cry from the ecstatic appreciation of the physical senses represented by the Goddess, and the common people did not accept it easily. The soldier with the raised swords who stands behind the "holy man" in the Motherpeace image symbolizes the force used throughout history to "convert" people to the new religions.

Linking the figures that Tarot calls the Hierophant and the Emperor, Godwin observes that "the monk's path, like the warrior's, is based on a dualistic view of the cosmos . . . a duality of spirit and matter, which is manifested in the human being as a gulf between soul and body." The Hierophant represents this dualistic view of the light-skinned Indo-Aryan invaders who imposed their leadership upon the darker-skinned indigenous peoples living in India, the Middle East, Africa, and later upon those in the Americas and the South Seas, dividing the world into "good and bad"—light and dark, male and female, spirit and matter.

The Hierophant represses "occult energy" and its uses. The divine oracular power of the priestess was a gift of her female-lunar cycle: when she bled and when she raised the *kundalini* fire, she could see into the future and her words became full of numinous power. This inner, intuitive vision (the human conscience) later became conventionalized into the morality represented by the Hierophant, which depends on written laws and codified rules of life. Feminist Mary Daly points out how important this control is, stressing that the "perpetual War" of Patriarchy is "waged primarily on a psychic and spiritual plane."

The biblical Ten Commandments are a good example of the Hierophant's handiwork. Like much of the Old Testament, they were written with the express purpose of overriding the prevailing religious faith of the times—of the Phoenician Astarte (whom the Hebrew scribes called Ashtoreth), the fire Goddess of the Canaanites. And the single most important commandment has been: "Thou shalt have no other gods before me," stressing the jealous nature of this upstart male deity who would not tolerate any of the diverse manifestations of the Old Religion. Ishtar, the Sumerian Great Mother, became the Great Harlot, the Whore of Babylon, or as Aleister Crowley has called her, the Scarlet Woman; the temple priestesses who had performed the sacred rites for untold thousands of years were domesticated into "temple prostitutes." The people who worshiped the Mother Goddess in any form, in her sacred groves or around her *asherim,* her pillar or "graven image," were massacred by the new "righteous" warlords, whose first commandment—Thou shalt not kill—was conveniently ignored.

From Tiamat to Lilith to Pandora, from serpent-sea monster to demon to wicked witch, woman became the villain, the personification of evil. The dark side of life—death, destruction, violence, irreverence—all the things actually embodied by newly established male leaders, were projected onto women who were now called unclean, material, instinctual, gross, sexual, and inherently wicked. In the Motherpeace image, these diatribes written against the feminine are represented by the leaden gray scroll of the Hierophant.

In 1979, Mary Daly published *Gyn/Ecology,* a lucid, astonishing account of the abuses done to women in the name of patriarchal religion and its ongoing effort to exterminate the Goddess in women and in nature. In late 1978, I worked three weeks on drawing the Hierophant image—a painful effort to make graphic the complexities I saw in the traditional Tarot card as well as in my feminist interpretation of it. Shortly after the drawing was finished, I was sent a copy of page proofs of *Gyn/Ecology* and was startled to find that Daly's hypothesis and the Motherpeace image expressed a common vision.

In the course of the religious takeover, what had been a cauldron surrounded by women became a chalice held aloft by a single man. Daly asks the question: "What happens, then, when the cauldron of women-identified transforming power is stolen, that is, reversed by christian myth into the chalice, a symbol of the alleged transforming power of an all male priesthood?" In her view, as in the Motherpeace Hierophant image, "patriarchy asserts its power over others in the name of the male god by using the ancient symbol of nonhierarchical gynocentric trans-forming energy."

In order to reclaim the ancient Goddess-power that belongs to us, Daly argues, we must move into the "background" and "exorcise" or expel the terrible lies of patriarchal culture and religion that exist in the "foreground." The Hierophant forbids direct access to holy wisdom, damming up the magico-religious power of the water in the background. The water represents emotions, feelings, the unconscious, the moon, the female. Women—once portrayed by artists with arms upraised in direct communion with the Mother—are forced to their knees in front of the Hierophant who doles out religion as if it were crumbs for a beggar. In matriarchal times, the hands of the High Priestess had been open, signi-fying creation and power. Where the Hierophant offers his synthetic communion, he points two fingers alone, symbolizing what Godwin calls "thought, logos, and teaching."

The open scroll is another sign of the "Logos" or male "word of God" and represents written law, divine scriptures, "sacred" books. Symbols of the Goddess-religion were unabashedly expropriated by the incoming priesthood and distorted or suppressed. Godwin points out that the mysteries functioned by use of symbols, which "elude the limiting precision of words, a precision which pins the ideas like butterflies to a single plane." The Hierophant represents subtlety lost.

Some of the oldest writing extant tells the story of Innanna's shaman-ic journey to the underworld. In later versions, the protagonist was no longer a shaman seeking visions, but a Hero sent to slay the Goddess herself, who is personified as a monster. Later mythology loses even more connection with the original material, thoroughly reversing the earlier concepts, yet cloaking this reversal in religious robes. Consider, for ex-ample, the origins of communion. The idea of ritually shared food goes back to the hearth fire, which served as the first altar. The flesh and blood of the Goddess were originally experienced in the throbbing flesh and pulsing blood of her worshipers. As explained in Chapter 4, the first blood laid at the altar of divinity was the menstrual blood of the priestess. The later religion dropped the female menstrual blood and replaced it with human and animal sacrifice. This taking of life, so often erroneously attributed to "Goddess-worship" or "matriarchy," is anathema to the Mother and her principles of natural life and natural death.

Wine is another substitute for the earlier blood offerings, and Christ is often credited with the change from human or animal sacrifice to the use of wine instead. The wine and wafer of Christianity, however, continues a long tradition of alcohol consumption that was quite widespread by the time of Christ. Godwin calls attention to a Persian Mithraic text, "amazingly reminiscent of Jesus's words," which states that "he who will not eat of my body and drink of my blood, so that he will be made one with me and I with him, the same shall not know salvation." And it was the Dionysian Mysteries, so similar to the Christ-story, in which alcohol was mixed with narcotics, leading to the eating of raw flesh of animals torn apart at the moment of "ecstasy," certainly a sickening corruption of the gentle ecstasies of the Mother.

One does not have to adhere to a patriarchal religion in order to feel the effects of the Hierophant on everyday life. Women only recently won the vote. We still do not control our own fertility. Opponents of the Equal Rights Amendment cite "God's laws" as the main reason why women should not have full legal equality. As Mary Daly exclaims: "Patriarchy is itself the prevailing religion of the entire planet."

However, the Hierophant is not identical with the Emperor. Although the church has often given its ideological support to the state, most religious traditions also include a potential critique of state power and, in particular, of violence. Quakers call it "speaking truth to power." Behind the absurd spectacle of priests blessing both armies in a conflict and telling each one that "God is on its side," the church has tried to draw distinctions between "just" and "unjust" wars, to mediate disputes, and to suggest limits on the methods used in fighting.

At this time in history, the church has the opportunity to awaken its members, and others, to the ethical consequences of persisting in a nuclear arms race. A growing number of Catholic bishops and priests have questioned the morality of continuing to pile up nuclear arms, and have urged that both sides in the race stop, negotiate, and then reduce the stockpiles of warheads. In at least one case, a bishop has refused to pay the portion of his taxes that supports the arms race.

Since the church exerts a strong influence over its members, when the Hierophant takes a stand for peace, many other people will begin to question their acquiescence in a suicidal arms system. Political leaders could not easily withstand a widespread, sustained protest from the church against their policies. In this way, the Hierophant might help stop the Emperor from carrying his self-destructive methods any further. For the church to lead the way in a serious struggle against the arms race would represent a long-needed "karmic cleansing" that could function to align church behavior with its holy precepts, a union of body and mind with revolutionary implications. The Hierophant might then function as the teacher and revealer of sacred truth that the name implies.

When you get the Hierophant in a reading, it means you are dealing with conventional morality and patriarchal law in some way. You may have a run-in with authorities—the courts or the church or temple—or you may just come into conflict with a parent or critical figure. Someone is acting as judge and moral preceptor, possibly standing between you and your feelings, or even you and your deity. It is important to remain strong in the face of this kind of social opposition, or you'll end up on your knees like the women in the picture. Somebody is trying to tell you how things are supposed to be, and you may start believing them. Maybe they cite written law or biblical references to scare you into acquiescing to the "fear of God."

On the other hand, as in the case of the Emperor, maybe the Hierophant is you. Is there some way you are trying to be a good girl or boy, keeping to the rules and regulations, even if it means going aginst your own true self? The internalized rules of a culture are strong, its taboos generally embedded in the unconsciousness of the body. What your parents or teachers told you about right and wrong stays with you your whole life, unless you develop an independent conscience of your own. You are acting now in a conventional or programmed way—from your conditioning rather than from the true feelings of your heart. Probably there is some fear operating that you aren't even aware of.

Try to figure out which rule you're afraid of breaking, and see if you can get in touch with who will punish you if you break it. Is it really your mature conscience that is telling you to be careful, or is it one of the early imprints that do not reflect your own values and that you want to let go of? If you find yourself somehow forbidden to enjoy life in some way, ask whether you are being controlled by the internal "judge" or "priest."

Just as the image of the Hierophant can sometimes make you aware of unreflective conscience, so it can also help you ask whether you are acting like a priest or law-giver yourself. Maybe you are getting a little inflated, taking on more responsiblity than you need to, telling people "where it's at." Watch yourself for signs of being a know-it-all. Especially if you are implying that someone's actions or nonactions might be "bad," you might like to ease up a bit, and let the other person have a say.

The Hierophant is a bore. He's overbearing and pompous, feels superior to others and tries to keep a lid on what's happening. He's probably against dancing, singing, and making love—certainly he would not want you using Tarot cards, which he would call "a tool of the Devil." When he's in your psychic realm or your physical space, you need to get out from under his thumb.

CHAPTER 8

LOVERS

Joining Together

Traditionally an image of duality and choice, the Lovers represent the *yin* and *yang* forces of the universe and their natural attraction for each other. "Love," or the coming together of these complementary forces, occurs on many levels. On the social level, the Lovers symbolizes marriage. In its deeper, esoteric form, the image refers to the *hieros gamos* or *sacred marriage* of the initiation mysteries, the coming together of opposite qualities within a being, which leads to wholeness.

The union of male and female is recognized by all cultures as necessary for continuation of the species. In Indian Tantric practices, this union is ritualized and performed in special environments. In the Eleusinian Mysteries, as well as some other ancient religions and traditions, the *hieros gamos* was facilitated by the Hierophant; and to this day, one needs a priest, rabbi, minister, or judge to be officially married in our culture. But the underlying significance of an "alchemical marriage"— whether sexual or not—is always the union with what is divine in us and in the universe. In the Motherpeace image, this union is not yet accomplished, but only envisioned and desired—what is active at this point is the attraction force itself.

The Lovers image is attributed to the astrological sign of Gemini, the twins, and represents seeing things in pairs. Occult science teaches the doctrine of soul mates, which embodies this idea most clearly. On the physical plane, each human being has at least one opposite or "twin" aspect somewhere on earth with whom one's soul longs to unite. When these people find each other, they know it and connect. (In fairy tales, they fall in love and live happily ever after.) On the more vertical axis, the soul mate doctrine says that the human soul exists even before it comes to

Lovers (VI)

earth through physical birth into a body. In this process of physical incarnation, the body-personality becomes separated from its opposite spirit self, thus creating a need to reunite with the spirit-body through yoga or meditation practice. When the two are brought into harmony, a blissful union takes place and the being is One.

In Tarot the Lovers card usually refers to a sexual union in process. (In the Motherpeace image, the lovers are drawn as androgynous or abstract in order that traditional male-female characteristics may be considered in terms of qualities rather than gender.) Tantra teaches that the merging of humans through the "sexual act" causes a dissolution of ego-boundaries and the experience of ecstasy. The Indian Shiva-Shakti statues of sexual intercourse or the Tibetan *Yab-Yum* pairs are demonstrations on the human level of a union that is divine. And as the *I Ching* explains, "between the two primal powers there arises again and again a state of tension, a potential that keeps the powers in motion and causes them to unite, whereby they are constantly regenerated."

In modern cultures, the coming together of Lovers is necessarily laced with mental ideas and stereotypical sex-role responses ingrained in us by our cultures. In the Motherpeace image, the patriarchal foreground in which loving takes place is represented by Greek vases that portray some of the "scripts" by which we live—scripts that began with patriarchy and that are still being used five thousand years later in the form of movies, television shows, books, and plays, the mythology of our day.

Greek vases began to be painted around the seventh century B.C. in Corinth; in Athens, a century later. Athenian vases in particular are precursors of modern-day European and American romantic mythology. The vase on the left of the Motherpeace image portrays a popular myth, the Hero slaying the Amazon Queen—in this case, Achilles murdering Penthesilea. In an early version of this scene (found on an Athenian amphora painted in 540 B.C.), Achilles is hooded in black and the Amazon Queen is using her sword to fight back. In a later interpretation (which actually appears not on an amphora as pictured here, but on the inside of a small wine cup, painted in 460 B.C.), the Amazon is no longer even defending herself. Now she has no sword. J. J. Pollitt tells us that "as Achilles looms over the falling Amazon and begins to deliver the mortal blow, their eyes meet. His thrusting arm seems to freeze as anger, duty, and pride begin to conflict with love and regret." Does Penthesilea fight back? Well, she "grasps him feebly, partly imploring, partly resisting. In her case fear and pride, and perhaps also love, mix."

The darker side of cultural romanticism is this early connection between sex and violence that began as rape during the patriarchal transition. This glorification of rape and its perverse association with sexuality is an ugly reminder of the violent roots of our culture.

The vase on the right shows a couple in which the man is not doing violence to the woman, but momentarily adoring her, which may seem to reflect the old Goddess culture at first glance. However, Athenian women were given the "power" to be adored, not to exist on an equal footing with men. Once married, the woman shown on this vase could not expect to receive romantic attention from her husband again. He might only be sexual with her for purposes of procreation, saving his passion for *heterae* and young boys.

The pink sludgy energy in the foreground represents the combination of love and unconscious desires and fears we bring to a relationship. It is thick with thought forms about what might happen between two people who come together in sexual exchange. In the words of occult writer Alice Bailey, "the glamour of the pairs of opposites . . . is of a dense and foggy nature, sometimes colored with joy and bliss and sometimes colored with gloom and depression as the disciple swings back and forth between the dualities." How long does this alternation last? "Just as long as the emphasis is laid upon feeling," and more precisely, it persists as long as we are lost in ideas about what we are supposed to feel, rather than moving from our own true heart feelings. As long as we come to each other governed by patriarchal ideas and by a certain image of what love is and how one might be in it, we have trouble touching cosmic joy.

It is when two souls reach out to each other in vulnerability and spontaneous trust that the second stage of loving begins. In the Mother-peace image, this is suggested by the black and white geometric images coming together. Now there is a sense of something greater than ego—what beckons is more than the conscious mind rationally understands. When two people can trust themselves enough to let go into the event of loving—to surrender to the force of the unknown, the Void—then they will begin to build together the divine body of light that represents their union.

In Buddhism, this "subtle body" is the *Vajra* or "diamond body," invincible and eternal. This "we" of our coupling is an entity in its own right and begins to have a life of its own. Behind it in the Motherpeace picture, the two beings stand poised on the threshold of ecstasy, the precipice where they will drop off the mundane. Under the overarching garland of red roses, which signify passion, the Lovers merge. As they leap into open space, self comprehends other as Self without separation, and all love given immediately returns in the continuous circling of energies between the partners.

This rapture, represented by the orange ball of the western sun, is the prototypical healing circle. To be a channel for the moving energies of love opens one to profound caring and the universal healing promised by yoga and any other form of cosmic celebration. The psyche is cleansed and the cells regenerated, as old pain releases and the heat of loving burns up the karma of the past. This blissful state of consciousness is well-represented by the number Six, which always signifies a peak experience of some kind. Expressive and expansive like the sun, six can be understood as the moving of the consciousness from the power center to the heart—a momentary uplifting that prefigures the more permanent integration to come, which is represented by the Sun (discussed in Chapter 21). Making love is a rehearsal for the ultimate union of oneself with one's Self.

What is necessary for modern lovers wishing to enter this sacred space is, first of all, a cleansing of the many violent thoughtforms and images that distract one from the real energy of Eros and Psyche—heart and soul. In *Sexual Secrets*, Nick Douglas and Penny Slinger describe how the Lovers are made ready for their journey, in Tantra and other Eastern disciplines, through focus on preparatory fasts and purification rites designed to clear the body of "poisons" and "toxins" that cloud the nervous system and make it difficult truly to feel. Next they prescribe meditation practices and forms of breathing together, touching, and relaxing, so that the energies of the two can become transformed and ready for merging. Finally, desire is allowed to swell, kindling the sacred flame of passion and longing that exists within us all.

When two serious Lovers come together in mutual respect and reverence for the sacred energy, a union takes place in which they understand without words the true loving nature of the world. They experience their bodies as temples of the Goddess wherein their hearts may open without doubt, criticism, anger, or egotistical needs. With practice they can achieve great sensitivity, and each time they come together, old patterns drop away and the new forms become more accessible. Tantric sages suggest that one may cure all illness through this means and achieve "longevity," as well as the deepest possible understanding of mysteries that lie beyond words.

When you get the Lovers in a reading, it suggests that you are either working on a partnership in which you are already involved, or preparing to begin a liaison with a new partner. Being a lover is on your mind. Feeling the pull of the attraction force, you face a choice. Probably the question is something like: "Are we going to be lovers, or not?" If this question comes with passionate excitement, sit back and take a deep breath—you are about to embark on a journey to a deeper place. Since somebody else is almost certainly involved, it means you are asked to face the unknown, to trust love and risk losing yourself in another.

The thing to remember about "the power of sexual surrender" is that you give yourself up to the Goddess—not to some other human being. Yes, you feel attracted to this person, and yes, you want to merge with him or her. But the yielding required of you as you leap into space together is a surrender to the divine force of love itself. The energy is transpersonal—that is, it is greater than either of your two personalities. It is not even the particular lover who counts, but the act of loving itself.

This is not to suggest that you needn't love your partner. On the contrary, sex works much better if you do. When you engage in "casual sex" with someone you don't like, it hurts your heart. Likewise, scripts involving violence or victimization serve only to deepen the gulf between you and your higher Self, and between you and the divine spirit of the universe. You may "get off" on rape or dominance fantasies, but they deaden your ability to really feel. The sensations will be temporary, and the long-term emotional pain hardly worth the momentary zing.

Anytime your ego dominates a sexual interaction, it will stay at the physical-mental levels; this is okay, but ultimately it is less than satisfying. When your heart opens, you'll feel a rush of "higher" force lifting you out of the usual mental set and into a more spacious environment. Whereas the ego wants to control everything, based on ideas and the dominance of one partner, the heart wants the two-in-one of absolute union—the bliss of universal oneness in which all your cells pulsate together. Yearning again and again, you return to the Garden each time you and your lover meet on sacred ground. You reenact the essential spiritual drama—that all life is really One in spirit, linked in love.

CHAPTER 9

CHARIOT

Winning One's Own Way

The Chariot represents the winner of a victory, a triumphant Amazon warrior. Whereas the Lovers image was about merging and union—the two-in-one of the sacred marriage—the Chariot represents the independent thought and action of the Virgin, one who can move out of relationship and into work. The charioteer is the Greek Athene, Goddess of wisdom, who, according to Robert Graves, came from Lake Triton in Libya. Originally, "before her monstrous rebirth from Father Zeus's head," she was the Libyan Triple Goddess Neith. Neith, who some scholars think is the oldest Goddess in the world, was Goddess of the upper heavens and is the same as the Egyptian Sky-Goddess Nut, pictured in the Motherpeace image.

Neith also, like the Greek Athene, calls up the light or the dawn (*Ahana* in Sanskrit) and represents the intellectual light of the mind. She later became the Goddess of wisdom, again like Athene. In this respect, she is the same as the Indian Goddess Ushas whose name means to dawn, to awake, or to know. A Vedic hymn to Ushas says: "This auspicious Ushas has harnessed her vehicles from afar, above the rising of the sun, and she comes gloriously upon men with a hundred chariots."

Nut's body across the top of the Motherpeace image represents the night sky and contains thirteen stars, linking her with the moon and the lunar number thirteen. The crab—in astrology the emblem of Cancer, the cardinal water sign—links the Chariot to the High Priestess and to Artemis the Archer, ancestor of the Libyan Amazon driving the Chariot. The Amazon's bow and arrows reiterate this connection. The crab also

See color illustration on Plate 2 and on front cover.

symbolizes a kind of protective armor that the Amazon wears into battle, symbolic of the psychic protection afforded by the Moon Mother to her worshippers.

Amazons are frequently portrayed in Greek and Roman art of the classical periods and are generally considered to be fictional. However, Herodotus and others wrote of the presence of real Amazons during the transitional period between matriarchal and patriarchal worlds. The Amazons seem to be fighters, who took up arms, and who are frequently portrayed as valiant archers and warriors living apart from men in all-female tribes. Many of these stories of Amazons relate to northern Africa and especially Libya, but it is also true that earlier all of Africa was known as Libya. Amazons may have been more widespread than has been thought.

Phyllis Chesler calls the Amazons the "Universal Male Nightmare," and says that, at one time, Amazons existed on every continent. Acknowledging that the mother-daughter bond was at the heart of matriarchal society, she calls the Amazon the Daughter—as Artemis is the daughter—and refers to her existence as a rebellion against both matriarchal and patriarchal power. The daughter rejected pregnancy and motherhood and its confines as much as she rebelled against being dominated by men. Many modern lesbian-feminist women identify with the Amazon figure, the archetypal presence of Athene, or as she was later called, Pallas Athene.

Traditionally Pallas Athene, as her two names suggest, personifies two sides to her character. Pallas suggests her function as Goddess of storms (she carries the storm-shield of her father) and Goddess of battle. As Murray puts it, she was "valiant, conquering, frightening with the sight of her aegis whole crowds of heroes when they vexed her." But the other side of her character is soft, gentle, and heavenly; she presides over battles not for the sake of blood, like her counterpart Ares, the god of war, but for the sake of victory, peace, and prosperity.

Athene, like Neith, instructs mankind in "all that brings beauty to human life, in wisdom and art." Murray sees her as a "divine personification of mind, always unfettered in its movements." In peacetime, she is always the Goddess of skills and handicrafts—weaving, spinning, and embroidery—of "clearness like that of the sky, and of mental activity." She is the Goddess of healing art, as well as of "taming horses, of bridling and yoking them to the war-chariot." She is later the Roman Minerva, also a warrior Goddess of wisdom and "serious thought," as well as the protectress of art and industry.

Christine Downing's chapter on Pallas Athene in *The Goddess* is the best I've found, both in its complexity and intelligence—marks of Athene herself. Downing sees Athene as the prototype of the artistically creative woman who calls into question "the alternating pull of work and relationships, friendships and solitude, ego and soul, femininity and creativity." Unlike traditional views of Athene as completely cut off from women and from her own female self, Downing finds in her a deeper character—androgynous, at ease with men as well as women and virginal (unto herself) with both. She is the active "anima" figure who imparts soul into pieces of work, and who embodies in herself the quality of spirit—cool, detached, even aloof.

For Downing, Athene represents the way our creativity is "released, distorted, and inhibited by the power of the father—not primarily his outward power but his power in our own imagination." She is "Zeus's inspired daughter," but as Downing points out, chronologically she predates him. Downing, like Chesler, emphasizes that Athene is not a mother, but a daughter in character, "not a goddess of procreation, but of creation . . . the worker, the maker, and as such connected to soul, to soul-work." In particular, Athene seeks to express soul outwardly. Thus she is "the goddess most identified with the work of civilization, the work that makes us human." Yet her daughterhood—her virginity—differs from that of the untameable Artemis of the Wild. "Athene is not a virgin in order to be alone, but in order to be with others without entanglement. She represents a 'being with' that fosters mutual creativity that is based on soul and spirit rather than on instinct and passion."

Like the Chariot, Pallas Athene directs her will from a strong, central self—balanced and whole. This center is represented by the double-headed axe she holds in her right (active) hand, symbol of matriarchal power and a balanced *yin-yang* personality. A symbol also of the sun, the axe itself was worshipped, much as spears were in some cultures. In this context, the axe represents the ruler of the universe, and the Charioteer is definitely the ruler of her own universe. She has taken control of her life and can handle her "vehicle" or personality.

The number of the Chariot, Seven, is usually considered a sacred, mystical number, embodying a sense of completion and accomplishment, as in the magical seven planets of the ancients and the seven notes of the musical scale. To the Pythagoreans, as Graves tells us, seven was the "letter of female enchantment" and belonged to Athene. There are seven *chakras* in the Hindu system of energy and psychic work, and the Chariot represents a balance in and control over the energy system. Seven is ruled by Saturn, the planet of caution and tests, limitation, and discipline. In an account given by Sybil Leek, Saturn teaches patience and restraint, "applying the brake on our lives" so that we can assess situations.

On the Charioteer's shield is the head of Medusa the Gorgon Queen with her snake-hair, her eyes wide, and her tongue sticking out. Graves says the Argives described Medusa as "a beautiful Libyan queen decapitated by their ancestor Perseus after a battle with her armies," and identifies her with the Libyan Snake Goddess Lamia or Neith. The Gorgon's head is "merely an ugly mask assumed by priestesses on ceremonial occasions to frighten away trespassers," another reference to the secrecy necessary for the magical work she is about to undertake. The red face on the mask links her to Kali as well. Graves links Perseus "the destroyer" to the first wave of Achaeans who broke the power of the Argive Triple Goddess. Although in later mythology Athene is said to have helped Perseus destroy Medusa, in earlier times she was one and the same with her. As Downing explains, Medusa was at first "merely the double of Athene herself, personifying the darker side of her character . . . her shadow side."

In the Motherpeace image, the goats pulling the Chariot are a hybrid animal, winged, mythical, two-in-one. They, like the stag, are an animal of Artemis, Lady of the Beasts, and represent the early domestication of animals by women, which both Athene and Artemis represent. One goat looks up, the other down, symbolizing the occult dictum: "As above, so below." They link within themselves the earth and sky, and in this way reiterate Athene's qualities of balance and integration.

Across the sharp division between the earth and sky seen in the landscape—green (new growth) and the sky-blue (spiritual presence)—the tree of life stands joining them together, just as the human being links the visible and invisible worlds of physical matter and spiritual entities. What the Charioteer learns as Adept or Initiate is that duality is only illusion, the way things seem to be.

The Chariot represents groundedness and the ability to accomplish tasks on the physical plane. It also traditionally symbolizes a victory of self-discipline. When you get the Chariot in a reading, you may find that your mind has achieved greater control over the unconscious parts of yourself. This control is not prohibitive and stiff, like that of the Emperor, but involves bringing unconscious contents to the surface of consciousness for the purpose of accomplishment. In this work, you may act like the kind of warrior whom Carlos Castaneda describes, the one who confronts monsters and turns them into allies.

Although you may be in relationship to someone else, rather than solitary like the Crone or Hermit described in Chapter 11, you are autonomous in the way you relate and are in no way dominated. You do not lose yourself to another, nor do you lose power to someone else. You relate from a position of strength and independence. You have under your control the attraction force of the Lovers image described in Chapter 8, having already yielded to it in the past. Now your mind turns to work—what is central and important to you in terms of creativity and output. Whatever you need to do to accomplish your goals, you do; you set your mind to the task and focus until it is accomplished. It is important, then, to be sure your goals are positive and that you don't ride roughshod over another.

You are not necessarily cut off from your emotions, but you may not be focused on them at this time, and you might not pay attention even if they call. You may think that the feeling realm would be a distraction from the work you need to do, and you may therefore choose to stay away from it for a while. This will be okay, as long as you don't pretend the feelings are not there. Sometimes it takes a firm will to push ahead on a difficult task and, like Downing's Athene, you may feel emotional involvement to be "entanglement." Whatever your goal, your focus will pay off.

However, if you carry the tools of the warrior—axe, shield, and protective armor—into matters of relationship, you will no doubt run into trouble, for love generally requires a softer approach. But if it is creative or artistic work you are doing, then calling in the Goddess of wisdom will aid you immeasurably. This is a time in which you are keeping a strong division between your work life and your feelings, but you have the ability to bridge the gap and connect the two.

The Chariot belongs to the activist—whether you are engaged in struggle against the nuclear arms race or some other manifestation of patriarchal destructiveness. When Athene battled Poseidon for rulership of Athens, she was able to cause an olive tree to grow from barren rock. The olive tree is the symbol of peace. Like Athene, it may be your task to help peace take root in a hard place. The Chariot suggests you can do it, so go ahead and try. You have leadership abilities at this time, as well as courage and a strong will. You can harness the energies you need to accomplish your task, just as the goats are harnessed and ready to move in the Motherpeace image.

CHAPTER 10

JUSTICE

Setting Things Right

Justice represents the laws of Nature, as well as the relentless workings of Fate—the slow, regular turning of the Wheel of Karma. In the words of Ecclesiastes, "To everything there is a season, and a time to every purpose under heaven." In the Motherpeace image, Justice suggests the connections among people and animals and trees, connections that once came automatically. As Jane Roberts explains, "each natural element had its own key system that interlocked with others, forming channels through which consciousness could flow from one kind of life to another." A person understood herself to "be a separate entity, but one that was connected to all of nature." When this kind of connectedness was broken by the overdevelopment of the ego, it became necessary to formulate a system of "ethics" that would summarize what people once knew without the need of words or concepts. "Initially language had nothing to do with words and indeed verbal language emerged only when man had lost a portion of his love, forgotten some of his identification with nature, so that he no longer understood its voice to be his also."

The figures in the image are the three Fates in their Scandanavian aspect as the Norns or Nornen, the "spinners" who hold the threads of destiny in their hands. In the words of Neumann, "they spin the thread, tear it off, and determine what is to come." Standing under the sacred ash tree (called the Yggdrasil), they dispense the Justice of the Triple Goddess. They speak the "language of love" and can easily identify with the various forms of nature to whom they speak. Words are not necessary, for the Fates enjoy a direct cognition of "the other." Most powerful of all the Norse deities, the Norns pronounce destiny over all (even the gods); and no one can undo their blessings or their curses. (Fairies who

71

Justice (VIII)

bless and curse newborn children in fairy tales like "Sleeping Beauty" are a late version of the Fates.)

From the roots of the great ash tree spring fountains and wells from which the Norns draw the water they use for sprinkling the Tree of Life, which Newmann calls "the place of conception, growth, birth." They are the old wise women, "learned in the old customs, the ancient precepts of right and wrong." Rather than viewing each expression of nature as an "object," the women participate in the total reality around them. One touches an animal, and through that touching, becomes the animal enough to feel its truth and its life. Another touches the tree with one hand and water with the other, bringing them together for nourishment and harmony, balancing between the two and becoming one with them. The third sits quietly and enters into the still reality of a crystal, nature's most perfect form, seeing herself and the future within its clear facets. All of these activities are ways of "knowing" without needing to conceptualize. "The emotional reaches of one's subjective life, then, leapt far beyond what you think of as private experience," says Roberts. With this knowing, one would naturally not casually kill an animal, cut a tree, or pollute a river, since to do so would be to hurt oneself.

The Greeks called this concept of connectedness *Themis*, and saw it as an abstract principle of Law and Justice. Jane Ellen Harrison traces Themis back to her origins as the daughter of the Earth Goddess, Gaia, "the oracular power of the earth itself." The first "ordinances" were prophecies, divine oracular decrees by the priestesses—utterances that later would become codified by someone like the Hierophant discussed in Chapter 7. As the daughter of Gaia, Themis was "earth-goddess with an unshakable power," the power of absolute "steadfast" law.

Modern Hopi Indians believe that, in both the natural and the supernatural worlds, there is a fixed order and life is cyclical. Like the ancient Egyptians, they understand that we must remain in harmony with this universal order and maintain it with our blessings and rituals. If harmony lapses, then life will not "progress smoothly" and humanity will not prosper. Then, says Patricia Broder, "they must recognize their errors and restore order as quickly as possible." This is "karmic adjustment"—if something has gone wrong, it must be made right, immediately.

When all of humankind was still "under the sway of Themis, of the collective conscience," this obligation was "so utterly dominant," in the view of Harrison, that people were "scarcely conscious of it." However, as the hold of the group slackened, the field of religion "is bit by bit narrowed" to "the god as individual." By Homer's time, Themis had come to represent social contracts among people. While the male godhead was becoming the powerful deity, she had become an abstraction. The Greek Themis, like the Egyptian Maat, held a pair of scales for weighing the truth of situations; but Themis also carried a cornucopia, her connection to Gaia. She was the mother of the seasons, who, like the Norns, "determined the proper moment for the fruitful earth's budding and exhaustion, proper times as well for human events."

The Egyptian Goddess Maat also went from Goddess of wisdom to an abstract principle of wisdom: Inner Truth. Maat, too, carried scales for weighing hearts of the deceased to decide whether they could go on to the afterlife or had to "undo the errors of the recent lifetime." Ann Forfreedom describes the way that the Egyptian people ascribed to the "principle of Maat," wherein if things weren't working right, people felt a right of redress. Peasants there created the first general strike in history when they didn't have enough food, considering it "divine will" that the situation be corrected.

An aspect of Themis is Nemesis—Goddess of divine vengeance, who turns the wheel of retribution and makes whatever adjustments are necessary to set things right again. We experience Fate in our lives when it seems to step in and cause certain events to take place that "punish" us for our wrongdoings. Occult science and astrology teach that the universe moves in cycles, some of them very long as compared to our human lifetimes. Most religious traditions contain some sort of "revelation" concerning the end of the current world cycle and its meaning for our lives.

The prophecies of the Hopi and the Tibetans, as well as the biblical revelations, all agree that "man" will go too far and the earth may be destroyed as a result of selfish and willful actions. Most of them similarly agree that this has happened before.

In Tarot tradition, however, the Justice card belongs to Libra, cardinal air sign of social justice and balance, symbolized by the scales. Libra is ruled by Venus (Goddess of love) and considers everything in terms of its relation to others. Libra loves beauty and harmony, and wants to bring the world to a peaceful coexistence. In this way, Libra is Themis—the cords that draw the human race together, and the urge to connect each of us with the all. A blessing on a single one of Earth's children blesses all; a curse on one hurts us all.

When you get the Justice card in a reading, you are coming to consciousness about your place in the universal scheme of things. Perhaps you are in telepathic contact with other people or life forms at this time, maybe you can feel the whole earth speaking. Like the tree in the Motherpeace image, you may be especially close to the earth right now, grounded and rooted in her wisdom. Listen for the oracle, sign, or omen that will guide you to the next stage of growth. You feel a sense of connection, ancient in its power, with whatever lives.

There is some way you can feel karma working in your life. Maybe you are winning a lawsuit or custody case; maybe you're moving into a new position or career, or have some new sense of yourself as powerful and moving through life with purpose. Like the women quietly listening and communing beneath the tree, you may feel a particularly strong sense of equilibrium at this time. Perhaps some conflict in your life has come to a resolution, or things have worked out after a period of imbalance. Things are setting themselves right again, and you can feel your own peace returning as a result of this adjustment. You may feel like breathing a sigh of relief knowing the struggle is, in some sense, over for the moment.

You are moving to accept your reality and responsibility for your past choices. You may feel more mature than usual, at home with your decisions, blessed by a self-confidence that is wired to the universal will. You are flowing with the natural cycles of life, following natural laws. Whatever you have been waiting for is about to materialize, what you have needed is taking place. You understand that what is happening is based on past actions that have karmic results.

If you don't feel entirely at ease with your situation at the moment, then ask yourself what seems to be out of balance. If you have made a mistake with consequences that are manifesting now, then forgive yourself and go on. This is a lesson for you to be guided by. If someone has hurt you or things seem unfair, let go of the hurt and let Justice prevail. Once you accept your fate and understand what brought it about, any dis-ease will flow away and you will feel at-one-ment again.

Sometimes the balancing that nature provides for us doesn't feel so good to our personality selves. Maybe you've been ignoring your responsibility in some area, and suddenly this is brought home to your consciousness somehow. Maybe you have a deadline on a project you haven't completed, and suddenly you must work overtime to finish it. Or perhaps you haven't spent enough time alone with yourself and nature, quiet, reflective, and self-nurturing, so you get sick. Nature works in calm, quiet ways, giving us what we need rather than what we want sometimes. The Justice card means you can tune into the "rightness" of your situation if you make the effort to understand it fully.

CHAPTER 11

CRONE

Turning Within

The Crone is the old wise woman who watches over our dreams and visions, who whispers secrets to our inner ears. As Nor Hall puts it, "the old woman, who is regarded as the teacher of 'song, story, and spindle,' is Wisdom herself, spinning and weaving the thread of life." The Crone is the Hag who knows how to call down the power of the moon, to converse with spirits and work magical spells. She is Hekate, Greek goddess of the underworld and mother of the witches, who predated Olympian gods and probably originated in Thrace, a province known for its magic. "Hekate, Daughter of Night—the dark of the moon who dwells in caves, walked the highways, stood threefold at the crossroads, and made love on the vast seas—was the force that moved the moon."

As Hekate is the dark of the moon, the waxing moon is Artemis. Hall sees Artemis-Hekate as a split figure, whom she calls "the medial woman." What is her function? To assist people who are no longer where they were and not yet where they hope to go. "As midwife to the psyche she is constellated in 'emergency' situations where a spirit, a song, an alternative, a new being is emerging—whenever things appear to rise spontaneously from the depths of the unconscious."

Initiate, seeker, and hermit, the Crone represents a stage of life in which wisdom is sought—a time of introversion and spiritual seeking. "The initiation is an active entry into the dark terrain of an unknown self where we still search for the lost daughter, the feminine source of life."

Biologically, the Crone represents the menopausal phase of a woman's life, where she can begin to think seriously of spiritual meaning,

See color illustration on Plate 3.

and embark on a quest that had previously been out of reach if she was engaged in the usual female functions of childbearing and rearing. As the initiate, she represents any period of turning to inner questions. "To be an initiate is to swaddle yourself against the world for a while, to be a candidate (dressed in pure white) for an entirely new experience of spiritual significance."

The Crone represents a spirit friend who knows her way in the spirit realms. "Lamplighter" of the dream world, she signifies a turning away from the external, social space of people and parties in favor of the inner, darker realm of the unconscious psyche. Like the Vestal Virgins in Roman times, she walks along the way barefooted, a pilgrim, radiating humility and inner strength. Vesta (or Hestia), Goddess of the Hearth, was a sister of Demeter and, like Artemis, obtained from Zeus permission to remain single—virgin—all her life. Unlike most Roman women, vestal virgins were, Murray explains, "inviolable, free from paternal control, and had the right of disposing of their own property." The Crone is related to Vesta in other ways: she has gained control of the sacred fire. In ancient Rome, the vestal virgins kept the sacred fire going at the city hearth. The Crone keeps the inner fire burning.

Like accomplished shamans and wise women everywhere, the Crone contains both male and female, active and receptive, sun and moon within her. She has learned the power of energy retention and transmutation —she can choose how to spend or store her energies. In the words of Hall, "introversion is the turning in of psychic energy, the sinking of libido into its own depths." The Crone is probably celibate, but not necessarily sexually inactive—just temporarily without a partner, possibly by choice. She represents a "time-out" in relationships, and a turning inward that will heal and rejuvenate her.

The Crone is the spinster, the creative spider-woman who weaves the world from her own substance. "Weaving a cocoon out of the substance of one's own life is the necessary prerequisite for the emergence of psyche: in withdrawing we prepare a way out." Part of the process of weaving the future depends on divining what lies ahead (as well as what lay in the past). The Crone is the soothsayer, the "conversation woman" or "spaewife" who wore hooded garments and traveled around foretelling the future. As the divinities "diminished in grandeur and power in the eyes of men," says Hall, "the medial powers of the old hooded wise women were repressed and came out in twisted and tortured forms of witchcraft and sorcery."

Thus we arrive at Hekate's bad name and the maligning of witchcraft in general as a dark, "black" art. But going down into the unconscious and coming back out again are necessary, vital parts of the soul's search for meaning, which is what the Crone and her nighttime skills of divining and foretelling the future represents. "Out of the dark wait and expectation comes the birth moment . . . the song, prophesy, or poem is always a breakthrough." As Queen of the Dead, Hekate was ruler of regeneration. It was Hekate to whom the ancients prayed for protection and long life, since it was she who controlled both life and death. Hekate's holyday is Hallomas or All Hallows Eve (Hallo-een), October 31st, when the spirits of the dead are said to walk the earth and the boundaries blur between life and death. As mother of the witches, Hekate represents magic and the working of spells for good or ill. In some circles Halloween is recognized as the Witches' New Year.

According to Monaghan, "While Hecate walked outdoors, her worshippers gathered inside to eat Hecate suppers in her honor, gatherings at which magical knowledge was shared and the secrets of sorcery whispered." In another sense, "Hekate suppers" were ritually prepared food that was often left at crossroads, particularly at places where three roads came together. Murray tells us that worshipers would arrange a statue of Hekate "so that she could look down all three roads at once." In many traditions, Hekate has three heads herself or a hound with three heads as her mascot.

The statue in the Motherpeace image is based upon a pre-Columbian terracotta from Veracruz, Mexico, her arms raised in the traditional priestess posture. In her arms the goddess of the night-sky carries a waxing moon (promise of rebirth and the end of a dark period) and the wishing star as she flies across the sky. The staff on which the Crone leans is the "distaff" or spinster's pole, representing the female maternal line (as opposed to the paternal spear). The wind whistles secrets to the Crone and she listens carefully for messages from the realm of unseen, invisible powers. Wind is *pneuma*, spirit, breath, and signifies a moving energy with insight.

The purple cloak of the Crone represents her authentic power, the ability to heal herself and project healing power to others. Through "having to complete nearly impossible tasks," the Crone earns her healing power. "Turning away from a world to discover whether you are really alive is unquestionably painful," says Hall. "But it is in the conscious acceptance of loneliness—when there is nothing else to do—that a natural process of healing occurs."

Mary Daly gives a subtle, energetic account of Crones, Hags, Spinsters, and spiders. In her rich sense of the word, the Crone represents the archetypal "separatist" who pares "all that is alienating and confining" away from the self. "Crone-logically prior to all discussion of political separatism from or within groups is the basic task of paring away the layers of false selves from the Self," says Daly. "Paring away, burning away the false selves encasing the Self, is the core of all authentic separations and thus is normative for all personal/political decisions about acts/ forms of separatism."

Daly defines the activity of spinning as a form of "creative boundary living," which women in Patriarchy desparately need to do in order to escape from the victimization so prevalent and enter into a new landscape of integrity. "In essence," says Daly, "the Spinster is a witch." Like the Crone of Motherpeace, she seeks transformation. Like a silkworm, she spins fibers around herself and later emerges as something new.

The Crone listens with the inner ear. "Hags hearing into the labyrinth beyond the foreground hear new voices—our own voices," says Daly. "We learn to sense our own new position and motion; we learn delicate balance." What distance do we travel? "From the entrance of the labyrinth deeper into the center of the homeland, of the Self." Through this inner listening, the Crone becomes not only an initiate, but also a teacher, a way-shower to others. "As she travels, she makes her knowledge visible. To other Spinners, her Network is a paradigm of creation. To her enemies it is a lethal trap."

What the Spinner, Hag, or Crone is hearing is not "the Word" but rather a "hearing forth" of new words:

We hear the call of our wild. We play games to end their games. Those who have been called bitches bark; pussies purr; cows moo; old bats squeal; squirrels chatter; nags whinny; chicks chirp; cats growl; old crows screech. Foxy ladies chase clucking biddies around in circles. The play is part of our work of unweaving and of our weaving work. It whirls us into another frame of reference. We use the visitation of demons to come more deeply into touch with our own powers/virtues. Unweaving their deceptions, we name our Truth.

Nine, the Crone's number, always symbolizes wisdom and a sense of sacred magic. Nine multiplied by any number reduces to nine (for example, nine times three is twenty-seven, which reduces to two plus seven, or nine.) In classical times, there were nine Muses, and nine is the sacred number of the Moon Goddess, signifying culmination and wholeness. The Crone is a woman whole within herself, an example to all of us of what it means to be more than female, more than male. Her active inner life shines out to touch others with the wisdom and knowledge she gains on her journey. Eventually she may re-emerge into the world once more, but for now she has retreated into herself for the joyous experience of gathering her energies and restoring herself.

When you get the Crone in a reading, it almost certainly means a time of solitude. Usually this inner time comes as a blessing, but at first you may feel a sense of loneliness. Mostly this comes from enculturation, which tells you that it's bad to be alone. If you can relax and enjoy this opportunity, you will gain from time spent in self-study. Learning to hear with the inner ear can be frightening at first, since the messages you get probably won't match up with what you've been taught. Hekate is a great truth-teller (soothsayer) and once you are in contact with her, your own truths will begin to surface.

You are at a crossroads, a time of decision and renewal. Hekate takes you down into the unconscious and guides you through it, showing you where your troubles are and offering choices and possibilities you may never have previously dreamed of. Sometimes this experience comes at around the age of twenty-eight or twenty-nine, when a person experiences what astrologers call her "Saturn return." Like Hekate, Saturn is the great tester, the task-master, forcing a person to get serious about her life.

It is time to learn about the magic and healing powers of divination and prophesy, maybe to use the Tarot or *I Ching*, maybe to keep a dream journal. Your healing skills may be developing, so be aware of new sensitivities in yourself, messages from your body about nutrition and natural medicine. You may be influenced by the Moon in a noticeable way, so tune in to Her cycle of waxing, full, and waning. You may come into contact with a teacher or guide, either on the spiritual plane or in the "real" world.

Sexually, you will probably experience a partnerless period, which you have the power to enjoy and profit from if you stay open to your body and its energies. Celibacy does not mean "no sex". You may wish to take yourself as a lover as seriously as you have ever felt about anyone else. Learn what you like and how you like to be loved, and you will eventually know exactly what you want in relationship. You will come to it whole, instead of needy; energized, instead of drained.

CHAPTER 12

WHEEL OF FORTUNE

Going the Great Round

Tarot historians believe the word Tarot itself derives from the Latin word *rota*, as in "rotation," and reflects the ancient sense of life as a moving wheel. At the hub is the still axle, but elsewhere the wheel is always cycling through external events. In particular, the Wheel of Fortune is identified with the zodiac. More than in any other chapter, therefore, we here describe the Goddess in terms of astrology; and in order to sketch the rich round of symbols, we allow more space than for any of the other Major Arcana.

From ancient Egypt, we have the famous round zodiac of Denderah, found on the ceiling in the Temple of Hathor. This zodiac was a late rendition (300 B.C.) of a design from a much more ancient temple on the same site that was destroyed. Its purpose was to organize and record astrological data, which Fix calls "the product of a long and careful observation." Fix posits that this zodiac, like many such monuments, was oriented around the circumpolar stars (Great Bear, Dragon, and Little Bear) and that "whatever took place inside the pyramids had something to do with the circumpolar stars." What took place there? Perhaps a version of the great mysteries celebrated by ancient paleolithic cave dwellers and African rock artists. Even today, the Dogon people in Africa still celebrate and revere the secret wisdom contained in a sort of code in ancient star maps.

In Denderah, the mysteries were enacted in the Temple under the wheel of Hathor. The images on this zodiac were pictures of the stars, maps of magical flight and shaman travel. In trance, the ancient Egyp-

See color illustration on Plate 3.

tians traveled to the "death realms" while alive, and lived to tell about it. Upon returning, they could provide information in the way of symbols and images that would help the next initiate go safely on the journey to the stars and back. In my view, what these initiates did is similar to the psychic travel of the headless women on early cave walls, or of shamans around the world.

The Wheel also represents the calendar wheels and stone circles found at many places in the world. The calendar was originally a lunar clock, which eventually came to include solar cycles as well. Stonehenge is a good example of assimilation of the two, the Druids having apparently brought together the old religion of the Mother and the newer religion of the Father and combined them in a fairly friendly way (unlike so many places where the transition was ruthless).

In the Motherpeace image, the Wheel of Fortune pictures the zodiac as it is presented in an astrological "natal" chart with twelve "houses" ruled by the various "signs." Each house contains an illustration from an ancient Goddess-worshipping culture. In this chapter we examine the dozen illustrations in turn, starting with the woman against a red background on the left and moving counterclockwise.

The first house is Aries, cardinal fire sign. The woman with her hand on her hip is a copper figurine found at Mohenjo-Daro, India (dated between 2400 and 2000 B.C.). Art historians generally refer to her as a "dancing girl" (sometimes "slave girl"), but I have seen her more accurately portrayed as a "divine *yogini*," which places her as a teacher of the sexual mysteries and makes her a representative of the ancient Tantric religion of India. In India today, it is still considered auspicious to get this teaching from an authentic priestess of the Goddess, a guru who is skilled in the magical arts of Tantra and can lead the Initiate along the path of surrender and transcendence that she represents. Although Kali has been distorted into a Terrible Mother archetype who devours or represents physical killing, she actually represents death of the ego and the regenerative power of the sexual mysteries.

House two is Taurus, fixed earth sign of the bull. A striking image of male potency, the bull in ancient times could also call to mind the fertilizing aspect of the Goddess, who included all aspects of sexuality. In the Motherpeace image, the woman is shown fertilizing the community by giving birth. All over the ancient world, the female is pictured in the act of giving birth, her fertility praised and revered. This particular image is pre-Columbian—similar to the well-known Aztec Earth Mother, Tlozolteutl, shown in the birth-giving posture with her teeth gritted in labor.

A lovely pre-Columbian statue from the earliest levels of excavation in Mexico shows a female squatting and pushing down on her large belly, as if helping herself to give birth. A similar squatting figure comes from the Belgian Congo and shows an African woman with her hands pushing down on her very ripe belly. On a wall in Chaco Canyon, New Mexico, I personally saw a series of four petroglyphs of a mother in the process of giving birth. Clearly this image is full of "numinous" power the world over. Judy Chicago observes, in connection with her latest artistic endeavor, "The Birth Project," that images of birthing women are notably absent from Western art. She wryly suggests that if men gave birth, there would be thousands of images of "the crowning," the moment of emergence from the birth canal.

Near the bottom of the wheel, the third house belongs to Gemini, air sign of the Twins, representing the brain with its right and left lobes and the duality present in all things perceived by the human mind. The figurine here is an "eye idol," a variation on the squatting mother image of the Fertile Goddess. Whereas Old Stone Age figures of the squatting Goddess lacked distinct facial features, in the Neolithic (agricultural) period the eye motif began to appear. This particular example is one of hundreds of figures found in the "eye temple" of Tel Brak in eastern Syria (about 3500 B.C.).

Some examples of the "eye goddess" in Spain from the Neolithic period contain eyes in the abstract, carved on bones and pots. A famous gate at Malta is carved with spiral eyes. So is the stone door to the Neolithic burial chamber at New Grange, Ireland. In Egypt, the eyes of Horus represent the sun and moon, and the single eye—*uzait*—is a potent symbol frequently represented there even today. A Sumerian seal stone from the third millennium B.C. links the eye Goddess motif to Ishtar, the Sumerian-Babylonian Great Mother.

Fourth house of the zodiac is Cancer, cardinal water sign of the Great Mother in the form of nourisher, giver of life and love. This statue, holding her breasts, offers the gift of mother's milk. In the Motherpeace image this figure is inspired by a clay figure from Susa (now Iraq) in the third millennium B.C. Similar figures have reached us from Cyprus and Mesopotamia (twenty-fourth century B.C.) and from Crete (2000 to 1200 B.C.). From the city of Ur, around 3000 B.C., comes a terracotta statue of the Goddess holding her breasts.

Oftentimes the Mother is shown offering her breast to a child, as in Isis and Horus statues from Egypt or pre-Columbian effigy pots found in the Americas. Esoterically, the transformation mystery portrayed by these figurines refers to the nectar secreted by the female breasts during Tantric sexual practices—a secretion recognized as imparting healing powers through its subtle essence, which her partner can literally taste during lovemaking.

Fifth house is Leo, fixed fire sign of the sun and house of creative powers. Against an orange background, a pre-Columbian figure is portrayed with a sun radiating warmth from her belly. Thought to be a precursor of the later Mayan "sun cult," she emphasizes the female sexual-generative power. I consider this statue a Shakti image, so many of which have been found in India, and which represent the fiery female creative power, shifting and changing, dancing like the eternal dance of life itself. In the Indian cosmology, Shakti is the female active power (projected from the mind of the male god-head).

In some forms of yoga, this Shakti energy is encouraged to find union with its opposite Shiva energy, creating ecstasy and balance through sexual union—a marriage of head and heart. In other schools of yoga, the sexual energy is deliberately harnessed and "transmuted" or raised into the higher centers, for use in creative or spiritual work.

Sixth house is Virgo, mutable earth sign of the Virgin—not in the restricted sense of "chaste" or "having a hymen intact," but in the ancient sense of the word: a woman who is autonomous, sexually and emotionally free, whole and self-contained. The female figure portrayed in this house is taken from a fresco in the Egyptian palace at Thebes from the Eighteenth Dynasty. The fresco, like the later Cretan frescos at the palace of Knossos, shows women together celebrating their religious rites through ritual body movement and dance.

Although this figure, like the one used to illustrate Aries, is frequently described as a "dancing girl," she is doubtless an acrobatic priestess performing an ecstatic ritual in the tradition of the ancient Goddess religion. Rather than gyrating for the entertainment of men, as the modern title implies, she is worshipping in the exclusive company of women.

The earliest portrayals of women dancing are found in African and European cave paintings that date from at least as early as the Old Stone Age. In every culture where the Goddess is revered, women dance in ecstatic celebration of the sacred energy that can be felt and enjoyed in the body. As evidence we have, in addition to the dancing female figures pictured in the prologue, small terracotta figures of women dancing in a ring around a boy (Spain), around a male musician (Mexico), and the Goddess herself (Boetia). Later representations are found in Greek art of the Maenads—the wild dancing women of the Dionysus rituals.

All these figurines show women empowered by spirit, bringing about an integration between the physical body and that realm which is often considered to be removed from and "higher" than the body. The same religious paradigm that separates spirit (good) and body (bad) also tends to align spirit with male and body with female, creating the unfortunate hierarchy that characterizes Patriarchy all over the world. By the same token, the female archetype of "Virgin," which includes sexual and spiritual freedom, is split into the modern-day archetypes of "virgin" and "whore."

Against a violet background, the seventh house is inhabited by Libra, cardinal air sign. In the Motherpeace image she is Aphrodite on her white goose, taken from a Greek cup (470 B.C.). This image is a variant on the portrayal of the Goddess as a winged creature, half human and half bird, able to fly to the spirit realm. Artemis is frequently portrayed with wings and occasionally with birds alongside her. Some of the most beautiful versions of Isis show her winged and somewhat austere, as if slightly removed from earthly thoughts and immersed in the cool spiritual world of inspiration. This concept reaches into shamanism and the ability of the spirit body to journey to the "other world" and back again, gathering information, bringing the sacred back to earth, communicating with spirits. The English Mother Goose of children's nursery rhymes is a late derivative of this Aphrodite figure.

Eighth house is Scorpio, fixed water sign of the female warrior or healer, seen here as a Gorgon (a winged version, relating her to the previous figure). Widely connected to Amazons as well as to witchcraft, the Gorgon as Artemis is frequently flanked by beasts—lions, leopards, or birds—and as Isis, Hekate, or Medusa is connected with the snake. Gorgons and snakes are frequently attributed to the idea of the Terrible Mother, the Goddess in her destroyer aspect. Their main role, according to Graves, is to protect the secrecy of women who practice the ancient witchy arts of healing and magic. The Gorgon tongue sticking out of the mouth, as in many images of Kali, says "Stay away," and warns against intrusion on the part of those who are uninitiated.

Sagittarius rules the ninth house, portrayed here as another version of the "eye Goddess" in an elevated form as a divine bird, a very widespread and ancient way of expressing the power of the Goddess. This bird-headed Goddess, a Sumerian figure from the third millennium B.C., emphasizes the generative eye of the womb, reflecting unity of body and mind. In this figure, religious power comes together with physical or sexual powers. The Sumerian figure resembles many Hebrew and Canaanite "idols" of the Bible, the Goddess as Ishtar, Astarte, Anath, or Ashtoreth. She is frequently shown standing frontally holding flowers or plants, her *yoni* marked with distinctive lines forming a downward pointing triangle in her abdomen. Now and then she stands flanked with animals (particularly as Lilith, who later becomes a "demon"), which links her with the Lady of the Beasts, Artemis, and later Diana of the Witches.

Tenth house is Capricorn, cardinal earth sign, marked by the Tree of Life and flanked by the traditional twin beasts of Artemis. In this case the animals are goats representing the fertile, earthy aspect of the Goddess and her consort Pan, the hooved goat-god. The goat is probably the oldest beast of Artemis and points to women's early domestication of animals that gave milk for their essentially vegetarian diet. In some places, the goat (or antlered stag) alone is understood to represent Artemis or Diana of the Witches. The ancient goat Mother is the she-goat Amalthea.

The Tree of Life and the Tree of Knowledge in the Bible are late versions of earlier, more graphic forms of the Goddess. The "tree cult" of the Semites was a disguised worship of Asherah (Goddess who "shelters, protects, nourishes the animal world") in the form of great World Tree, not dissimilar to that of the Buddhist religion. It is possible to follow the worship of the Goddess from groves of her sacred trees to the biblical *Asherim* or pillar resembling a tree (which also symbolically resembles a sign for priestess). As the priestesses were persecuted for worshipping under the Old Religion, the religion itself went underground into more abstract symbolic forms, like the biblical Tree of Life. This motif surfaced again in the Middle Ages during the witch burnings as the Alchemical Tree, and is studied today as part of the Jewish Kaballah—the Tree of Life with its ten *sephira* or emanations.

Eleventh house of the zodiac is Aquarius, fixed air sign bringing light and love to the New Age, which we are now entering. The Goddess depicted against a yellow background is the "many-breasted Artemis of Ephesus" from the last millennium B.C. Originally one of the wonders of the world, this famous shrine of Artemis or Diana was founded by a tribe of Amazons when the matriarchal society went through its tumultuous effort to stay alive during the transitional period. Artemis of the Thousand Breasts was known in particular for her power of healing diseases, and people visited her religious shrine for many centuries.

The feeling in this particular version of the Artemis theme is unusual, compared to pictures of her as a strong warrior Goddess. This statue has a more nurturing quality that may remind us of the Chinese Kuan Yin, the Tibetan White Tara, or the Christian Virgin Mary, whose early title was "Many Breasted Mother of All." From Siberia to Greece, Artemis carried the theme of shamanism or the power of the female group. During the bloody transition, there seems to have been a splitting of her image in response to various forms of female enslavement. Although the fragmentation of the matriarchal cultures meant that the group no longer carried out its seasonal rituals as a community, still the worship continued for millennia, in secret caves, distant islands, and often at "patron" healing shrines to which pilgrimages were made.

Twelfth house is Pisces, mutable water sign of the ancient Fish Goddesses, calling up images of the Moon and the later "foam-born Aphrodite," whose most famous temples were built by the sea. The Motherpeace image is a mermaid, the "snake-legged Scythian Goddess," probably a version of Medusa. The mermaid motif is widespread in time and space. Graves links "mermaid" to "merry maid" (as the High Priestess of the Witches is sometimes called), to the Goddess of the Eleusinian Mysteries in Greece, and to the Moon-Goddess Euronome, the original Pelasgian Goddess of All Things, and likewise the Sumerian Nammu who created the whole cosmos ("She whose waters are all the universe").

Graves quotes a second-century mythographer who says that Artemis was "unsuccessfully pursued and finally escapes in fish form." I believe this myth refers to the escape made by priestesses of the Goddess and their tribes in ships that carried them out of the Mediterranean. There are stone inscriptions written by Libyans, Celts, Phoenicians, and Iberians in North and South America, singing praises to the Goddess and signed by her priestesses and priests. These inscriptions date from prehistoric times, long before Columbus "discovered" America.

From the Elamite fish-tailed Goddess figurine (third millennium B.C.) to the Exeter Cathedral carving of a mermaid in Britain and the pictoglyphs of sailing ships on the walls of Chaco Canyon, New Mexico, the ancient Sea Goddesses have left their mark. "The original Mother, she who created all the universe, was always a body of water . . . the original amniotic fluid that once bathed all the surface of the earth."

One of the earliest Wheels of Fortune was inscribed with these words: "The Tarot speaks the Law of Hathor." Hathor, the Egyptian Goddess of change, evolved from the earlier Mother Goddess Isis, one of whose symbols was the Wheel. The circle itself, of course, is an ancient symbol of the female, symbolizing wholeness.

Robert Graves connects the Wheel with the Celtic Goddess Arionhod and her silver wheel, representing the in-and-out maze of death and rebirth, and the ancient revolving doorway between this world and that one. Celtic inscriptions of this double spiral, such as those at New Grange in Ireland (2500 B.C.), reflect this idea of the ever-turning Wheel of Life.

In Buddhist thought, the Wheel of Life is *Samsara*, the never-ending, going-nowhere wheel of illusion that represents the physical and emotional world of the senses. Buddhists believe the solution is to get off the wheel by transcending the physical and emotional worlds.

In contrast, Goddess religion suggests a coming to terms with the Wheel by reaching out for understanding of cause and effect, and by directing one's life accordingly. Fortuna (Goddess of good luck), Hathor, Isis—these are positive images of the Great World Mother who gives life, guides us toward wholeness, and welcomes us back at the close of life. She can be represented by Time, as if the Wheel of Fortune were a "clock of destiny" picturing the transformations that one can expect throughout the course of life. Goddess religion sees us not as prisoners on the Wheel—the Buddhist vision—but rather as participants in our Fate and movers through our individual and collective destiny.

When you get this card in a reading, it suggests your life is in the hands of the Fates—Fortune is smiling on you, and you may as well surrender to the flow, because something remarkable—a big event—is taking place. As if you were on a ferris wheel carrying you up to the top of the world, you are swept into prominence in some way. Although Fate does not in any sense control our lives, when something has been wished for and worked toward, it is the Goddess Fortuna who decides on the timing of the event. The Wheel of Fortune signifies a high point, a wish coming true, the manifestation of something anticipated.

The Motherpeace image emphasizes the cyclical nature of time and change, rather than focusing, as traditional Tarot has, on the "highs" and "lows" one might expect. Every point on the zodiacal wheel is positive and potentially "fortunate," each position having a particular meaning or impact for your life at any given time. Perhaps by meditating on the twelve houses and aspects of the Goddess presented in this chapter, you can locate your present position on the Wheel and gain a deeper insight into the transition you are presently undergoing. Likewise, you may wish to compare your astrological "chart" with the Motherpeace Wheel and make planetary correspondences.

CHAPTER 13

STRENGTH

Finding Magical Helpers

In Tarot tradition, the Strength card represents matriarchal conscious-ness and in contrast with the patriarchal dominance of the Emperor de-scribed in Chapter 6. The Strength embodied by this card represents mind-force, the strength of the woman-who-tames. She is the Lady of the Beasts, the Mother Goddess as both a friend of Nature and a civilizing force. In traditional Tarot decks, she opens or closes a lion's mouth; in the Crowley deck, she is "Lust" riding a lion and radiating the full female sex force. All the Great Goddesses are credited with bringing both sexuality (fire) and language (alphabets) to their people. This is true of Sarasvati in India, Ishtar in Mesopotamia, Isis in Egypt, and Brigit in the British Isles, to name only a few.

In the Motherpeace image, Strength is represented by the pre-Celtic Bride (Brigit), Queen of the land of Faery, sitting on the emerald mounds of Ireland with her animal friends and the unseen "little people" whom she represents. She was the Mother Goddess, the Quickening Triple Muse, whose holiday was (and is) celebrated in February—Candlemas, the Feast of the Flame. In Ireland, as Bride, she was worshipped by priestesses who tended her sacred flame, much as Roman Vestal Virgins kept the hearth-fire burning for the benefit of the city. After the advent of the Christian empire, Catholic nuns kept her flame going until the Middle Ages, when witches were burned all over Europe and the flame of Brigit was called "pagan" and snuffed. Today the flame of St. Bride burns once again in Kildare, Ireland.

In the Motherpeace image, the animals around the red-haired Irish

See color illustration on Plate 4.

"Banshee" express her many roles. The hare she touches with her right hand symbolizes the moon, the earth, and the power of the nighttime consciousness. In China, the hare is the Moon Goddess bringing fertility and health. The white rabbit of Alice in Wonderland represents mystery and magic, a land of unseen and fantastic spirit friends, the astral plane of the imagination. When Alice slips down the rabbit hole, she is practicing shamanism, whether she knows it or not. She falls into the other world, enters into trance, and experiences a magical journey of the psyche akin to shaman travel.

The coiled blue Indigo snake near the priestess represents her oracular power. A type handled by South American snake-charmers, this sinuous vertebrate also calls to mind the python of ancient Delphi as well as what yoga tradition calls "the coiled *kundalini*." When the Goddess Kundalini awakens in her secret place at the base of the spine, she rises up through the *chakras* or energy centers toward the head, activating the spiritual life. When the heart center opens, fire radiates out into the world, as it does from the left hand of the priestess in the Motherpeace image.

Snake Goddesses appeared all over the world. In Egypt, for example, the earliest hieroglyph for Goddess is the same as that for serpent—a raised cobra. In India, the Goddess is the sleeping Kundalini who becomes Shakti on awakening. In the pre-Celtic British Isles, Brigit or Bride was intimately connected with the serpent. When St. Patrick drove the "snakes" out of Ireland, for which we recognize St. Patrick's Day, it was the Goddess-people he was persecuting.

Despite the Catholic takeover, however, the fairy tradition has remained strong in Ireland and exists side-by-side with the church. As a result, Irish people, especially outside the cities, remain in touch with magic and the healing power of "the green." This magical power comes directly from the earth and her creatures, both worldly and otherworldly —those animals who live in the woods as well as the magical sprites and elves who live under the hills and crannogs.

The wolf, similar in many aspects to the dog and often substituted for it, represents Sirius, the "dog star," and the mysteries of the Triple Goddess. In the Motherpeace image, the steely gray wolf represents a twilight time between the worlds, the hour of the wolf, "when most people die, when sleep is deepest, when nightmares are most palpable, when ghosts and demons hold sway . . . when most children are born." In Tibet, the wolf attends a priestess of the famous Green Tara. Images of Tara were carved on rock walls in Tibet and, according to Stephan

Beyer, are considered to be "among the most potent protections for an individual, a dwelling, or an entire district."

Paintings of Tara for ritual use are done by the waxing moon and completed on the day of the full moon, "when the moon's power of increase is at its most potent." A Tibetan ritual describes Tara "seated in the posture of royal ease . . . and behind her is a halo of an undimmed full moon." The use of menstrual blood in Tibetan ritual is interesting in light of the connections between Tara and the Strength card. Tibetans believe, says Beyer, that "the easiest way in which a woman may subjugate a man and gain his love is to burn a cloth stained with her menstrual blood and to mix some of the ashes surreptitiously into the man's food or drink; or she may simply use a drop of her menstrual blood in the same way." In Tarot, the Strength card traditionally refers to the power to get what one wants through strength of mind and force of will.

Near the top of the Motherpeace image, a lion and bull sit on the mound under the oak tree. Like the snake and hare in the foreground, they indicate a blending of fire and earth. Artemis is frequently shown flanked by two beasts, and both the lion and bull have been sacred to the Goddess in ancient cultures. The roots of the tree extend down into the earth, visibly reaching between the feet of the two sacred animals, and the leafy branches reach out and shelter the woman and her twelve creatures.

What is Artemis doing in the wilderness? According to Nor Hall, Artemis offers to "teach us how to make contact with the unconscious and survive." In undertaking this task, she "has no fear of the dark, or of wild animals, or of places uninhabited by men." A shaman, she invites us to accompany her to this underworld—the other world—where we might receive the gift of consciousness and healing.

On this journey, the initiate gains an animal friend or helper who stays with her indefinitely and provides energy and power to the human form. In exchange for this gift of power, the human being must "dance" the animal in some way, give it body, dramatize it. This seems to me very close in spirit to the lifelike pictorial representations of animals in Paleolithic caves of Europe or rock shelters of Africa. Surely they served a similar purpose of being taken into oneself, the way monks in Tibetan ritual "gather in" Tara through detailed visualization techniques.

With her animal circle of twelve like a modern witches' coven, the Motherpeace figure of Strength sits on the mound of earth called an *omphalos* or navel of the world. In ancient Greece, Delphi was an *omphalos*, as were all the early oracular centers. From this position she prophesies, as the Druids did, or the Pythoness, the sybil, enchantress or seer of old. According to Robert Temple, "the omphalos is the place of Omphe," which means the sacred voice, the holy sound. *Omph* also connects to the sacred OM of the Sanskrit language and to sacred music, traditional sacred names and the "never-to-be-spoken word of god."

As priestess of the full moon, Strength recalls the Goddesses of sexuality and Tantric teaching. From Sumerian Ishtar to Indian Kali to Irish Bride, the Goddess was revered for her power of fire—her sexual flame. She was respected not only for her knowledge of sexual secrets, but for her unabashed sexual assertiveness and external expression of the sexual energies.

The full moon inspires the oracular priestess to poetic prophecy— orgiastic, ecstatic speech that flows like a river or bubbling spring. "A sibyl's raving is uncontrollable," says Hall, "in the way a murmuring spring, fountain, or river is uncontrollable." Originally the full moon was the "sabbath" in the days of the Babylonian Ishtar. *Sabbatu* means "heart rest" and represented the day of Ishtar's menstruation, which coincided in Babylonia with the full moon. Once celebrated monthly, like the female "period," the "sabbath" later became a weekly event, following the four quarters of the moon. So saying, Hall brings us back to the power of the female menstrual cycle and the sacred menstrual blood. "The first flow of a young girl was especially potent for healing extreme illness," says Hall. "Also, a naked woman 'in this condition' who runs around a field can kill the insects on it, thereby insuring the growth of the crop."

The Strength card represents the power of healing by the laying on of the feminine force, the Indian *tapas*, the heat that heals. The scorpion in the extreme foreground of the Motherpeace image links Strength to Scorpio, fixed water sign of healing and regeneration. This inner Strength is so powerful, wild animals are tamed and the world of unseen forces is explored through it. We touch this Strength when we dream, enter trance states, and practice healing or psychic powers.

In the Motherpeace image, a tiny wren in the oak tree sings to the full moon, representing the ability of the priestess to sing the truth, to make poetry and music, to bring language and communication from "the other side" to this one. The raccoon is her friendly familiar, its paws across her calf, its face masked like a shaman. The three water birds in the foreground exemplify her shamanic abilities to fly and swim. Like her, the birds are rooted in the water (feelings) but fly above the earth and breathe air (*prana*) into their lungs. Their flying reminds us too of migration and cyclic change.

Like the spider among the branches, the priestess spins out of her own substance webs of life and transformation. What she hears within, she is able to translate into something tangible in the external world. What she sees outside, she can take into herself in the form of wisdom and knowledge, understanding how things work and what is to be done. It is this ancient, magical art that is revered in the Old Religion—the power of the priestess to "draw down the moon" on behalf of the welfare of the group.

When you get Strength in a reading, it means you are experiencing yourself as ready and able to get what you want in life. Grounded and centered in your experience of energy, you know from the heart what you need. Since your own needs are not cut off from the needs of others, you are probably able to provide energy for others at this time, consciously lending a hand. You may be reaching out to heal or touch another life, and you do this with passion and a sense of caring. Your moral Strength is alive right now, your courage and sense of conviction powerful as you express your feelings openly and move others in this way.

Just as the priestess in the image is surrounded by the green of the fairy world, so there is magic afoot in your life at this time. Try wishing for what you have always wanted—now is the time it may manifest. The animal friends around the priestess attest to the help you can get from the various worlds around you. Try tuning into the animal world. Perhaps the time is right for a "shaman journey" in which you could enter trance states and find an animal spirit-helper. The earth is a source of power for you now. If you can take time to sit quietly and feel the magnetic power of earth—her rocks, plants, trees, rivers, hills—you will benefit enormously. Your psychic powers are ready to open, your dreams may become more vivid, you may hear your own oracular voice.

Like your heart-feelings, your libido is strong now. Setting your sights on what you want in the way of a lover or sexual partner, go after it, the energy is there for you. The overhanging tree of life behind the priestess reminds you that the Goddess protects and nurtures. Her open arms embrace you. The full moon shines her light on your endeavors.

CHAPTER 14

HANGED ONE
Accepting Initiation

The "Hanged Man" is one of the many traditions that belonged originally to the Goddess and was later taken over by a male god and changed to suit his new religion. "Artemis, the Hanged One," had a sanctuary in Arcadia in ancient Greece where the cypress was sacred to her and where it still represents resurrection. (In the Motherpeace image, the trees are swamp cypress.) Artemis, of course, is not the only divinity who hung from a tree. In Norse myth, Odin (who had replaced the Goddess Freya) hung himself for nine days and nights from the Yggdrasil (the Tree of Life described in Chapter 10). In the more familiar Christian tradition, Jesus was hung from the cross at Calvary, entombed for three days, then miraculously resurrected.

In psychic terms, all three of these stories represent an initiatory process involving some form of burial followed by a leave-taking of the soul from the body, and then its return. "Under a variety of circumstances," says William Fix, "some conscious sentient part of a human being normally resident in the physical body can temporarily leave it, journey far or not far at all, return to residence in the body again, remember and report its experience."

The Hanged One fundamentally represents the voluntary surrender to a death and resurrection process celebrated in shamanism. The earliest written history of such an event involved Ishtar, who, Fix says, "triumphed over death by venturing into the after-death realms and then returned to the land of the living." In a similar spirit, Paleolithic cave-dwellers crawled into tiny, difficult-to-reach portions of caverns in which they experienced their visions and painted magical symbols on the walls. Egyptian priests were interred in sarcophagi, Native Americans in kivas,

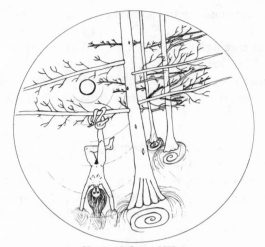

Hanged One (XII)

Indian yogis buried alive for several days, Irish Neolithic people in underground chambers like New Grange, prehistoric Ohio residents in underground "serpent" mounds, and the ancient Greeks in their dream temples and sacred caves. In popular culture, the latest version of the Hanged One was the hero of the movie *The Empire Strikes Back,* who, by hanging upside down long enough, received "the Force."

The Hanged One is a Pisces card—mutable water, ruled by the Fish Goddesses and the planet Neptune of spiritual power. Twelfth sign of the wheel of the zodiac, Pisces represents a death or letting go, once a person has thoroughly experienced an entire cycle of life. In this sign, and in the Hanged One, the human being submits to a renunciation of the personality and a deliberate turning toward the soul or higher Self. Pisces rules the feet, by which the Hanged One is suspended in order for this change to come about. Pisceans are tuned in easily to the feelings of humanity and thus, in the words of healer Richard Moss, "discover that words like trust, balance, surrender, allowing, and love are more than words, they are reality-defining energies." The collective consciousness of the Hanged One is the part discovered "as the ego boundaries of personality or individual self-consciousness begin to dissolve into realms of a greater Self."

As the boundaries relax, an inner light radiates from the head of the Hanged One, as from the head of all shamans. In writing about Eskimo culture, Rasmussen has described "a mysterious light which the shaman suddenly feels in his body, inside his head, within the brain, an inexplicable searchlight, a luminous fire, which enables him to see in the dark, both literally and metaphorically speaking." With this inner searchlight, "he can now, even with closed eyes, see through the darkness and perceive things and coming events which are hidden from others."

The goal of meditation is to experience divinity—as the Goddess or God, or the great Void, the mystic All. A Chinese nun devoted to Kuan Yin told John Blofeld how she prepares a space within which this Goddess will appear:

With your mind you make everything empty. There's nothing there, you say. And you see it like that—nothing, emptiness. . . . Then there's the sea and the moon has risen—full, round, white. . . . You stare at the moon a long, long time feeling calm, happy. Then the moon gets smaller but brighter and brighter till you see it as a pearl or a seed so bright you can only just bear to look at it. The pearl starts to grow and before you know what's happened, it is Kuan Yin Herself standing up against the sky . . .

Once this happens, the nun explained, she saw Kuan Yin no less clearly than, in ordinary reality, she saw Blofeld. "If you keep your mind calm by just whispering Her name and not trying too hard, She will stay a long, long time." After Kuan Yin and the moon and sky would vanish from the blissful inner sight, the nun said, "Just space is left—lovely, lovely space going on forever. That space stays long if you can do without you. Not you and space, you see, just space, no you." It is for this experience of "no you" that yogis meditate with discipline, in order that the ego can disappear into the greater Mind. Once a person has experienced this "death" of self, a sort of "rehearsal" for physical death, then the latter ceases to frighten one so much.

In yoga, an excellent technique for opening the head centers and uniting them with the heart is the headstand, a position similar to the Hanged One. Standing on one's head causes changes in the hormonal system as the pineal and pituitary glands are stimulated. Coming down from the headstand, one feels refreshed and somehow "transformed." Discussing the breaking of boundaries he experiences in meditation and healing work, Moss describes the powerful energy that seems to awaken within his body. "Sometimes it is localized in the chest, the head, the lower abdomen, but often it is a diffuse activation," he says. "In this sense the word body is no longer accurate because there is the feeling of extending outward beyond the body surface, not only through the energy that seems to be radiating both within and without, but through one's thought."

Mircea Eliade tells us that the first initiatory experience usually involves the opening of the novice's head for "the spirit to enter." Thus the Hanged One, suspended in a state of utter abandonment, radiates light from the head centers and is open to what Hall calls "the strange fertilizing powers of the imagination." Moss links this new energy to the opening of the heart and the experience of "unconditional love . . . a state in itself . . . quite beyond words." He reiterates what the Chinese nun said, "When it is there, you are not."

Women have sometimes objected to the harsh ascetic disciplines of Eastern religious schools that seek to transcend the earth, sometimes to leave it altogether. Frequently such schools of thought disparage women by comparing the female to the earth, making clear their determination to escape both. In contrast, the Hanged One is a surrender to what is essentially feminine—receptivity and the feelings of the heart, suggested in the Motherpeace image by the open space of the Void and by the full moon. Criticized for their "spacey" ways and devalued for their natural use of "intuition," women may find that they are able to surrender to this energy of the Goddess with little effort. Training and techniques may help, but some women may require less of them than yogis have found necessary, and to this extent the process would take less time. Many women seem to be able to meditate and experience surrender very naturally, without difficulty. Letting go of control is less difficult for women precisely because we don't control so much in the first place.

In Tantra, as in western witchcraft, this power is recognized and acknowledged. In the Motherpeace image, the Hanged One is suspended by a snake, symbol of the Goddess within, or in Hindu tradition, the *kundalini*. What's needed is a surrender to the unconditional love awakened by the snake. Moss calls it "the yes that leads to infinity."

This Piscean surrender to an ocean of feelings is not possible by conscious or rational choice alone—one may have to develop a "one-pointed consciousness" until the ego forgets itself long enough for an experience to happen. For some people this happens through meditation on an image or an idea; for others, through mantra or the continuous chanting of a sacred sound; and for still others, through making love and the intense ability to focus on pleasure or sensation so characteristic of the sign Pisces. What is sought is abandonment to pleasure or ecstasy, a "dissolving into" rather than "trying hard."

In a coven of witches, this magical surrender is sought together through dance and song, trance and breathing and celebration. Starhawk speaks of "divine ecstasy" and the "orgasmic process" of creation that comes out of such blissful sharing "in the primal, throbbing joy of union." What patriarchal, ascetic religions have sought to obscure is that witchcraft draws its power not from "the devil," but from shamanistic experience and, more broadly, from ecstasy. In Starhawk's words, ecstasy is "the source of union, healing, creative inspiration, and communion with the divine—whether it is found in the center of a coven circle, in bed with one's beloved, or in the midst of the forest, in awe and wonder at the beauty of the natural world."

To experience such joy, especially in the company of other humans, requires a "transparency" that Moss describes as "releasing into dimensions that are broader than those reflected to us through the content of our experiences." To know this joy alone, in meditation or yoga or silent communion with nature, is to become transparent to the Goddess herself. It may bring tears or laughter, as the recognition of ecstasy sinks into the consciousness of the simple everyday human mind. It is a death of self that one learns to welcome for its healing and regenerative power, for the times when "I am not" end up being the times "I" like the most.

When you get the Hanged One in a reading, what it means is not that you are going to die, but that you are going to lose yourself. Unlike the Christian tradition, the Hanged One does not imply crucifixion or pain, but rather a sense of ecstasy and surrender to love. Think of a spider suspended by its own silken substance, yielding in trust to gravity. You are suspended in time, right now. Maybe this means you need to meditate or find your calm center from which light radiates. It definitely means "stop action" and "allow" to happen. If you fight this need, you will go in circles, because your psyche is struggling to assimilate something. Turn inside yourself, yield, wait, and see what happens.

Probably your ego fears losing control, maybe your mind is saying phrases such as "Trouble . . . watch out . . . take care . . . do something." But you need to still the mind as much as possible and listen to another part of yourself, the heart, that deep still center from which visions come. Find the female part of yourself, allow the irrational to surface, let the full moon hold sway, breathe deeply. The Goddess within wants to talk to you. You must be quiet so you can hear her.

You may want to do something to literally turn yourself upside down temporarily, in order to change your perspective. Think how small children love to be turned upside-down by a strong adult. It makes them laugh and squeal with delight. Maybe you can stand on your head (only if it is not difficult for you; otherwise you must learn in stages). Maybe you can hang upside-down on a trapeze or bar, letting the blood rush to your head and feeling the rush of strangeness and change that happens almost immediately. Maybe you need something less "drastic" than these measures, like just lying down and closing your eyes, in order to allow your consciousness to get quiet and to focus on inner vision.

In any case, imagine yourself being suspended by a strong adult or mythical figure. Imagine letting go in trust to that person and feel your own breath relax and deepen. Let your lungs expand and your heart open. Imagine taking this trust into your daily life and allowing things to happen without your control, without being sure what will take place. Feel your heart's appreciation of this loving, healing energy that exists all around you. Let each in-breath truly be an in-spiration. With each out-breath, let go some more, telling the universe what you're letting go of—whether it be tension, control, dominance, fear, doubt, or hatred. You will feel yourself becoming empty of tension and full of light. Make a gradual return to your ordinary consciousness.

CHAPTER 15

DEATH

Letting Go

Death is change. In shamanistic terms, Death is the period of time when the body is still and cold, the door opens, and the soul crosses the threshold between this world and the beyond. In one sense the shaman lies in trance, as an accident victim might lie in coma: if the soul does not return to the body, then death is complete.

Like the night, Death is dark, quiet, lacking sunlight and the warmth of life force. But night is paired with day, as *yin* with *yang*. The sun will rise again. A dance of death and life pervades our universe, describes it. From the point of view of the body, Death is an ending—one's time on earth is finished. But from the point of view of the soul, physical Death is the beginning of a new journey, an expanded state of being, in the formless worlds.

The Death force is usually attributed to the planet Pluto, named for the Greek god of the underworld who abducted Demeter's daughter Persephone and took her down into darkness each autumn. A planet of regeneration, Pluto changes us from the deepest place inside, and is related to the sign of Scorpio in the zodiac. Scorpio represents transformation, death, and mysticism—the three central experiences of the shamanistic mysteries. Through the process of facing death, through meditation or dying, one comes to know the soul more deeply. Scorpio rules the sex organs, the deep unconscious, and the ability to channel healing energies. Sex, death, and meditation are frequently connected in Eastern religious doctrine.

In Tarot the number of the Death card is Thirteen, the magical lunar

See color illustration on Plate 4.

number of witchcraft and the ancient religion of the Goddess. A year is composed of thirteen lunar months. It was patriarchal culture that deleted the thirteenth month, contrived the solar calendar we still use, and put an aura of bad luck around the number thirteen. Once the most sacred of the numbers, signifying the end and the beginning, the number thirteen now makes people so nervous that a hotel can't even have a thirteenth floor, because hardly anyone will risk sleeping on it. The thirteenth fairy brings a curse, and Friday the thirteenth is as unlucky as a person can get. All of this speaks to the distortion that has taken place in our culture over this issue of Death.

When Death comes naturally, at the end of a long and fruitful life on earth, one greets it without fear and with a minimum of grief—the work is done. But when Death comes too soon, as it does so often in the world today, leaving the soul unfinished, the task undone, then we feel fear, grief, and frustration.

Our ancient ancestors understood the body to be the temple or habitation of the soul during a lifetime on earth. They greeted each new soul with ceremony and reverence, and respected and loved the body—the house—during the life in every way possible. But the "fertility" Goddess was also the Death Goddess, and at the end of life, the body was respectfully prepared for burial, which was seen as a return to the Earth Mother. As Downing says, "to die is to return to the receptive, generative Mother. The earth is womb. . . ." The body was wrapped in a fetal position and buried in communal tombs with friends and relatives who had gone before. These round "bee-hive" tombs characterize matriarchal civilizations.

One of the easiest ways to mark the influx of patriarchal culture is the absence of these communal burials. Obsessed with status and individuality, patriarchal culture established social classes and maintained these distinctions in their burial customs. Kings were buried lavishly, with efforts to preserve their bodies, an idea unthinkable to earlier cultures. In the Motherpeace image of Death, the skeleton has been bound for a simple return to the Mother, once covered with red ochre to symbolize her regenerative power, then left to her loving embrace.

Bones are magical and respected by "primitives" and magicians all over the world. A contemporary shaman, Brooke Medicine Eagle, received a shaman song that points out the magical, divinatory power of bones: "I found some dry, bleached bones today, and gathered them to put into a bag for casting to ask the future, when modern means have failed me." Our ancient Paleolithic ancestors kept track of their menstrual cycles on bones, creating the first lunar calendars corresponding to the menstrual cycle. Because of the amazing endurance of bone, we still have samples of these early calendars from the Old Stone Age.

Like the trees that let go of their leaves each autumn season, Death comes in cycles. Everything is born, lives, and decays. Even ideas arise, live for a while in a certain form, and die. The key to understanding the Tarot Death card is the universal transformation process. Nothing ever really dies, it only transforms. All matter has the ability to change its form, to become something else. In every process of Death, there is simultaneously a rebirth. This is a central message of the Goddess religion—Death and Life are shifting poles of the same phenomenon, a revolving door between the worlds.

As bones are revealed by death and decay, so the process of renewal within one lifetime is symbolized by the snake shedding its skin. In the image of Strength described in Chapter 14, the snake took its place in a large circle of helper animals. In the Motherpeace image of Death, however, the snake takes center stage. When the snake sheds its skin, it acts as if with instinctual consciousness of rebirth, with acceptance of the process. It finds a pair of birch trees through which to crawl, in order to facilitate the shedding process. Like the witnessing consciousness of the human soul, the snake watches itself in the process of Death and rebirth.

In contrast to the snake, humanity fears losing the old skin, even when it has begun to constrict our growth. More comfortable with the old, we fear the unknown, the future. Therefore, when Death rears its "ugly" head, we turn away, avoiding it at all costs. Physically, as a culture, we make a tremendous, almost unbelievable medical effort to prolong survival of the body, as compared with our reluctance to live in ways that would enhance vitality. The soul needs harmony and connectedness. It wants to feel loved and truly "known" by others. It is wounded by stress, destruction, and hatred.

If we could become like the shedding snake, we would allow the old ways to fall away, the inner, bright skin to emerge. The Death that currently asks to happen in the world is the death of patriarchal culture, war and violence, a death of greed and the power of the few. In the Motherpeace image, the new skin of the snake is red and yellow, full of life force, like the will power and passion of the human individual in the face of annihilation. Psychics and religious figures tell us we are now entering a New Age of understanding and wisdom, the power of the reborn Self to have an effect in the world.

The encounter with Death and "mastery" of it are central themes of shamanic initiation everywhere. Always the purpose of the descent into the underworld or the ascent into the other world is to confront this force

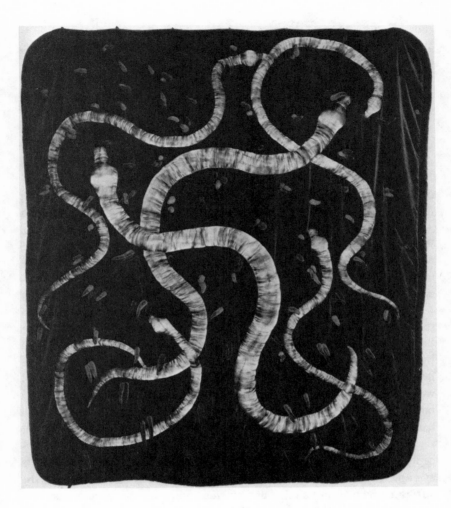

called Death—to meet it, come to understand it through experience of it, and to fear it no longer. Moving back and forth between death and life, between the opposite poles of experience, is the initiatory experience: in the words of Joan Halifax, "to open the mystery by becoming it, to transcend death by dying in life, to pierce duality by embracing the opposites, to reunite the fractured forms." Shamans call this the "great task" and once it is accomplished, they are permanently empowered. With this power, a person can heal, bless, and envision the past, present, and future of all things.

In the Genesis story of Adam and Eve's displacement from the Garden, it was, of course, a serpent who offered knowledge of good and evil, life and death. This knowledge was accepted by Eve, who offered it to Adam. For this breach of the rules, the two of them were expelled from Paradise by the jealous, rigid Jehovah. Our return to the Paradise of the Mother and the Tree of Knowledge would amount to a relearning of the mystery of Life and Death—a basic understanding of the relation between the two.

In patriarchal culture, however, we combine a denial of Death with a terrifying readiness to use death as a threat. Like our counterparts in the Soviet Union, we live just a half hour away from the ruin of civilization by nuclear rockets. Polls show that much of the population falsely believes we have a defense against these rockets. On a personal level, too, we deny Death when it threatens us, pretending we can keep it away by ignoring it or refusing to understand it consciously. In this way, Death has power over us, as if it were a Terrible Goddess with a lust for blood.

Eastern religion teaches that Death must be understood and accepted, so that when one approaches it, one approaches with the mind's eye open. In this conscious manner, the experience of Death will not be a frightening one, but a relief and a joyous reunion with the ancestors and the one light of the universe. Within the teachings are techniques for purification and cleansing of "bad karma" or the ill effects of former actions that keep us in darkness. The *Tibetan Book of the Dead*, like the *Egyptian Book of the Dead*, informs humanity of the ways in which the dead can be aided in the journey to the other side. Rather than clinging and crying, trying to hold back the loved one, the group or family sings, chants, prays, and sends off the soul to the spirit realms with joy and thanksgiving.

This very sane approach to death and dying is being picked up in our culture by New Age healers such as Elisabeth Kübler-Ross, a modern shaman herself, who helps people understand and accept the broader, more spiritual aspects of the death process. Her approach is to cleanse the psyche of "old business" such as fear and blockages, what Hindus might call "bad karma." With the cleansing comes a freedom to see, understand, and "rehearse" death in life and therefore come to accept it without fear. If accomplished early enough, this frees the spirit in life to work toward change and transformation of society as well as the individual. For example, this understanding would enable us to go beyond despair about the arms race and to work, our hearts out, against it.

When you get this card in a reading, it almost never signifies physical death, but acts as a metaphor for some experience of dying and rebirth in your life. Perhaps a relationship is ending, or it is time to move on in some way. The death may involve pain and loss, causing you to grieve and feel bereft, making your heart hurt. But the change is essential and final, and the rebirth is already taking place. The central message of the card is to tune in to the process of rebirth and allow your old skin to drop away, the new one to emerge. In what way are you changing? How are you being reborn?

With any luck, you can witness your change as you go through it, much as the snake watches and helps itself shed the old skin. You may want to ritualize the Death in some way, to make it more real and give it form as well as support. Perhaps you can have a ceremony of letting go or saying goodby. If a part of yourself is dying, see whether you can speak to it, then relinquish it with love.

If some old pattern is being replaced by a new and better method of coping, acknowledge this and focus on the positive. If the Death is happening in a relationship, there is a helpful process of psychic cleansing that you can use to affirm and speed the process of letting go. You can do this with or without your partner. What you do is to take some quiet time and remember the relationship fully, allowing your tears and pain to release. You may want to look at old pictures, listen to old music you shared, gather together objects given to you by your former lover. Let the feelings flow freely and completely. At some point you will have a sense of completion (or exhaustion).

Then breathe deeply and find a quiet place of meditation inside your mind. Visualize or think about the cords or ties that have connected you to this other person. They appear like electric cords or cords to a switchboard, from your body to the other person's form. You can look at each separate cord and decide what it represents, then pull it or cut it. Or you can simply take a look at the whole thing, and cut all the cords at once. As you pull or cut the cords, make a strong affirmation, such as: "I am letting go of so-and-so with love. I acknowledge the Death of this relationship. It is completed."

Then sit and meditate on the Motherpeace Death card for a while, letting the image of the snake shedding its skin sink into your psyche. Feel your fears about Death sliding away with the old skin and allow your new self to emerge like the gentle changing of the seasons. Use this process whenever Death enters your life, and you will know the power of the shaman who has mastered Death and fears it no more.

CHAPTER 16

TEMPERANCE

Grounding Cosmic Energy

In Tarot tradition, the Temperance card represents the empowerment of Alchemy, the process of blending the parts of the self until fusion is achieved and the "philosopher's stone" is made. For me, Temperance also refers to the culmination of shamanic initiation, an integration of the emotional forces with the physical—a blessed union of opposites within and without. No longer a novice, the Temperance shaman has come of age. All learning has turned into technical prowess. The shaman has mastered the fire, no longer fears Death (or anything else), and is Mistress of the Spirits. Once having been involuntarily possessed by spirits, the shaman now understands and uses the process of actively "raising the fire" and calling in the spirits. She is an open channel, cleansed and purified by past process, ready to handle tremendous forces and energies. She does not swing from one extreme to the other, but rides the wave in perfect union with it—stays in what Buddhists have called the Middle Way, straight to the heart.

An old !Kung Bush-person "curer" tells the story of the *n/um* or "healing medicine" that the shaman-healer receives in a successful initiation. The "curer" gets the power while engaged in a "trance dance" such as the one depicted in the Motherpeace Temperance image. "*N/um,* residing in the belly, is activated through strenuous trance dancing and the heat of the fire," says Joan Halifax. "It ascends or 'boils up' the spinal column and into the head, at which time it can be used to pull out the sickness afflicting others."

At first these energies seem wildly out of the ordinary and can throw a person off balance as channels open and consciousness changes radically. Here is the experience of contemporary healer Richard Moss:

*Every cell can be alive and vibrating as if one were electrical or inde-
scribably blissful, and it seems to fluctuate of its own accord until there is a
gradual stabilization. Basic to this is an inner kind of balance that cannot
be described and must just be learned moment by moment. Physical symptoms such as tremor, weakness, extreme sensitivity to heat and cold, muscle
spasms may occur. Yet if one comes into harmony with the current the sense
of strength and vitality can be nearly superhuman. But even when there is
inner peace the initial energy can simply be too much for the body—something like putting too much current through a wire.*

Most native cultures have activities and a context in which to ground
this amazing emergence of cosmic energy from within the body. Modern
American culture has none of these outlets or structures, and people who
open to psychic power sometimes "go crazy." Because no one understands how to help, they end up in mental institutions. The solution is
really very simple—the energy, like lightning, must be grounded. The
first step is something to keep the psyche in touch with the physical
plane. Dancing, running, swimming or any other form of physical activity is good. Meaningful sexual activity is wonderful, because it "earths"
the energy at the same time as it uplifts the emotions.

Aleister Crowley calls the Temperance card "Art," which suggests a
genuine possibility for channeling these tempestuous energies. Creating
something with the mind and hands is a perfect union of spiritual and
physical energy. In cultures where divinity is part of daily reality, art is a
form of prayer and the making of art is integrated into life. In ritual,
making music or art is often a part of the general healing that accompanies the dancing (or for which the dancing is done). After the dance raises
the energy and heightens sensitivity, the receiver of energy makes art or
does a healing, or both.

In Tarot, the Temperance card represents Sagittarius, the balanced
ability to channel and ground the cosmic energies that at first were so
difficult to handle. Temperance is the archetypal "curer" calling in the
healing spirits. Centered in the flow of energies—sun and moon, hot and
cold, day and night—she becomes what Halifax calls "a master of thresh-
olds, a mediator between polar opposites." When she succeeds in unify-
ing them, as Moss has said, a change "occurs simultaneously at all levels
of the structure. . . . Transformation is radical. When it occurs, it effec-
tively integrates and alters one's nature at every level all at once."

The Temperance priestess personifies the innate female arts of healing and magic—sexual power danced to its peak, its orgasmic point, and

Temperance (XIV)

transmuted into healing energy. She is woman as witch, her ancient power intact and fully expressed. It was for this knowledge that nine million witches were burned during the Middle Ages.

In ancient Goddess-worshiping cultures, the entire community participated in healing ritual, dancing, chanting, and loving together, without a need for an individual shaman. Later, when these early cultures had been fragmented and disconnected and the Goddess lost her unified power, illness became more prevalent and individual healers were needed; religious activity was separated from "secular." Certain people embodied more of this ancient magical power than others, particularly some old women who became known as witches, and some old men who became known as shamans. Although there were female shamans and male witches, generally speaking the words came to be split by gender with the usual patriarchal associations of good (shaman-male) and bad (witch-female). The two types of healers embody the same powers, yet their status is very different in most cultures.

The millions of women who were massacred during the Middle Ages in Europe were often charged "specifically with possessing medical and obstetrical skills." Although it was the Christian church that suppressed and annihilated them, the Witch-hunts "coincided" with the rise of the male medical establishment. Healing knowledge that had been the province of women since ancient days became largely a male domain. With the development of forceps, the new profession of gynecology crystallized. Women who had been able to trust the wise midwives for the safe and effective knowledge of birth control, abortion, pregnancy, and delivery, were suddenly thrown into the "care" of males who considered them unclean, contaminated, and disgusting, unworthy of proper treatment and deserving, perhaps, of whatever pain they experienced. The new doctors quoted biblical passages about "original sin" to convince women they were supposed to endure pain during childbirth.

Even today in America midwifery, the oldest female art, is illegal or severely restricted, as shown by the arrest of midwives in Santa Cruz, California, in spite of their impeccable record of low complication rates and gentle birthing methods. Under the system monopolized by gynecologists, what is happening to women and their offspring? Infant mortality and morbidity rates are extremely high for a "developed" country. The rate of Caesarian births has swung up sharply. And surgeons show a remarkable avidity for relieving women of such organs as breasts and uteri, precisely the symbols of our ancient power.

What can women do? In many so-called primitive cultures, where a patriarchal religion predominates, groups of women form "possession cults," as anthropologists call them. In these groups, women practice their religion of magic under the guidance of the elder female healer who teaches the younger women her skills. The women enter the "cult" when they become ill because they are "possessed" by a spirit and need help from the healer who has long since become a Mistress of Spirits. After a while the possessed woman not only is cured, but learns from her mentor how to invoke the spirits into her body (or a pot or fetish) and how to handle them. In other words, they learn to master the spirits of dis-ease.

The main feature of this widespread female religious practice is "ecstasy." The women become possessed through the invasion of spirits into their bodies, and then become ecstatic by dancing them out in order to heal themselves and others. The entire female group is allowed to come together and celebrate their ecstatic power regularly within this framework, which the men of the tribe find acceptable. Through this means, the women gain some power in relation to their husbands and have dialogue with them through the voice of the invading spirit and the intermediary of the shaman-healer. It is an effective means of combating the otherwise blatant oppression and inequality. The men fear and respect the powerful magic of the women and concede certain gains to them through this process. The women, although considered "peripheral" by scholars who write about them, experience the deepest of religious feelings on a routine basis and must be much closer to certain sacred truths than those of us who are supposedly liberated.

The "orgiastic" tendencies of women are alternately encouraged and feared by men and their culture. In ancient Greek times, for example, the Maenads (and later the Bacchantes) met under the full moon to dance in frenzies that ended in violent dismemberment of animals and, some even say, of children. If this is not simply metaphorical, the actions may have been a result of narcotic substances being added to communion wine by that time in history. Did these practices stem from severe repression of the natural female sex force? When women worshiped the Goddess through the "erotic celebration" symbolized by the fiery waves in the Motherpeace Temperance image, there was no war and no rape. When we do not dance for the Goddess, energies get stuck and either sink into depression or explode like a volcano. Temperance, like the Volcano Goddess Pele quiescent, reminds us of our natural abilities to balance and harmonize the energies of earth and sky, body and mind, woman and man. Through the rhythms of the dance, the Temperance priestess has lost her self and found divinity in the oldest form of worship known to humanity, the sacred dance of energy.

When you get this card in a reading, it means you are in balance. The natural movements of energy around and within you are in harmony and integrated. You are not fragmented or disconnected from yourself. A Tantric fusion has taken place, through which opposite parts of yourself have come together. You may feel yourself in a heightened state of consciousness, able to absorb much more than usual and to assimilate it naturally within your being.

You may be experiencing a union with another person, or perhaps with nature or the world around you. If you get this card in relation to someone else, then you have reached the union that was sought in the Lovers card described in Chapter 8, but is only now achieved. The fusion is molecular in nature, transforming you on a cellular level, changing you from the inside out. You may be able to feel the healing taking place. Your cells may tingle, your ears ring, your heart pound. The energy is running strongly through you, healing and renewing. You are probably experiencing a new sense of courage and well-being.

This card carries with it an enormous power—an electrical current of energies pulsing through your body and soul. It is essential to stay grounded and conscious, being aware that the energy is coming through you, but it is not you. It is a gift to be managed with clarity and love, not to be used selfishly or against others.

You may find yourself called on at this time to heal someone or apply yourself on behalf of someone else. You have the ability—the gift—of healing and can feel free to channel aid to someone else, as long as you stay neutral and don't attach your ego to this power. If you get taken up in a "mythic identity"—if you begin to believe that you are this power, that you are the Goddess—you will no doubt run into trouble. But as long as you remain respectful of the energy coming through and its universal source, you will increase in your abilities to heal and create beauty in the universe. It is an opportunity for supreme centering and equilibrium, for pure power and focus of energies. Feel free to use your power wisely.

CHAPTER 17

DEVIL

Denying the Spirit

In Tarot, the Devil is a complex card full of paradoxical meanings. "Devil" is a concept invented by religious patriarchs and later used, in the Middle Ages, to help rationalize the killing of nine million witch-healers. The name "Devil" became attached to Pan, hooved god of the forest, who embodied forces of Nature and, particularly, of positive male sexuality. Pan's sensual nature and earthy qualities derived from his earlier forms as Dionysus and Bacchus—the mystery gods of wild women and ecstatic abandon. In magic circles, Pan was invoked as the male principle to bring fertility and abundance to the earth, in much the same way the Goddess is called.

After medieval witch-hunters accused women witches of copulating with the Devil in their sacred full moon rituals, pagan Goddess-worshipers were forced underground. Many died anyway, forced to confess to crimes invented by the perfervid imaginations of the celibate Catholic priests who defended their faith with torture. In many cases they took literally what were metaphorical descriptions of the shaman power embodied by wise women and healers, such as the ability to "fly."

In Jungian terms, we could regard the Devil as the collective "shadow" that patriarchal culture has projected onto women, who, most men appear to agree, "should be kept in their place." Modern feminist women reject this image of themselves and look for the true roots of "evil." In the Motherpeace image, the Devil symbolizes the "bondage model" of social organization, the philosophy of "power over" as a way of life. In

See color illustration on Plate 5.

place of the natural laws of the universe, this model establishes dominance and hierarchy.

At the top of the pyramidal structure so loved by Patriarchy is the Big Man, who may take the form of the Emperor familiar to us from Chapter 6. Next in line are his immediate subordinates, who maintain their status by doing his bidding. Preeminent in the picture is the exchange of gold between the higher-ups. On the left, a mother on the lowest step is having to sacrifice her own child to the chain of command. On the right, soldiers guard the Big Man and fight off an Amazon who has broken her chains. Everyone in the hierarchical set-up is in chains; the differences are only in where they sit, or stand, or kneel.

On the inner blocks of the pyramid are murals taken from the Sumerian city of Ur. From the king's "royal standard," these images depict the basic hierarchy of patriarchal structure, with its scribes and priests near the top. Next come the soldiers and nobility, shown in one frieze portraying "war" and in the one under it, "peace." Note that the peacetime scene includes racism and slavery—the catering by some of the population to the "needs" of a few white men in the upper echelons. At the bottom of the heap are portrayals of women: instead of the ancient daughter/mother/crone of the Goddess, we now have (from left to right) Daddy's good girl, Daddy's bad girl, and Daddy's cast-off hag.

The clock at the top of the structure forms a backdrop for the enthroned male authority figure (the owner, the boss, or proprietor) as a sign of bondage to work. Everything is done for the personal gain of a few at the expense of the many. In basic terms, this image of the Devil suggests a state of greed and selfish egotism, an untenable pattern if human civilization is to continue. It represents the "sin of separatism" discussed by Alice Bailey and other esoteric teachers who understand that human connectedness to one another and the earth is the only hope for humanity's survival. The mentality of the Devil cuts itself off from others and says "me first" and "anything to get to the top."

Capricorn, the cardinal earth sign attributed to the Devil, represents manifestation and the attempt to scale peaks. As such, it is a very spiritual sign of the Earth Mother. But with the patriarchal competitive ideal, and the creation of a mountain of status, Capricorn's ambition turns to physical gratification, power, and wealth. This winter earth sign represents the longest night of the year, Winter Solstice, and is known for its negativity. Without connection to what is spiritual, the human ego becomes immersed in the unreal; and since it pays attention to nothing else, the ego dismisses any other way of thinking as "unrealistic." Just as the ego dominates the heart, the rational mind dominates the irrational, intuitive forces, and lives by the slogan, "If you can't see it, you don't have to believe in it."

However, there lives in each of us an invisible, untamed spirit. Even if we cannot feel it or relate to it, it is there in us—originally and essentially—wanting expression, yearning for freedom. The witches and pagans of old, and other Goddess worshipers, understood this simple reality and created a context in which the untamed spirit could express itself regularly through the body and mind of each individual. The Devil represents the repression of this free spirit by Church and State, to which it poses a threat to authority and order. Any release of this spirit, whether inadvertent or intentional, is considered either sinful or criminal, punishable by God or the secular "authorities." The force of the Emperor is used to carry out the laws of the Hierophant, and the system created for this purpose is represented by the Devil.

The outcome of this repression of the wildness within us is robotism —dull, mechanistic, monotonous ways of living. And the extreme reaction to such servitude and lack of meaning is violence and aggression, often "unexpected" and always misunderstood. When the free spirit makes itself felt through a normally well-behaved individual, it feels as if "the Devil made me do it."

The gloomy gray-brown color that surrounds the figures in the Motherpeace image is the background of funk and doubt that hierarchy creates. A mentality that assumes a winner and loser in every situation makes for pessimism and eternal lack of trust. In a culture based on these premises, relations between people often take the form of dominance-submission interactions lacking in love, simple affection, or caring. In sado-masochistic pornography we can glimpse the sickness of our culture manifest in a distorted version of what might be the most satisfying and healing experience of human life—lovemaking. Once sexuality is removed from the sacred realm of "religion" or worship of what is divine, it becomes at the very best, harmless, a mundane activity. Once sexual expression is no longer connected to respect for life and the universal love of the Mother, it takes on the negativity and power struggles of secular life. The battle of the sexes, manifest most blatantly in rape and other open violence to women, is also painfully enacted in the bedroom between ordinary people. In a society that respected the Goddess, would we have so many women who do not experience orgasm, or so many men who suffer impotency?

On a broader social level, the individual feels increasingly unable to fight the effects of "military-industrial complexes" that are bringing disaster to the earth at an extremely fast rate. The nuclear arms race is out of control and threatens to throw biological evolution back, in the phrase of Jonathan Schell, to the level of insects and grasses. And for what? The aims and desires of the men at the top of various nations involved in disputes over power and control are almost out of reach of the average human mind's ability to comprehend.

To throw off the forces symbolized by the Devil card takes an enormous effort, an almost unimaginable mobilization of personal and collective power. To break free of the chains that bind us to old habit patterns and stuck ways of thinking requires an Amazon consciousness, a Medusa-like focus on victory, the discipline of Athene.

The first step in breaking out of bondage is to protest—to say "no!" The saying of "no!" by an individual who has habitually acquiesced in oppression releases energy in itself. It requires courage and conviction, a strong belief in Self, and an impulse toward freeing the wild spirit within. This simple, even limited protest or boycott sets up a chain-reaction that can be felt by the entire being. When this activity or saying "no!" to what is happening is enacted on a group level, such as antinuclear protest, people begin to feel the potential power that exists for change. The forces of the Devil card—the powers that be—may throw us in jail for civil disobedience or react with physical brutality, but the shared focus of the group, the collective knowledge of doing what is right, sets up a very powerful vibration of energy that moves out into the world beyond the immediate situation and effects other changes.

Saying "no!" on an individual basis to private thought forms that cripple us emotionally is equally valid and empowering. Every person who has given up an addiction—thrown away their television, stopped drinking, smoking, or using hard drugs—knows what effort and victory mean. The Devil may exist in some form in every one of us, but it can always be exorcised. What is needed is profound choice—the exercise of free will and human affirmation.

When you get this card in a reading, the message is that you are in bondage to some power. You are in some way subscribing to the dominance-submission mentality, and the issue of power is at stake. Maybe you are abusing power in some way, exercising your will over others, letting your ego take the reins and your ambition lead the way. Maybe it seems as if others have control over your life and there is no point in doing anything, no reachable goal, no positive outcome. If so, you may feel trapped in a negative thought pattern, defeatism, and a gloomy out-look on life.

Whether you are the person wielding the power or the one feeling the effects of submission to authority, your soul is in need of liberation. Find yourself on the pyramid pictured in the Motherpeace image—which fig-ure are you at this time? In what way are you playing the master or the victim? Then ask yourself some basic questions about your situation. Are you getting pleasure from this power structure in some way? If so, you are not likely to want to give up the "rewards" you anticipate or experi-ence. To release yourself from the bondage inherent in the Devil card, it will be necessary to confront your reality on a very deep level. You must truly look at the supposed rewards you reap from whatever game you are involved in, whatever situation holds you captive, and try to see beyond its "unreal" and addictive aspects into its totality.

Once you pinpoint where you are on the pyramid, what your game is, and how it hurts you and others, you will want to get rid of the pattern of behavior or thinking that keeps you enslaved. To do this, you need to see yourself—feel yourself—interacting in more positive and life-affirm-ing ways; and then to affirm your intention to break bad habits and create positive methods of doing what you need to do. Be specific and actually focus your imagination on such change. You need to begin to believe in the possibility of doing things differently—in inherent sanity and justice, natural law, and universal love.

It is an occult truth that positive energy is more powerful than nega-tive, that simple good can overcome evil; but it must be mobilized. Once you can truly see yourself transforming, transformation will begin to hap-pen. Personal power of choice is not "power over." It does not depend on dominance. To be power-full is to express the life force and to work for positive change—to cast out "the Devil." The force of negativity shatters under the all-seeing eye of truth.

CHAPTER 18

TOWER

Shattering the Structure

The Tower in traditional Tarot interpretation is representative of destruction and cataclysmic change—an earthshaking stroke of illumination and the end of false consciousness. It is tempting today to interpret this card in literal terms, as the karmic end to the cycle of patriarchal existence we have endured for five thousand years. This period of time is referred to by Hindus as the *Kali Yuga* and defines a degraded, evil period that is currently coming to an end. Whether the end will be a brutal and total annihilation of life, or a radical change in the consciousness of the human race, remains to be seen.

Kali is the Hindu Goddess of Death, represented by fire and the sword. Although she is personified as terrible and grotesque, with a lust for blood (and, in particular, a nasty urge to cut off Shiva's head), Kali really represents the cutting edge of truth and the fire that burns away falsity and the misdeeds of the past. Kali was once the Great Mother who had the powers of creation and destruction at her command. As the Goddess of Fire, she represents a sexual fire as well as enlightenment, and even in her reduced form as Goddess of Death she is powerful and respected, even feared.

The Tower in Tarot is a symbol of Kali's cutting off the head—ego death, the end of mental control—a motif we have seen in the earliest cave art. Kali symbolizes truth and the raging fire of intuition, life force expressed through the oracular power of seeing into the future, the divine shock of knowing. Sitting at the top of the Tower, a priestess catches the lightning with her bare hands, representing the power of the shaman to

See color illustration on Plate 5.

channel intensities of energy that the ordinary individual could not bear. Her eyes are open and she radiates fire from the head—electrical fire, the force of *manas* or creative power.

Behind the priestess is the dark sky and the ocean, feminine powers of intelligence and wisdom. Below her are the members of her community, waiting for her to reveal the oracle that will guide them into action. On the ground is a Hopi migration symbol—double spiral and two spiders—and a lot of driftwood burning. The message is that a change is taking place, a significant movement from one place to another, and a burning away of what is old and has drifted into shore. When lightning strikes wood, the wood burns; when illumination strikes the human mind, old concepts are put to flame. Waiting to take the people out to sea are the ships that will carry them from the old world to the new.

In the sky, the full moon completely eclipses the sun—it is not night, but only the passing of the lunar orb in front of the solar, the temporary triumph of the night force in the middle of the day. In all "primitive" cultures, a solar eclipse is regarded with awe and a sense of danger as a miraculous visitation from spiritual realms. The Tower is ruled by Uranus, the planet governing change and illumination and associated with the astrological sign of Aquarius. The New Age is the age of Aquarius, and the Tower represents the lightning-swift changes taking place in consciousness as well as form. As long-predicted by psychics and people close to the earth, such as Native Americans, old structures and ways of thinking are shattering in the world today. The crystallizations represented by the Devil are beginning to crack, as the illusions of the past five thousand years are called into question.

The people in the Motherpeace card are Libyan in origin, on their way to America and other places far away from the patriarchal invaders of the second millennium B.C. Representing all people who worship the Goddess—the feminine force of life and Nature—these involuntary exiles are fleeing invasions of destructive, aggressive human beings who would eliminate them and their beliefs. According to Harvard professor Barry Fell, peoples of the Mediterranean area came to all the Americas during the second and first millennia B.C., thousands of years before Columbus "discovered" America. They left stone carvings and inscriptions in Egyptian, Phoenician, Libyan, and Iberian scripts that speak of the Goddesses Tanith, Astarte, Beltis, and who knows how many others?

Perhaps many of these early visitors were involved in trade with Native Americans who, according to Jeffrey Goodman, have been living here for at least two hundred thousand years. Others probably were exiles, driven out of their Mediterranean homelands by patriarchal invaders who swept through between 3500 B.C. and the birth of Christ. During this transition period between Goddess-worship and Patriarchy, migration was inevitable. Most of the people in the world share a common mythology of cataclysms. Although such destructions usually take such natural forms as volcanoes, earthquakes, or floods, they are almost always assumed to be "karmic" in nature. That is, people believe the disasters have been brought about by "the gods" in retaliation for the wrongdoing of the human population.

The Hopi view of natural balance, the Egyptian idea of social justice, and the Indian concept of karma all agree that natural laws govern the universe and "man" is able to respond to them. When human beings stop being responsive and begin to do things their own way, trouble starts. As humanity drifts farther and farther away from the divine source of guidance and wisdom, the forces depicted in the Devil image come more and more into play. Eventually there must be a break—the inevitable "retribution."

Many people today believe that we have reached one of these "retribution" periods of cataclysmic upheaval and change. Global pollution—such as burial of nuclear and chemical wastes in the body of the Earth Mother—and human interference in weather and growth cycles may bring the karmic cleansing or "great purification" spoken of in the prophecies. Human destruction of the ozone layer already accounts for an increase in radiation from the sun, as well as climatic changes on earth. Or "retribution" may take the form of a major nuclear "exchange." A former Special Assistant to the President for National Security, considering which factors had so far averted a nuclear war, started his list with "luck." The danger is so great that most of us are numb to it and act, on the conscious level, as if it were not there, or as if nobody could possibly do anything about it. In contrast, New Age teachers, like ancient oracles, suggest the possibility of free choice. With the simplicity of children, they ask what sense it makes for the human race, through its own "defense" establishments, to destroy itself. It is questions such as this, more than the intricate calculations of "arms control experts," that will help people grasp the stupidity of the war system.

The possibility of transformation is the message of the Goddess, the feminine force of healing. Kali, with her sword raised and her red tongue hanging out, challenges us to mobilize our energy and learn to act right. Let the old forms shatter, she demands; let the truth shine through us and destroy what is false. She cuts away the past and invites us to create with her a future that is tolerable to the human soul, where quality of life is more important than mere existence. Kali is a vision of outrage—she represents the part of us that knows we must have more dignity and truth, or die.

To look away from the truth manifesting in the Tower is to get lost in destruction, to go out with the old forms and ideas. To stare truth in the eye is to take power back into ourselves in response to the almost unspeakable situation that presents itself and the deeply human need to change it. The awakening that Kali presents to us is painful, bringing nightmares and hideous visions of what may come; but the fire that she represents is the awakened and activated *kundalini* energy, an electric shock of very high voltage that brings with it the ability to sustain that very force.

The message in the Tower is "we can do it," and the deeper implication is "we have no choice but to try." The earth is moving, the oracle is speaking, and the return of the Goddess into body and soul is imminent. The destruction of the old always precedes the building of the new, but one can choose which side to be on. The spiritual truth of Kali carries with it immortality and a living awareness of the eternal nature of the soul. With this awareness comes a victory over death and the forces of death and destruction. A fearless courage is born. "Life will triumph!" That is the banshee shriek of Kali (and of the Irish Calleagh, whose name is pronounced the same). Those who have ears to hear will never be the same again.

When you get this card in a reading, brace yourself—you're in for a change. A radical shift is taking place in your life, a flash of illumination. Whether you like what you see or not, you see it. You may not want to move, but the structure is falling out from under you. Prepare yourself for the future, for the past is slipping away before your eyes and things are becoming very clear.

The change may be something that happens to you—an event or situation that transforms you. You may suddenly know your marriage is over, your job is ending, or a new lover has just entered your life and is going to shake everything up. You may have a sudden lucid understanding of your own destructive patterns or addictions and the need for immediate and radical change. These understandings may be momentary, like a lightning bolt, but the effects are far-reaching and will endure. A moment of luminous anger or understanding transforms you from within.

When your *kundalini* awakens and your spiritual centers open, then you will feel your own shaman-power and the ability to know what is really happening and what to do about it. You will not get lost in the particulars; you will transcend the momentary; and like the priestess in the Motherpeace Tower, you will find yourself raised above mundane levels of life. You may experience very high levels of creative energy. It is your task, then, to interpret what you have seen and heard at these high altitudes where the sacred and profane intersect. What makes you so clear is the fire from within meeting the fire from without. It is control over these fires that makes you powerful.

At the same time that your "high self" can understand and handle what's happening in your life at this time, your personality self may be freaking out. Like the group of people waiting at the foot of the Tower for the advice of the oracular priestess, your personality needs help and guidance during the stress of this transition. Take time to appreciate the difficulties facing you, and be especially cautious with your health and welfare right now. Eat well, get plenty of rest, and don't leave yourself open to accidents or illness.

If possible, open up to the power offered by the Tower card. There is great joy in what Kali holds out to us—profound bliss in the understanding of the soul's immortality and the body's divinity. When these energies move through you, you can experience them physically as well as spiritually, as they reveal to you the highest experiences of spirit simultaneously with the deepest pleasures of the body. It is no accident that Kali is both sexual guru and destroyer, for she slays whatever stands in the way of true appreciation of what is real. She does not ask to escape "the wheel of life," but rides it consciously from the center. When you let her into your life, you will experience an increased sensitivity to everything in existence along with a heightened ability to handle whatever comes your way.

CHAPTER 19

STAR

Opening to the Goddess

The Star represents the calm after the storm. The raging fires of the Tower have subsided, a light rain falls, and grace descends like the mist itself. Immersed in the magic mineral waters of Mother Earth, bathed in starlight, the priestess opens herself to the healing power of the Goddess, and her cares begin to dissolve. As she reaches out through prayer to touch the oneness of all life, the same light that radiates from the stars in the sky glows from her.

Pink flowers float in the pool, blossoms opening in love. In a ritual for women of the Yucatan Peninsula in Central America, a hollow is made in the earth and a woman bathes there naked in water up to her breasts. Other women cover the surface of the water with flowers and dance around her singing and praying in order to heal her and to demonstrate, as Kay Turner says, the "nurturing effect of tribal sisterhood." Modern Dianic Witch Z. Budapest suggests a similar cleansing ritual for a victim of rape. Women gather around her in her bath and bring her flowers, bathe her, sing to her, and generally re-affirm her beauty.

In the words of a Navaho ritual chant, which needs to be said aloud slowly:

> *The world before me is restored in beauty.*
> *The world behind me is restored in beauty.*
> *The world below me is restored in beauty.*
> *The world above me is restored in beauty.*
> *All things around me are restored in beauty.*

See color illustration on Plate 6.

My voice is restored in beauty.
It is finished in beauty.
It is finished in beauty.
It is finished in beauty.
It is finished in beauty.

In this lovely prayer to "Changing Woman," a chief deity among the Navaho, we experience—just as in the Motherpeace image of the Star—an appeal to the transformative power of the Goddess, the one who can truly finish us in beauty. The Star signifies that redemption is possible. In this respect it recalls the Tibetan White Tara, savioress who redeems through her holy, healing touch, and who is sister aspect to the Green Tara described in Chapter 13. Tibetan prayer to Tara is believed to grant all attainments and remove all terrors. As in the case of the Navaho Liberation Prayer already quoted, try speaking the prayer instead of merely reading it silently. Say:

Homage to Tara our mother:
great compassion!
Homage to Tara our mother:
a thousand hands, a thousand eyes!
Homage to Tara our mother:
queen of physicians!
Homage to Tara our mother:
conquering disease like medicine!
Homage to Tara our mother:
knowing the means of compassion!
Homage to Tara our mother:
a foundation like the earth!
Homage to Tara our mother:
cooling like water!
Homage to Tara our mother:
ripening like fire!
Homage to Tara our mother:
spreading like wind!
Homage to Tara our mother:
pervading like space!

Like White Tara, the Chinese Kuan Yin is Goddess of mercy and compassion, the compassionate light, the healing heart, and the force of purity. Like the Chinese nun quoted in Chapter 14, I have felt the touch of Kuan Yin. In my experience, it is as if she were placing her hands over my body and channeling divine energy through to the very center. She cleanses and releases all pain, bringing hope and joy back to the heart in time of need.

The idea of cosmic power reaching down and blessing our earthly lives is as old as the rain. Like the pre-Columbian water pitcher and washbowl, the receiver of the spirit is an open vessel and represents the archetypal feminine. She is in a state of ecstasy, full of faith and open to the universal force of healing love. Immersion in water is an ancient healing practice, and the power of mineral waters or hot springs cleanses and purifies body and soul. Pain releases and fear lets go, opening the pores to love. The water surrounding the body feels like the Mother's loving embrace, and the woman's own hands touch her body, soothing and stroking, transmitting the healing energy.

Over her head soars an eagle, symbol of spirit. The eagle flies higher than any other bird, high enough to "touch the sun." The golden eagle is a symbol of peace, and its flight through the lavender mist of the Star card seems to reflect the spiritual flight of the woman who bathes in the healing waters. An eagle flying overhead is a sign of shaman-power, sometimes taken as a call to that vocation. To the shaman, the eagle is a messenger, bringing instructions from the spirit of the night. As Halifax says, "When shamans get power, it always comes from the night."

All healing requires an openness to universal energies and the ability to "step down" these energies to the physical plane, so that the physical body benefits. The healing force enters the crown *chakra* at the top of the head, where, according to Huichol shamanism, the soul lives. This energy lights up the head and spiritual centers, whereupon the healer brings the force down through the heart and hands. This is the age-old power of the laying-on of hands, which natural healers have used for millennia and which the nursing profession is gradually rediscovering.

The Star is like Justice, but taken to a higher level. Now there is a conscious submission to Fate, a loving gift of the self to the spirit of life. No more unexpected karmic adjustments, no more confusion about what is right and wrong. Now the being gets in touch, through the body and the feelings, with how things are flowing and what the purpose of life is.

Aquarius, the astrological sign attributed to the Star, is the fixed air sign of the "water-bearer" and represents the healing force in the universe, as well as universal friendship, psychic sensitivity, and group understanding. Like the healer in the Motherpeace image, Aquarians tend to be visionary in their outlook. Another astrological sign often attributed to the Star is Aries, cardinal fire sign of the Magician, which represents the inner fire and spiritual will of the human being making contact with the divine forces. The Aries fire boils up from within and reaches out to meet the Goddess halfway, like the eagle flying towards the sun. As healing power touches this priestess, her own fire awakens and responds with equal intensity to the force she receives.

The stones surrounding the pool in the Motherpeace image form a protective circle around the healer. Within the magic circle, work can take place in safety and with a consciously directed focus. One of the cardinal rules for the practice of magic or psychic work of any kind is to make a protective circle around oneself for grounding. Then the soul can fly like the eagle, while the body remains nourished and protected within the magical space.

Around the pool, the cattails and lilies of the valley reflect both the earthly and spiritual nature of the healer. The frog on a rock is a symbol of transformation and rebirth, much loved by Native American people. From egg to tadpole to frog to egg once more, this amphibian demonstrates the circle of death and rebirth and how to make transitions between the worlds. Blue morning glories reiterate this message. Although poisonous in excess, a part of the morning glory has hallucinogenic qualities valued by Native American shamans who used it for crossing the threshold between form and spirit.

In the upper right of the Motherpeace image is Sirius, brightest star in our sky and one of the nearest to earth, only 8.7 light-years away. Visually nearby is the famous star cluster called the Pleiades or Seven Sisters. The star named Sirius by the Greeks was earlier known by the Egyptians as "Sothis," who was the Goddess Isis. In turn, Isis was related to the Sumerian Ishtar, named for the planet Venus—the morning and evening star. Ishtar (or Venus) belongs to a cluster of Goddesses including Aphrodite, Artemis, Mary of the Thousand Breasts, and the Mother of Eleusis, also called "the Wise One of the Sea." This returns us to the theme of water and may remind us of the Hebrew concept of the feminine spirit that "moved upon the face of the waters." This spirit was later absorbed into the Christian idea of the Holy Spirit, which is symbolized by the Star.

The Star prepares one for initiation. A modern equivalent of this cleansing ritual might be the work currently being done to relieve "despair" about world problems. Johanna Macy posits that when individuals feel hopeless and afraid, but do not admit to such feelings. isolation results and with it, utter despair. However, when people share with each other the depth of their fears and feelings about possible disaster, and maybe cry together, the numbness begins to tingle like a cheek when novocaine is wearing off, and we can once again begin to feel.

When you get the Star in a reading, you know you have passed to a new level and something in you has opened to the Goddess. You are ready to ask for help, and you receive it. You trust in the ability of the universe to heal you and you are ready to begin the process of transformation. A grace comes over you which allows you to look forward to the future. You can feel beauty radiating through your very being, from the center out. Chances are, you are enjoying a rather peaceful, restful period, which helps you to feel your connection to others and perhaps to the divine spirit in the world.

Take time now to bless yourself. Do something nurturing and self-loving. Maybe you'll want to take a hot tub or a sauna, or just get into a hot bath, letting your cares flow away like the priestess in the Mother-peace image. Imagine yourself surrounded by dancing priestesses or, better yet, invite your closest friends for a ritual celebration of your new sense of self. If this is not possible, just imagine the presence of ancient female ancestors all around you and feel the caring inherent in the feminine spirit. If you have fresh flowers, take them into the bath with you, and let your beauty shine through. Feel the way you and the flowers are the same—open, living manifestations of life force.

This may be a time when you are aware of the Navaho Changing Woman touching your life, transforming you. Perhaps you will take a new name to signify the newness of yourself. All Witches have a special, spiritual, or ritual name. Listen for yours. It may be any name that comes to you—the name of a Goddess or a flower or anything else. It will be unique to you and have some symbolic significance, upon which you can meditate as you would a healing dream. Roll the name around in your mind, feel the changes taking place in you on many levels, and imagine yourself reborn, renewed, refreshed.

Buddhists and other Tantric practitioners visualize the Goddess in detail and then take her into their hearts. You can do this too. Find a picture or statue of some Goddess you like, or simply imagine the divine female presence in your mind and allow her to take form. You can use the Star image as your visualization, if you like, and begin consciously to work toward identifying so strongly with the image that you start breathing her into your own heart. Imagine that your ego becomes her ego, her mind becomes your mind. Feel her beauty in you and your beauty in her; let the separation disappear until you can feel that you are She, you are Goddess, you are love itself.

CHAPTER 20

MOON

Experiencing the Mystery

The Moon represents the core of the ancient female mysteries—the journey into the labyrinth or, as Nor Hall says, "the underground dwelling of the goddess." The labyrinth is the holy path to the center and back out again, the "moon-wheel" which, in the words of Monica Sjöö, spins in both directions, "bringing knowledge and energy for both creation and destruction." Very similar labyrinths are found as far apart as India, Crete, and Arizona; and a simplified version of the labyrinth, the double spiral, is found everywhere in the world. The spiral, like the snake, is always a symbol of the Goddess; especially of the feminine power of regeneration—the going in and coming out again. The way is marked by Ariadne, Cretan Goddess who had the spiderlike foresight to unroll a thread as she entered the labyrinth.

Like the Motherpeace images described in Chapters 13 through 16, the Moon represents the shamanic call, in this case the call to enter into the darkness. The labyrinth invites, and a boat waits to transport the spirit of the initiate to other realms. The "winged gate," which Neumann discusses, stands like a beacon at the end of the "tunnel" of vision waiting to be entered—the birth canal that awaits the soul at the end of the journey of development.

In Tarot tradition, the Moon represents unconscious desires and the fears that accompany the sense of losing control or falling into the unconscious realm of sleep and dreams. However, if one is afraid to enter one's own astral territory, one can never truly know oneself—and the mystery of initiation is about little more than this. The phantasms flying around

See color illustration on Plate 6.

129

in the Motherpeace image are visions and illusions that occupy the astral plane, making this a "dark night of the soul." The astral plane is crowded with unhappy ghosts and negative thought forms created by the human mind and projected into the space around us.

This realm of the unconscious is often dense with ugly visions and hideous creations of deluded consciousness, and the lost souls of people who have lived out their lives in discordance with natural laws of the universe. Only the strong can enter this realm and remain clear and protected throughout the journey—for others, danger lurks, madness threatens. For the human mind is likely to seize on the negative, if that is what it is accustomed to. The real confrontation that the Moon represents is the meeting with the "Dweller on the Threshold" of which occult and esoteric teachers speak. This is the giant force of accumulated evil or wrongdoings, the hideous part of the self that a person would rather not look at and would like to pretend doesn't exist, and which rises up at the point of real psychic growth. This "demon" must not only be looked at, but integrated into the being, in order to establish wholeness. In the dark realms of the imagination, it is crucial to envision the powerful good Moon Mother and let her be a guide. Like the woman in the Motherpeace image, one must travel these realms with the eyes shut and the senses open, like a bat with sonar rather than sight, letting feelings dictate the direction as one gradually enters the deep. For protection and guidance on this path, one may call on Artemis-Diana, the Virgin, or Hekate, the Crone.

In 500 B.C., the first Dianic witchcraft "cult" was formally established in Greece for the worship of the ancient Moon Goddess. Greek Artemis or Roman Diana with her bow and arrows represented the waxing half of the Moon cycle, from silvery new crescent to fullness. The Egyptian lunar Goddess Neith was portrayed in a similar way, as was the Irish Re. The Full Moon Goddess represented abundance and the fire of sexuality and union, personified by the Phoenician Astarte, whose iconographic forms resemble her dark sister Lilith, or the Greek Selene, the Cretan Pasiphae, or even the Egyptian Isis. In witchcraft, waning Moon was signified by the Greek Hekate described in Chapter 11, and also by the Sumerian Levanah (Hebrew Lebanah) whose name means Moon. Levanah is particularly associated with the menstrual cycle and bleeding at the dark Moon.

Although all these Goddesses are still invoked into coven circles by the High Priestess, it is the name Diana that is most commonly associated with witchcraft today. Generally, witches hold their ritual celebrations on or around the full Moon each month, and Diana represents the Moon Goddess in all her aspects.

As long as one can surrender to this lunar mode of consciousness, the journey will be creative and full of revelation. One can expect, like the orgiastic priestesses of old, that the trip will involve powerful and deep experiences of wisdom and understanding. One must give oneself to the darkness in order to fully emerge into the light of life represented by the next image, the Sun. Sjöö explains that "at the fusion of the Double-Spiral there is a vortex, and winds of dissolution; beyond is a Still Center and the bliss of Union." How does one achieve it? "Transcending the opposites, one can experience the shift from one pole to the other and contain, within consciousness, an active understanding of this process." In this journey, there is truly nothing to fear except fear itself. It is fear that creates demons and all the unpleasantness associated with the Moon card in traditional Tarot.

This night-force, with its phantasms and glamours and hidden, intoxicating elements, is most frequently represented by Lilith, an early Semitic Goddess who became the classical "demon" and now represents "woman as evil." In earlier forms, Lilith personified benign powers of the night, helping spirits collectively known as *lilim*, who offered "the greatest kindness to mortals."

Lilith's power is enchantment, and in European culture she became known for this above all, bringing the stigma of "demon" and "enticement" and "sorcery" to all women, because of men's fear of this power. Like the Moon itself, Lilith is connected to sexuality and the instinctual realm of desire and erotic dreams and fantasies.

In shamanism, it is necessary to accumulate "helping spirits" in order to succeed. Shamans have what are loosely called "spirit lovers" who represent the union they make with divine forces in the form of guides or spirits. In ancient times, these forces might have been known positively as "liliths" who came and made love with the shaman in the night; but in the Middle Ages they became "demons," who attacked and secretly stole something from men—their vital fluids—during their sleep, when they were most defenseless. No less disturbing, perhaps, to the medieval patriarchal mind was the link between the Moon and menstruation, the source of another vital fluid. As Sjöö points out, "shamanism— an ecstatic lunar cult—relies on the natural descent into body-consciousness that menstruation brings each month." Whenever men sought to suppress desire and "eros" itself, they put the blame on a figure such as Lilith. Projection of this kind was ultimately the cause of the destruction of some nine million women during the "Burning Times."

Today our problem is not so much witch-burning as the result of its success, and the success of propaganda against Goddess worship. However, despite the near-disappearance of the ancient rites, our dreams may allow us, as Hall argues, to experience the same "terrain" as the "actual experience of initiates." The celebrations and community acknowledgment of initiation may have been destroyed, but the experience is still being enacted all the time. Jung worked with this idea in much of his study and therapy, and Jungian psychology today reflects the idea that modern people experience initiation rites and symbolic ventures into the ancient mystery realms through the unconscious—mainly our dreams and our artistic expression. Through these avenues, a person is able to integrate experiences and the parts of the being until reaching wholeness.

In the Motherpeace image the sea-green reminds us of desire and the magnetic pull of the watery realms. The Moon rules all fluids, including the waters of the body and brain, so she has a very powerful influence over us, certainly as powerful as over the tidal pulls of entire oceans. She pulls us to her depths, and if we go in fear, we are likely to struggle, experience hysteria and paranoia, become a "lunatic," and possibly miss the revelatory experience itself. If we go without fear, we experience ecstatic and joyous entry into the labyrinth.

When you get the Moon in a reading, there is nothing to do but yield to the feelings. If you try to figure things out intellectually, you will fail. The Moon is a sign of unconsciousness—you may as well flow with it. If you can open yourself to being in the moment and not trying to figure out what lies ahead; if you can enter the darkness with eagerness and courage; if you can trust in the higher powers to guide you intuitively through the journey of darkness and the unknown, then you will learn from the voyage and gain consciousness as your initiatory gift.

To imagine the friendly darkness inherent in this journey toward consciousness, try to envision going down into the deepest chamber of a pyramid; or imagine the innermost sanctuary of a sacred cave of our Paleolithic European ancestors; or try to think what a Native American might have felt like in a pueblo, going down into the Great Kiva to await rebirth into sunshine. Finally, let your feelings float back to your own experience of growing in the amniotic waters until, finally, when the time came, you were born from the safe dark womb space into the light.

The Moon suggests a good time for dreaming. In order to deepen your understanding of the transformation in which you are engaged, you might try your hand at dream-work, keeping a journal and writing your dreams whenever possible, then working with them in any of a number of interesting ways. You may want to interpret them according to one of the popular symbol systems, such as those developed by Ann Faraday, Patricia Garfield, or Strephon Williams. Or you may already do this and want to reach further into your psyche through "dream yoga" or "lucid dreaming." The word lucid does not imply rationality, but an almost super-rational ability to enter into the dreamworld consciously and interact with your dreams as they occur. You may wish to share your dreams with a friend or lover, simply letting yourself feel what they mean in a noninterpretive way as well.

Another way of tuning in to the moon is to get into your "menstrual clock" and see how your personal cycle corresponds to the cycles of the Moon. Or you can chart your emotional and physical energies all through the month and examine these "biorhythms" in light of the Moon's phases of waxing, full, and waning.

CHAPTER 21

SUN

Raising Consciousness

The Sun represents rebirth—the emergence of the butterfly out of the cocoon. It symbolizes consciousness and the active, awakened understanding of, and appreciation for, life. Out of the dark womb of night, emerging from the birth canal of the kiva or underground chamber, the Sun represents the soul's appearance in all its radiance. Full mental understanding bursts onto the horizon of consciousness, and one sees what is, with joy and celebration.

What is the illusion banished by the dawn? In the Motherpeace image, human beings no longer insist that they are separate from each other and the rest of the planetary life. The Sun represents the knowledge that we are connected by the eternal rays of the life force, each of us part of a vast organism called "humanity" and the even greater body of the Earth itself.

In rebirth one feels a great happiness, a joy of being alive, an expanded sense of play. Less attached to desires and expectations, one enjoys a growing feeling of acceptance. The achievement of nonattachment does not imply lack of feeling or disconnection. On the contrary, it means stronger links with the oneness that is at the center of life, and at the same time a less personal sense of attachment to the little hurts and grievances of the personal daily reality. The inner "Sun" radiates to the outer sphere and heals the fractured parts of the being, bringing together and harmonizing the various subpersonalities under the guidance of the soul.

What this means to the ego is transmutation. The ego is not obliterated. Rather, it is lifted up. From the solar plexus or power center, con-

See color illustration on Plate 7.

sciousness is "raised" up into the heart from which it radiates in a more powerful and balanced flow of life energy. This "raised consciousness" is the higher octave of the zodiacal sign Leo and the key to healing and clarity in the New Age of Motherpeace. When conscious awareness is centered in the heart (the fourth *chakra*, corresponding to the chest), one sees the personality as the "vehicle" of Consciousness (or the soul). Personal concerns and petty desires no longer control or dominate the human being but are seen for what they really are—theatrics and a display of personal ego consciousness. This display might be attractive and dramatic, but it is no longer taken to be the central meaning of one's life.

The Sun does not judge or "put down" the personality or the concerns of the ego. It simply sees itself as part of the whole, of the group, for example, and this leads to a joyous explosion of appreciation and spiritual comprehension. Human personalities tend to become easily confused in the face of complexity and paradox. The central Self views things with a more holistic awareness, knowing how the other person feels, understanding all the parts of a problem, relying on interaction more than personal desires and needs.

What is this "Self" to which I have referred several times? Most people know they have an inner being of some kind, because every now and then it speaks up in some way and offers guidance or direction. If the ego personality dominates, then the advice won't be taken. As in the case of the Devil described in Chapter 17, the inner voice will be denied. Yet we know the voice is inescapably there. Once allowed to speak, the Self introduces us to worlds we had barely suspected.

There are many people who expect the New Age to be heralded by the return of Christ or of some avatar such as the Buddha or even, perhaps, the experience of a female messiah for a change. My sense is that those who look too hard for a human individual who embodies the wisdom we seek may miss the real happening and will therefore be disappointed. Occult teacher Alice Bailey, writing in the early part of the twentieth century, predicted that the messianic return to the world during this New Age would be in group form—the gathering together of evolved or advanced souls working for peace and healing.

Bailey called this gathering "the New Group of World Servers" and predicted that struggle within relationships and groups would eventually lead to a kind of purification that would teach humankind by example how to move forward into the New Age. Each group of workers or "servers" would come together around a "group soul," which, like a Sun, would radiate light and healing to the group. Individual egos would be overcome by its brilliance—the radiance not of a charismatic leader, but of a spiritual idea freely shared. Many people today feel the presence of these soul-lights, and are mobilizing in groups around a central guiding principle that overrides egocentricity and promotes life.

With rebirth into the sunlight of consciousness, humor begins. "All the world's a stage . . ." turns out to be true, and sure enough, each player has a role, a "vehicle" through which the deeper, truer Self may be revealed. In the Motherpeace image of the Sun, life is a circus and everybody is in the ring together. Dark and light skins touch, and community is born, balancing in an open form of free choice and joyous collectivity.

In the Kabalistic Tree of Life, the number six is the number of the Sun. There are sixes in the Sun card, too, starting with the three people in front, two in the second row, and the single one in the back, adding up to six and forming a perfect triangle of harmony. There are three animals and three balloons, another six. The Sun itself radiates like the central disc of *Tipareth* on the Tree of Life.

The play of animals is instinctual and free—unselfconscious and spontaneous. The play of free human beings—those who are not limited by the lesser needs of the personality, but have opened to the wider purpose and meaning of life—assumes the spontaneous quality of animal frolic. Animal spirits taken on during shamanistic journeys help the human being to become freer and more naturally joyful. Dancing the spirit of the animal loosens the tension of being human and opens the heart. The understanding that divinity is right here, in us, now—in everything and everyone—is extremely liberating. This is the philosophy of "immanence" or spiritual embodiment that the Goddess represents.

In Japanese mythology, among hundreds of thousands of national deities, the Sun Goddess Amaterasu is central; the imperial family traces its descent through her. The best-known story of Amaterasu is the day she fought with her younger brother, the Storm god. In anger, she withdrew into a cave, causing the world to become dark and uninhabitable. Only the Goddess of mirth was able to entice her with dancing and singing of bawdy songs, and—some say—lifting her skirts to show her female genitalia. When Amaterasu, who was amused, came out to laugh, the gods and goddesses had hung a mirror from a tree and she saw herself in it for the first time. Struck by her own beauty, she came out of the cave and began again to shine. This rebirth of the central Goddess is reflected in the happiness of the Sun card in the Tarot.

The Australian Aborigines also believe the Sun to be female and the first creator of life on earth. Most cultures that consider the Sun female see the moon as male, the opposite of the traditional Western view. In

Western culture, we are used to the idea of the Sun as male and the moon as female, a fairly old idea that is reflected in Goddess cultures of the Mediterranean, the British Isles, and northern European civilizations. In the West, the male Sun began as the son of the Great Mother—her child and, when he grew up, her consort or lover. The Great Mother gave birth to the Sun as her masculine counterpart who had been formerly contained within her. His yearly birth and death were celebrated in the agricultural mysteries from early times, frequently symbolized by the birth of the seed and the later harvesting of an ear of corn or the reaping of the grain. The times of the birth and death of the Sun are the Solstices—roughly June twenty-first and December twenty-first—the longest and shortest days of the solar year.

Later patriarchal Sun Gods usurped the role of the Mother as creator and generator of life force, and were accompanied by prejudices in favor of light over dark, white over black, and, of course, male over female. Solar calendars replaced lunar ones. Solar symbols of axe, sword, and the "chariot of the sun" evolved; and the warrior consciousness was born. Among its earliest casualties was the matriarchal consciousness of male and female contained within the One. The return of this consciousness is a goal of yoga and other spiritual disciplines designed for healing and spiritual growth.

In the Motherpeace image, a butterfly is superimposed on the Sun. Archetypal symbol of rebirth, the butterfly is one of Nature's most delightful and marvelous creatures as it moves out of the chrysalis state and into the light. Through a process of conscious transformation and rebirth, we can each experience the miracle of the butterfly—crawl out of our cocoons, unfurl wings, and soar into the heavens, utterly changed. During the New Age, the human race as a collective organism has the possibility of transforming in a similar way.

When you get the Sun in a reading, you can relax and enjoy yourself, it's going to be a good day, week, or year. You are probably experiencing a great deal of expansiveness and pleasure—your Sun is shining. Celebrate! In some way you have come out of a dark, lonely, or sad space, and are now feeling the renewal of energy and friendship. Life seems to open and offer you new directions. You feel yourself to be part of something bigger than your own individual life, and yet your individuality is freed up as well.

The Sun offers you confidence and the ability to put yourself forward in the world. A higher version of Leo, fixed fire sign, the Sun lets you radiate personal power because you understand your own place in the universal scheme of things. Say what you see, express yourself. Others will listen and you will provide a light of clear leadership. This should be a very creative period for you and the people around you. Allow your ideas to grow and change, dramatize your thoughts in some way, let your true colors show. It may be time to dance or sing. The bright yellow light radiating out of the Sun image blesses you with positive mental energy that enlivens others and activates possibility.

Because of the balancing of polarities within the Self that the Sun represents, it may mean different things to different people. For instance, if you are a man getting this card, you may experience a playful side of yourself opening up and the warm energy of love being expressed in new ways. Your heart may open and you may feel the healing heat of the Goddess. This will no doubt mean a relaxing of the usual controls and "performance anxiety" and a calm self-confidence that doesn't require proving yourself or thrusting forward.

On the other hand, if you are a woman getting the Sun card, you may be experiencing the expression of your inner "masculine" self in new ways—your powerful positive "animus" may be emerging. It might be a time of really expressing the power of your ego for the first time, demonstrating your leadership abilities and working out in the world.

Solar consciousness is not the rulership of the Sun King or the power of the battle axe; these are misinterpretations from the past. What the Sun represents for us is New Age consciousness, "rulership" of the heart, the coming to the fore of the central spiritual Sun. Whatever way this central loving Self emerges from you, it is time to rejoice. An open heart paves the way for peace and a world connected through joy and harmony. Sun consciousness may be the first step to putting down our weapons and joining hands in a great, global circle of healing. Nuclear war and global pollution hurt us all. The pain of one person starving is my pain and your pain. Ask not for whom the Sun shines: it shines for us all.

CHAPTER 22

JUDGEMENT

Healing the Earth

Judgement represents the return of Gaia, the Mother of Life, to earth. The Aeon, as Crowley calls this card in Tarot, is a symbol of the cycle of return, the time of healing and planetary regeneration. Occult and esoteric teachers speak of this return as the "feminine ray coming back into manifestation." Feminists and pagans see it as the return of the Goddess. Others see it as a return of the Christ-consciousness or the coming of a Messiah. In Gnostic literature, the Female Aeon is the "Great Manifested Thought," which suggests the power of the group-mind to overcome evil with good. All these descriptions carry a similar message: the life force, represented in the Motherpeace image by the Egyptian *ankh* symbol, will shine once more on Mother Earth and her children. A great healing force more powerful than any one of us will make itself available.

Will we take advantage of it? Peace is our need above all others, because without it, in an age of holocaustic weapons, we can no longer count on the continuation of our species. Along with technical negotiations about how to "control" weapons and how to resolve particular conflicts, the people of earth need access to healing energy. In the Motherpeace image of Judgement, the ancient symbol of *ankh* is also a symbol of Venus, Goddess of Love. A circle of spirit balances on the cross of the earth's four elements, and a rainbow of peace pours out of the diamond center of the heart.

When human awareness is raised to the heart level, one enters an altered state of consciousness that heals and generates extraordinary

See color illustration on Plate 7.

power. This healing light is becoming available to us now, as shown, for example, in the work of Elisabeth Kübler-Ross, who helps dying people make contact with their spirits; Helen Caldicott, the pediatrician who speaks out against the nuclear arms race; Joan Baez, who sings from her heart and strengthens the tradition of nonviolent resistance; and Mother Teresa, who seeks the end of world hunger and, meanwhile, cares for children who are starving and in pain.

Anywhere and anytime that people begin speaking and acting from their hearts to protest world destruction and work toward peace, Judgement is being felt. This card represents *bodhisattva* energies, the compassion and forgiveness of Isis (Chapter 4), Kuan Yin (Chapter 14), and Tara (Chapters 13 and 19). A Buddhist *bodhisattva* is any person who, having reached "enlightenment" or a state of true understanding, then pledges herself to work toward the same freedom for all of humanity. As long as part of the human race is still in chains or bound by negative forces, how can anyone be free? This is the worldview of the Goddess-cultures of old—a deep belief that the entire world community is bound together, that the destiny of one person is inextricably connected to the destinies of all the rest.

In Tarot tradition, the Judgement card represents the "judgement day" when the souls of the dead shall confront their Creator and be judged. In the Christian tradition, this scene includes punishment for the wicked and the heavenly reward for those who have been "good." In the Motherpeace image, however, Judgement really portrays a much more loving, all-embracing "moment of truth" when the heart can look with complete forgiveness on the personality, just as the Goddess looks with forgiveness on the Earth and humanity, in spite of our "evil" ways. Once one has truly seen and forgiven oneself, has lovingly accepted the personality and the ego and all the individual human traits one is ordinarily ashamed of, then the integration lifts one immediately into the sphere of the divine presence.

When one can see oneself with clarity and acceptance, then one is likely to see others in the same way; without criticism and with full acceptance of what is truly the human condition. This acceptance is an understanding of human beauty, rather than an accusation of imperfection, and is personified by Sophia or Divine Wisdom, called Helena by the Greeks. So, as Sally Gearhart suggests in her pioneering reinterpretation of a popular traditional Tarot deck, the Judgement card really points to divine understanding "beyond Judgement." The narrow criticisms of the past are released, one's "sins" are seen and let go of, and an angel of mercy descends like a dove into the heart, bringing the "peace that passeth all understanding."

In Tibetan meditation, the goal of the initiate is the building of a body of light that is called the *Vajra* or "diamond body." This diamond body represents the heart and the new, "purified" energy body that is created through meditation, yoga, and the channeling of cosmic healing energies. Old negative patterns of behavior and thought that have "tarnished" the soul in the past are overcome with powerful white light; illusions (or what Bailey calls "glamours") are washed away, and the human consciousness is "uplifted" and "refined" until love is the overriding force and can overcome "evil." In the Motherpeace images, a similar transformation occurs between Sun (described in Chapter 21) and Judgement. In Sun, divine rays of one's spiritual center have begun to illuminate the personality, but the personality remains up front. In Judgement, the personality recedes into the rainbow light of the central Self.

In contemporary Buddhist thought, this process may imply leaving the body or the planet; but in the Motherpeace image, it suggests a realization of the divinity present in both, a return in consciousness to the presence of the Mother, and a renewal of the peaceful culture once familiar to humanity. A return to this integrated, holistic world of Goddess means no more separation between what is "spiritual" and what is "material." Instead of making an effort to become "free" of desire or sexuality, one might hope to wrench apart the unholy merging of violence with sexuality, and to restore the natural sanctity of pleasure as an embodiment of the Goddess.

The assumption that evil is somehow rooted in Mother Earth is a harmful illusion. Evil exists in the universe and is manifested in the human soul's *separation* from the world of natural life and universal law. Western utopians who yearn for the landing of some extraterrestrial spacecraft to lift the "good guys" off the planet to some "better" place seem to be repeating the age-old mistake of the Eastern gurus who want to leave the body (planet) by spiritual means. Why this persistent urge to leave? What is the use of trying to escape the nuclear arms race on earth by constructing fragile "space colonies"? In any environment, a denial of the spirit will lead to disaster, although the technological means may differ.

What our ancient cave-painting ancestors understood was our holy purpose, the path of human consciousness as liaison between biological evolution and spirit. The Tarot in general and the Judgement card in particular emphasize the return of this awareness—the understanding of cause and effect, and the compassion and divine order that accompany that understanding. An advanced Libra card ruled by Venus, Judgement promises a cosmic rebalancing of the earth's forces.

Despite the concept of the "feminine ray," much esoteric writing and teaching neglects to deal with cosmic balancing of actual women, or to say what roles we must play in the return of the feminine principle. If particularly "feminine" energies are manifesting on such a high and vibrant level, what does it mean to be incarnate in a female body at this time? I believe it means female leadership in very tangible ways, an explicit challenge to old structures and philosophies that are almost completely male-dominated and male-supremacist in tone. In contrast, the Judgement card promises a return of the High Priestess described in Chapter 4.

The return to the Goddess implies a return of her many priestesses—powerful female transmitters of the energy of the "feminine ray." All over the world, women are being "tapped" with this power and beginning to manifest the Goddess in their work and daily lives. Men who respect and respond to this energy are also feeling the power of the feminine, which puts them into touch with a gentleness and sensitivity unrealized by most men in the world today.

Motherpeace is literally the "peace of the Mother." While those who are open to her influence are healed and released from past limitations by her regenerative power, those who fight this incoming energy may find it almost overwhelming in its power to destroy old forms. If so, they might experience the Goddess in her aspect as Destroyer. This means, for each of us individually, that the parts of us attached to negativity would be threatened and ultimately destroyed. As is the case of the Death image described in Chapter 15, consciousness must focus on what healer Patricia Sun calls the "new skin," and not on what is being lost in the transition. To focus on the past that is dying, at the expense of the moment of liberation, would pose a hindrance to the growth offered by Judgement.

For transformation, one must become open to intuition and healing messages from the biosphere—knowledge from the group mind, Gaia—guidance from Mother Earth herself. To cling to old patterns of behavior may mean extinction; and to value money or possessions at the expense of human relationships would miss the action. Fitfully, the Age of Individualism sputters to an end.

When you get the Judgement card in a Tarot reading, you can bet some important decision has already been made by your "high Self" or "oversoul." You may not even be consciously aware of exactly what has happened, but something has—and it alters your reality for good. You have been uplifted in some way, transported right out of the past and into a new present full of wonder. You are not angry, and are not blaming others, but taking full responsibility for a choice and for a new way of viewing reality. You are making wise judgements.

Likewise, you are in a new space of global vision and divine understanding. In some way you are tapping into the very highest energies and using them with balance and foresight. The compassionate understanding of your heart is ridding you of old negative patterns that held you back, and the same sympathetic understanding is having an effect on others around you. You have stopped judging people from a narrow, critical vantage point. Now you see them with deeper caring and clearer vision— you understand their foibles as well as their divinity, and you accept them as a package of both, like yourself.

Judgement portrays an end to suffering and the beginnings of spiritual "resurrection." Now is the time to make amends for past errors. If you have needed to be honest or frank with someone, do it now. If there is some unhealed wound between you and another, heal it now. Let your negative patterns dissolve in the rainbow of healing magic falling from the heart of the Goddess. Know that the positive forces in the universe are acting through you now and there can be no defeat; as Susan B. Anthony once said, "Failure is impossible."

Judgement is the card of the divine healer—the absolutely transcendent and nonattached channel through which flow the highest forces of the universe. You have an opportunity to manifest these energies right now. If you do, they will have lasting effects on your life. You might want to work with envisioning the New Age in your own specific way. Let the visions flow through you and manifest in some way that will also allow others to see them. Share your vision.

CHAPTER 23

WORLD

Casting the Circle

In the World image, we see Motherpeace herself, the Great Mother with her torch and tambourine, dancing the oldest dance. Around her the peoples of the World form a ring of energy, as blossoms are linked to form a lei of welcome. Ecstatic within the circle, the Great Mother represents what Arthur Avalon calls "the union of the quiescent and active principles of consciousness itself," and what von Franz calls the "magical union of the individual psyche with the whole cosmos." In sexual terms, she is the Divine Androgyne, integrating male and female energies. In terms of yoga and other forms of meditation, she symbolizes the liberation of consciousness that is not *of* bliss, but *is* bliss.

Within the eternal circle, the dance of consciousness continues uninterrupted. Taoists, stressing intuition and ecstasy, describe the "expansive power of Tao in the middle space" as "imperishable." For them, too, this power flows from "the mysterious Mother of all beings." As she comes and goes, she produces Heaven and Earth. "Thus acting, She is never fatigued." To Goddess-worshipers, such as Indian Tantrics, "immaterial Spirit is just as unthinkable as spiritless matter." When heaven's spirit and earth's matter are known to be One, then "cosmic consciousness" is attained.

The Indian understanding of universal law is based on the Great Mother, just as were the ancient cultures of Egypt or Sumer. Her creativity is the cause and effect of all existence. She is both Being (unchanging Consciousness or *"Cit"*) and Activity (incessant creation of shifting forms or *"Maya"*). By consciously making every human function a sacred act, one can enjoy the World and simultaneously be liberated from all worlds. "When the Mother is seen in all things, She is at length realized as She who is beyond them all."

144

World (XXI)

On reaching the consciousness inherent in the World image, one understands that "all that exists is here." As Avalon says, "There is no need to throw one's eyes into the heavens for it." A line from the Visvasara Tantra sums it up: "What is here is there: what is not here is nowhere."

The word "*Maya*" usually means "illusion" and is meant to disparage the entire state of existence (what most people think of as "reality"). But Tantra, and in the West witchcraft, recognize worldly existence as one form of what is "divine" and "real;" the other divine reality is "formless" and "unmanifest." The Mother represents both spirit and nature. "In herself She is not a person," says Avalon, "but She is ever and incessantly personalizing; assuming the multiple masks (*Persona*) which are the varied forms of mind-matter."

In the Motherpeace image, she is pictured as the Self at the center of the "selves" that make up the outer ring of the circle, consciousness among her "multiple selves." In particular, the World is "Consciousness veiling Itself" or Maya-Shakti, the spirit wearing forms like clothing. In this way, she is a symbol of yogic achievement in the sense of having control over all the "vehicles," from the physical body to the highest spirit body in which her consciousness can leave the physical plane and exist elsewhere at will.

In a temporal sense, the "cosmic dancer" is the essential Self who takes form again and again through reincarnation of the soul in different bodies during various lifetimes. Since hemispheres of the brain govern opposite sides of the body, the fire in her right hand symbolizes the active consciousness of the left-brain that lights her way; and the music in her left hand signifies the more creative, unconscious aspect of the right-brain. Clearly, she balances the two and utilizes them equally. Hall suggests the types of beings who might be able to move between these two worlds of dream and waking reality as if there were no boundaries: "poets, artists, muse(r)s, gossips, bees, elves, fairies, and children."

The ring of life around the central dancing figure also represents the coven or magic circle who worship the Mother together. At the center is the High Priestess who, on behalf of the group, channels energy or what Starhawk calls "the subtle current of forces that shape reality." In *The Spiral Dance*, Starhawk speaks of the "ecological circle" (which represents the interdependence of all living organisms), the "circle of Self" (site of the "inner journey, a personal vision quest, a process of self-healing and self-exploration"), and the circle of community. In a coven's dance, as in the cycle of Motherpeace images, "each gesture we make, each tool we use, each power we invoke, resonates through layers of meaning to awaken an aspect of ourselves." What is enacted on the outside must then be taken within. "The outer forms are a cloak for inner visualizations, so that the circle becomes a living mandala, in which we are centered."

The World represents bliss, the rising of the *kundalini* energy to higher centers in the body. The union of body and spirit that then takes place is a form of empowerment and ecstasy. The state of *Samadhi* can be gained through either mental or physical practice; but Tantrics believe that raising the energy through lovemaking results in a more perfect union than is possible through exclusively mental methods. In either case, body-consciousness is lost; but in *kundalini*-yoga the body (Shakti) is actively united with the quiescent force (Shiva) producing an "Enjoyment" that the mental form does not as easily offer. This ancient method of body-spirit union is what Goddess-worshiping priestesses enacted in the groves and temples of early matriarchal culture.

Without attachment, the figure in the World image lets go of the past and dances ecstatically into the future, in open space and to her own rhythm, within a circle of support. Like the Empress described in Chapter 5, she offers the gift of the matriarchal World: possibility of peace and the joyous celebration of life. From the World, we learn that the body is divine, a temple for the realization of spiritual truth. The earth is divine, the body of the Mother and the domain of her children. In Starhawk's wonderful phrase, "the Goddess does not rule the world; She *is* the world." In ancient days, the body of the Mother was revered in very physical terms, and in "primitive" cultures, it still is. Silbury Hill in Britain is the largest known representation of the Great Goddess, but her forms exist all over the world, in many ingenious ways. As Michael Dames puts it, "in prehistory, the land was not regarded as an 'It' but as a 'She.'"

The garland through which the figure of Motherpeace dances is made up of peyote buttons and flowers. With the help of magic substances in ritualized ceremony, she breaks through ordinary consciousness and reaches another plane. For Native American peoples, the peyote disc was the key to worlds beyond the mundane, a sacred means of travel through time and space. In the Motherpeace image, the dancer no longer needs peyote; she gets high on just being. Her mastery of the spirit world is accomplished. No chemicals are necessary to take her into sacred space. The simple breath of life is enough to set her free.

Eastern disciplines teach "breath control" as part of the sacred practices that lead to liberation. The World represents in-breath and out-breath in rhythmic cadence. In yoga practice, the stages of accomplishment are first, sweating; second, trembling; and finally, levitation. The World depicts this final stage of levitation, as well as the supreme achievement of total breath suspension.

The background of vibrant turquoise represents the world of the heart and the union of opposites in space. A favorite of Native Americans, this color was also prominent in the art of Crete and the murals of Pompeii. It suggests "ether" or open space—the archetypal feminine—and the abandonment of the security of the physical plane.

The unity reflected in the human circle around the central Motherpeace figure is multicultural and racially mixed, a symbol of true egalitarianism and interchange among peoples. Together we share the planet; we all breathe the same air. In one of Starhawk's "exercises" we are asked to "feel our breath as it meets in the center of the circle . . . as we breathe as one . . . breathing one breath . . . inhale . . . exhale . . . breathing one circle . . . breathing one, living organism . . . with each breath . . . becoming one circle . . . with each breath . . . becoming one. . . ."

When you get the World in a reading, it means you have in some sense mastered the three planes of mind, body, and emotions. You have come to know yourself in a way that makes you feel at home with yourself. How did you reach this knowledge? In Chapter 9, the Chariot represented a triumph on the physical plane, getting it together in the world.

In Chapter 16, Temperance signified a similar mastery over the emotions and energy realms, the achievement of control and balance so that your emotions and feelings no longer control you. Now, with the World, you have reached an even greater balance and integration—one happening in the spiritual world that both includes and transcends the first two realms. Your personality seems guided by a central sense of Self, your inner "real" Self, who works through all the "vehicles" of your life. You are in a state of knowing all your parts—and using them for the expression of your real self in the world.

You have reached completion on some work, the end of one phase and the very expansive beginning of another. You may not know exactly what the change means, but clearly it brings growth. Rather than a feeling of finishing something, you probably feel a beginning taking place. The whole World opens up before you—all possibility is offered and you feel capable of embracing whatever comes with this new start. As the Fool described in Chapter 2, you also felt this way, but then you were unconscious and unaware of yourself. Now, as the World, you know yourself and others—you have experience and consciousness—yet you come to understand that the Fool was right and there remains only openness and the pure impulse.

The World card represents transcendence, so the experience may be hard to define or put into words—you may feel elated, as if your spirit were dancing. You may sense huge and important insights, the wisdom of the world, yet be unable to articulate it. The experience of "cosmic" consciousness is shared by sages and yogis the world over, and they all agree on the difficulty of explaining it with the rational vocabulary. The overriding feeling may be one of paradox, and this may make you laugh and cry for joy. You know yourself to be an individual, yet completely the same as others.

Your understanding of how the World works allows you to step outside of time and feel yourself as a spirit who has eons of experience. You may feel miraculously untouched by human problems, yet fully competent to deal with the personal tasks of your life. Your understanding of what is real helps you deal with what is happening here and now on the physical plane—you know the overview, therefore you can focus on the minutiae with success. Nothing can overwhelm you, because you are only a grain of sand in the universal scheme. And yet, at the same time, you recognize your own unique individuality. You are therefore truly ready to work with others on solving world problems.

Color Plate 7

Sun (XIX)

Judgement (XX)

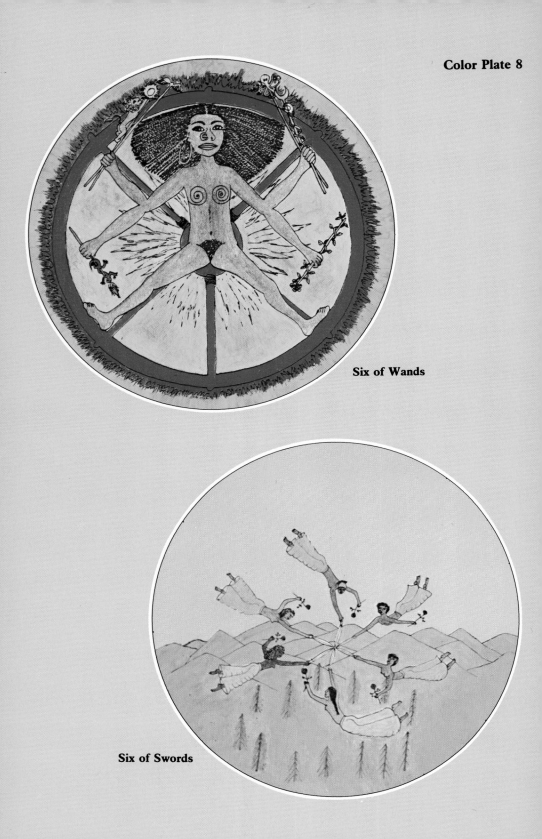

Color Plate 8

Six of Wands

Six of Swords

Color Plate 9

Six of Cups

Six of Discs

Ten of Wands

Ten of Swords

Color Plate 11

Ten of Cups

Ten of Discs

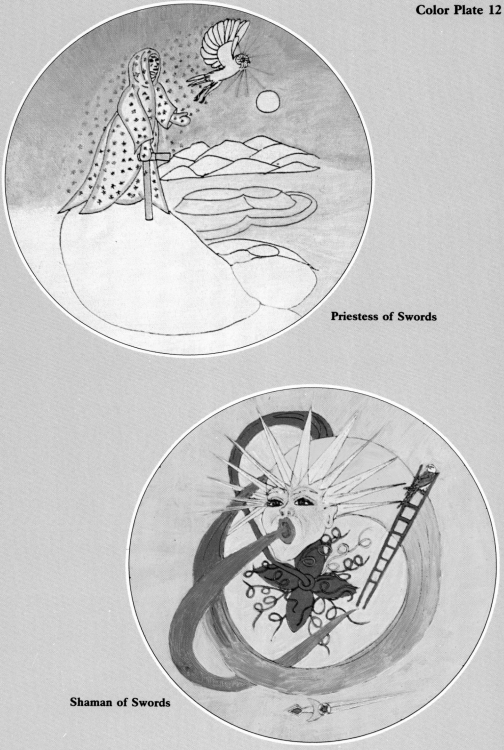

Priestess of Swords

Shaman of Swords

Priestess of Discs

Shaman of Discs

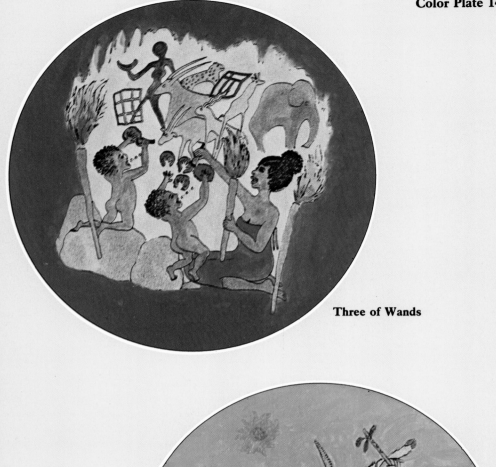

Three of Wands

Son of Wands

Color Plate 15

Priestess of Wands

Shaman of Wands

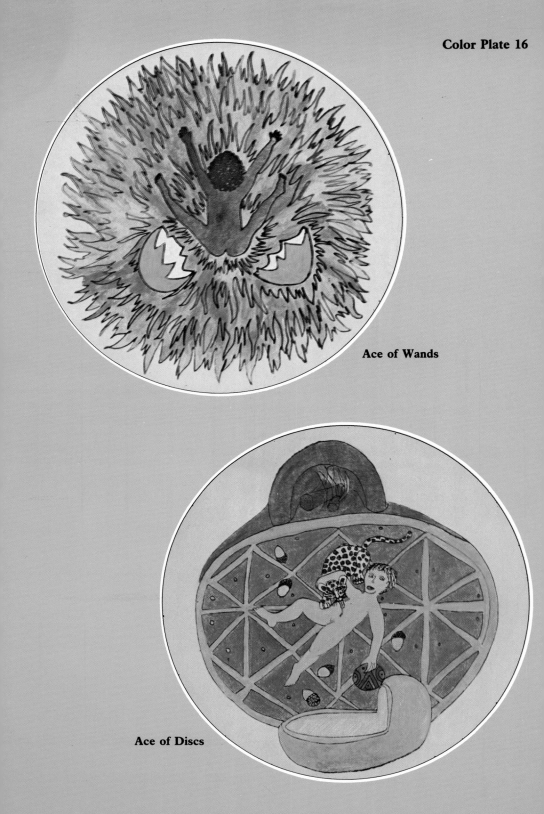

Ace of Wands

Ace of Discs

TWO

MINOR ARCANA

CHAPTER 24

INTRODUCTION

Dramas of Everyday Life

Now that we have gone through the entire cycle of the twenty-two cards of the Major Arcana, starting with the Fool and ending with the World, we can proceed from the cosmic themes they embody to the more familiar dramas of everyday life. Whereas the Major Arcana depict enormous forces normally beyond our experience, the Minor Arcana deal with events in the microcosm, the small world in which we ordinarily live. Although these events include such transient phenomena as thoughts, emotions, and bodily sensations, they are no less important to our personalities than the cosmic passage is to our souls. In fact, they are the stuff of the tangible world we share.

In the Major Arcana chapters, I focused on the soul and its development through cosmic or evolutionary phases, referring to environmental or planetary influences and mythic archetypes to which the human personality might respond. The second section of each of those twenty-two chapters began with the words, "When you get this card in a reading, it means. . . ." The purpose of that form was to note a pause in the theoretical or mythological discussion, and the beginning of a personal application.

In the following chapters on the number cards—Ace through Ten— the earlier division is unnecessary, because *everything* in the description pertains to the personality level. A reader may approach the Minor Arcana through projection into the Motherpeace image, as if she were the personality portrayed there, or as if she were participating in the action. In this way, reading the cards becomes like "dream work" in which a person identifies with all the aspects of her dream picture one-by-one in order to appreciate more fully how the self is a collectivity of diverse voices. In the "people" cards—Daughter through Shaman—mythology again becomes relevant, as it was throughout the Major Arcana. Therefore, I again add a separate "reading" after the basic description.

Precursors of our modern playing cards, the Minor Arcana are divided into suits symbolizing the four elements: fire, water, air, and earth. What cardplayers know as clubs were Wands (fire) in Tarot. Hearts were originally Cups (water), spades were Swords (air), and diamonds were Discs or "pentacles" (earth). Almost every culture in the world deals with the four elements, the raw "materials" that interact in all biological forms. Earth symbolizes the physical plane and the body. Water represents the unconscious and emotions. Fire stands for the energy of the life force, the passion that urges to action. Air represents the mental plane with its thoughts and ideas (such as we are now describing).

Each Tarot suit contains ten numbered cards in sequence and four "court" or character cards. As in modern playing cards, Tarot suits have a King and Queen, but the Jack is traditionally called a Page. In addition, the Tarot has a court card called the Knight, which got lost somewhere in the transition to playing cards. In the Motherpeace image, the King of European tradition becomes the Shaman, the Queen becomes the Priestess, the Knight becomes the Son, and the Page becomes the Daughter. The Ace and numbered cards remain the same and, although they carry new images, they preserve meanings they have always held in the Tarot.

In the Motherpeace images, the Minor Arcana are arranged in a number of meaningful ways. For example, they represent human evolution from prehistoric times through the present, an evolution that includes black and brown as well as white peoples; women as well as men; and old folks as well as children. In each of the four suits, the numbered cards can be read in sequence to tell a story about a particular group of people or period in history. The character cards—Daughters, Sons, Priestesses, and Shamans—reflect growth and development through phases of human life, as well as different manifestations of elemental energy. In Chapters 25 through 31, all of this material is organized to allow an orderly, gradual appreciation of its richness. Before considering individual cards, however, we will examine the special character of each of the four suits, following the sequence of cultural evolution.

Wands

The suit of Wands depicts energy and the force of fire. Wands can be sticks, batons, or clubs. They symbolize power and authority, urgency and action, and, on another plane, the life of the spirit. In astrological terms, fire cards are "ruled" by the three astrological fire signs—Aries, Leo, and Sagittarius. In the Motherpeace images, Wands are frequently torches, which represent the light and warmth generated by physical fire, as well as libido and the body-fire of sexuality. Although traditionally described as "phallic" and "male," wands also represent Shakti, the Hindu Goddess of active creativity and female power.

Fire is an ancient symbol of female power, often represented by the Tantric color red, color of menstrual blood. The sacred color red runs throughout the suit of Wands. As the energy builds and the numbers increase, the power grows. The Ace and Two are yellow with some red, the Three brings in more red, and so forth, until the Nine and Ten are ablaze. Red is the energy of Mars—most recently regarded as the "God of War," but once known as the divine energy of sexual passion.

Not every culture welcomes red. The Navaho, for example, consider it to be the color of "Evil." The Indian Kali, Goddess of Death, the Terrible Mother, is also red. Our own culture links red with anger and war. We have made Eros into a warrior; whereas the erotic once emerged from the realm of fire, we have transferred it to the world of air, the mental plane. Eros was hot, but much of modern eroticism has become cool and detached, a visual experience removed from the energy and healing heat of the wand—the risen snake.

In the Motherpeace images, Wands once again stand for what is passionate and energetic, the heat that moves through the body, causing action, regenerating cells. The people in the images are ancient. Often called "primitive" and "prehistoric," they are definitely prepatriarchal. They live in Africa and are socially organized around the core relationships of mother-and-child. They represent the discovery of fire, the invention of language and communication, and the evolution of culture, art, and religion.

The suit of Wands corresponds to the Magician in the Major Arcana. "Batons of Commandment" is the title given to the discovery of many "wands" from prehistoric sites whose use baffles archeologists. Are they "weapons" or "wrenches"? The artifacts show no sign of manual use. Were they used in some kind of ceremony? Perhaps the best clue is found in the practice of modern witches, as well as Native American shamans, who still focus their magical power with the help of a Wand or "prayer stick."

Swords

The suit of Swords represents mental activity and the powers of the mind. Because the mind so often engages in struggle and projection, the Swords traditionally represent more negative qualities than the other suits. In the Motherpeace images, they depict the Aryan race and the early patriarchal invaders of Goddess-cultures. It was the Aryans or Indo-Europeans who came into the Mediterranean and Asia Minor with their ideas that light is good and dark is bad, who forced indigenous cultures to give up their allegiance to the Mother, and who worshipped Sky Gods (and later, Sun Gods), who represented aggression, "power over," the God of spiritual "transcendence." However, the Motherpeace Swords also embody Amazon intention to fight back against these invaders, and the bold intellect of the Amazon warrior intelligence, ruled by the Goddess Athene.

The suit of Wands is set in the Stone Age; the suit of Swords is set in the age of yellow metals that followed it, when tools were made of bronze, and the finest ornaments were made of gold. Gold was (and still is) the favored metal of rulers and monarchs, representing power and authority, wealth and status. The lust for gold has been the root cause of many wars and massacres throughout history, and occult teachers such as Alice Bailey warn of the bad karma connected with gold and its misuse. Gold is intrinsically a very powerful metal, its vibration one of outward force. One wears gold when one wants to be effective in the external world. On the other hand, too much emphasis on gold leads to the unrestrained quest for dominance that we see all over the world today. Gold is a solar color and has become known as the color of Heroes—as, for instance, in connection with Jason's golden fleece. It is the King's metal, and leads to the "Midas touch" that severs itself from humanity and life.

The light yellows and yellow-greens that predominate in this suit reflect the mental powers encompassed by Swords. There is potential for abstract thought and conceptualization, the power of creating systems and seeing clearly into future time as well as knowing the logic of things. At their best, Swords connote the power of the mind to slice through falsity and promote truth. In this way, Swords represent the ego and its separative tendencies, the sense of "I" and "other" that marks the age of Patriarchy. They correspond to the activities of the Emperor of Chapter 6, whose ordering consciousness names and categorizes "objects" in the world.

Cups

The suit of Cups symbolizes the feminine element of water and the quality of receptivity. Cups are vessels—they hold feelings, emotions, desires, unconscious dreams, and visions. Cups are lunar, represented by the silver moon, and astral. Like the High Priestess of Chapter 4, they portray a female mode of consciousness—listening from within, an interior space where oracles emerge, an orgiastic style of religious expression, and a deep, feeling-level experience of what is sacred. Cups are archetypal symbols of the womb and of the Mother's breasts. Ruled by astrology's water signs—Cancer, Scorpio, and Pisces—Cups reflect generative energy, healing power, and the ability to know things psychically.

In the Motherpeace image, the suit of Cups is set mostly in the Mediterranean island of Crete during the transition from Goddess-worship to Patriarchy, in the second millennium B.C. The only images set elsewhere are located in North America and suggest a migration that took place during the late transition period when the Cretan religion and culture were being overthrown.

The Goddess-culture on Crete was widespread and evolved over a period of several hundred years. Archaeologists pay most attention to the late "Palace Period," which involved the patriarchal trappings of class division, with "kings" and "governors," along with their "mansions," taxes, bookkeeping, and the development of a mundane language of rule. The best-known ruin from this period is the palace at Knossos, luxurious and aristocratic. But there were many so-called palaces, including temples and granaries, all over the island. Most of them were connected with sacred caves where religious rites were practiced through the period of time that included the destruction of the "palace" culture. This destruction took place by means of invasions and human destructions, as well as by means of the enormous volcanic eruption of nearby Mount Thera around 1400 B.C.

The blues and greens of the suit of Cups represent the sea and the inner realms of the dream world. There is pleasure and feeling in this suit, stories of magic and moon-madness, snake-priestesses and flute-players. Water is the element of ecstasy and unconscious bliss, the deep enjoyment of the heart and the flow of love. Ruled by Venus, this suit belongs to Aphrodite, variously known on Crete as Britomartis, Dictynna, Aegea, or Rhea.

Discs

The suit of Discs depicts earth and the physical plane. Discs connote whatever is solid and "real" to us—the body, money, the physical world. In terms of yoga, Discs represent the first *chakra* or energy center, the place in us that focuses on survival, health, and physicality. Traditionally called "Pentacles" or "Coins," Discs represent the magic of earth and the ability of life to sustain itself. Corresponding to the Empress of Chapter 5—Mother Earth herself—Discs symbolize creation and procreation, barter, economy, and fruitful harvest. Further, as an extension of the Empress, the Motherpeace Discs celebrate a communal way of life in which the mother-child bond, motherhood, and group sharing are central, work is meaningful and appreciated, and everyone makes art.

Today this "matriarchal" way of life barely survives in, for example, some Native American tribes and the Bushpeople of the Kalahari Desert in southwest Africa. Even after being touched by white culture, some peoples have somehow retained their harmonious way of relating to the Earth and her creatures, ways that we seek to rediscover through ecology. These cultures keep up what they call "the old ways," including respect for women and Nature, the guardians and vessels of life. Motherpeace Discs depict Native American people engaged in practical, everyday activities that they approach with a sacred sense of meaning and purpose missing from most of the mundane cultural activities in the United States today.

Discs, of course, are circles, which Giedion calls the oldest symbolic form to emerge from the human consciousness as an objective symbol. Circles mean feminine reproduction and perpetuation, the beginning and end contained in a perfect form. In prehistoric or "matriarchal" cultures, circles are the dominant motif. Houses are circular, burial tombs are round. In Stone Age caves, archeologists have found hollowed out circular "breast" marks (cupules) in the walls, circular perforations, and colored spots or discs (usually painted red) that surround hands, breasts, or animals, or stand alone. They have also found circular discs, slabs of stone with perforations on them, which scholars assume must have been used ritually in some way. In the Native American way of living, as Evelyn Eaton shows, "the Sweat Lodge is round, the hole in the center containing the fiery rocks is round, the sun is round, the world is round, the bird's nest is round, life is a round between birth and death, and everything revolves in a circle, everything has its appointed place in the wheel of the Universe."

Like magical "Pentacles" of witchcraft, Discs represent what is sacred and secret, passed orally through symbols and the voice, or through magic languages such as the Runic alphabet. The religion of the Goddess is a religion of Earth that considers the planet and all earthly energies as sacred. Discs represent the tablet as transmitter of language and art, and the body as transmitter of what is holy and known in one's cells. Old as the hills, this body-wisdom is available to us still. It is our legacy as children of the Earth Mother. With it, we can heal ourselves; without it, we're dead.

Now, after this abrupt promise and warning, we are prepared to spend some time with each card in the Minor Arcana. In Chapters 25 through 27, we will look briefly at the numbered cards in each of the four suits. In general, these cards require little more than quick verbal sketches, in part because they refer back to the body of knowledge already developed in the detailed examination of the Major Arcana, and in part because each card in the Minors is illuminated both by its position in a suit and by contrast to the other cards bearing the same number. Then, in Chapters 28 through 31, we will discuss the "character" cards that, like the Major Arcana, call for detailed background and a separate "reading" in conclusion.

CHAPTER 25

ACES, TWOS, AND THREES

Cardinal Signs

The Aces, Twos, and Threes of each suit correspond to the "cardinal" sign of that element in astrology. Therefore the first three Wand images are Aries; the first three Swords are Libra; the first three Cups are Cancer; and the first three Discs are Capricorn. Cardinal signs are the initiating aspects of whichever element they represent. Like fire (or *rajas* in the Hindu system), they reach out and make direct contact with reality. They know where they are going. Geometrically, they correspond to a straight line.

Aces: Gifts

Corresponding to the number One and the Magician, Aces represent the point at the center of life, the beginnings of activity. Aces are gifts, first causes, roots. They represent the primary impulse that evolves throughout a particular suit.

Ace of Swords

The Ace of Swords represents force, particularly on the mental plane. Swords are air and pertain to thought forms and ideas. This Ace is the gift of intellect, the place where thought begins. In the Motherpeace image, the right hand holds the sword steady, takes aim, and points the will toward a goal. A choice is made to do something specific. The waxing moon signifies increase and fresh starts. Force of will pours from the

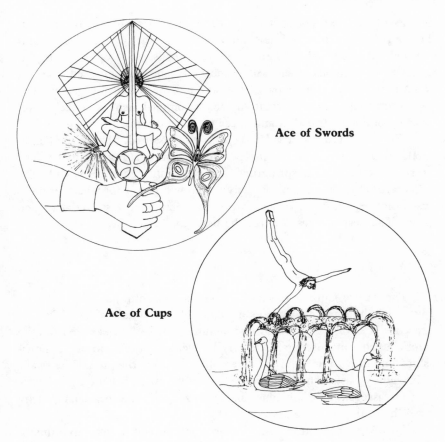

Ace of Swords

Ace of Cups

right hand as the mind holds a sharp, one-pointed focus. A decision to win has been made, an aggressive "yes."

On spiritual levels, this image represents the desire to build a "body of light"—the subtle body that houses the spirit and allows it to take flight, like the butterfly, into heavenly realms. The personality balances on a waxing silver crescent, denoting increase and protection. The sword forms the axis of this meditating *yogini*. It centers her and at the same time represents her. The meditation posture allows for second sight, clairvoyance, the gift of inner vision.

Ace of Wands

See color illustration on Plate 16.

The Ace of Wands is the beginning of fire—spirit, intuition, energy. The egg bursts open and the sun is born. From the center of fire, a figure leaps with joy, expressing hope for the future. A rebirth of the spirit is taking place; one is brand new like a baby, and the force of fire streams through the personality. This energy is expansive. It opens us to our abilities. It includes a sense of immortality and a heightened sense of what is possible. The yellow of the sun and the red of the planet Mars lend warmth and light for creativity and accomplishment. One feels alive, warm, confident, friendly, and eager to fulfill desires.

The passions are aroused and creativity is assured. Shakti, the Hindu Goddess of fire, is alive in the personality, stimulating creativity. The spirit awakens like the springtime—happy, healthy, and ready to begin. This card represents expansive activity and will-power for whatever one's goals dictate. It may signify active sexual energy and a strong attraction force. The heat of Eros is born; the heart may catch fire.

Ace of Cups

The Ace of Cups is the gift of love—a dive into one's deepest feelings, which are spilling over in abundance like a fountain of joy. After the grace in the dive, a gentle landing is assured, a friendly welcome from the depths of the unconscious. One may land either in the cup of self-nourishing and nurturing; or in the ocean of love, where the pure white swans skim lightly past each other on the gentle waves. Either way, good feelings are assured. The soft blues and greens signify that peace and purity dwell here, in watery calm.

This Ace represents a surrender to emotions and beauty, an influx of pleasure, inspiration, imagination. The silver cup is the vessel, the chalice, the grail—the archetypal feminine receptive mode. It promises a joyous experience of letting go into unconditional love, the spaciousness of the open heart.

Ace of Discs

See color illustration on Plate 16.

The Ace of Discs promises a gift of earth energy—the birth of something in material form. It could be a baby, it could be money coming. Whatever the form, it signifies something manifesting. Someone brings something, does something nice, or makes one feel good in some way. It may be the beginning of some new work or job, a brand new life, a new pattern emerging. The person learns to make ideas into physical reality.

The acorns on the rug speak of winter's long nights and cold days, the time to store what's needed for later. This Ace signifies a time of meditation, an inward pull of energy. The baby represents the inner mysteries and the birth of a "Solstice child" in December, celebrating the turning of the wheel of the year. The baby leopard represents the animal spirit that will grow up with the child. It may be the same leopard whose skin the Magician wears (after its death). The animal lends power to the human spirit, giving it the gift of bodily life.

Twos: Balance

The Twos are ruled by the Moon and, like the High Priestess, represent receptivity and magnetism. The two is the polar opposite movement to the one, which means it naturally pulls back from the outward or forward action of the one. Twos can be somewhat secretive or private—more unconscious than the one or the three, and quieter. All the twos signify polarity and balance between opposites.

Two of Swords

The Two of Swords represents an attempt to gain mental balance and peace. The mind wants to be still, to avoid dealing with whatever might be happening in the external world. One method of temporary escape and refreshment is to undertake a discipline of balancing, such as Tai Chi or yoga. In the Motherpeace image, the swords being used are as soft as feathers, creating an infinite space of calm. The woman may even be learning her *asana* ("the Stork pose") from the bird beside her; and since legendary storks bring babies, we can assume there is a hidden fertility in this card—a fertility of the mind, since Swords are mental, representing the element of air.

Behind the figure, on a deeper level, power is available. The ocean and the night sky are feminine symbols, and the full moon offers all its brilliant light and energy if the personality wishes to tap into these sources. For the moment, she declines. Perfect balance is sought—as well as grounding and privacy. This temporary withdrawal stills the mind and gives a person time to figure out what to do next. Since Swords represent quick-moving energies, the situation will no doubt change soon enough. Meanwhile, one gets a respite, a chance to take a deep breath.

Two of Wands

The Two of Wands depicts a visit from an ancestor-figure who brings a vision or message concerning the way to make fire. Making fire is an

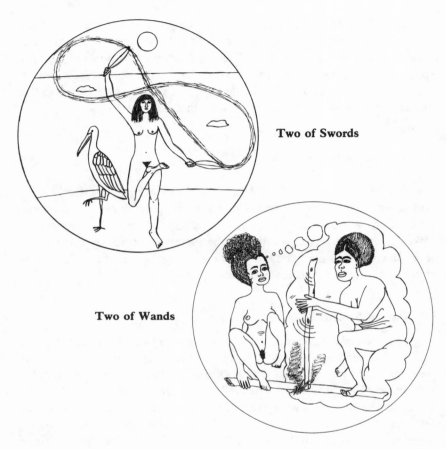

Two of Swords

Two of Wands

important thing to understand, since it is the means to everything in life. In most cultures, the discovery of fire is originally attributed to women. Perhaps the woman here is kindling the libido or fire of the body. Perhaps the fire of energy and action. In either case, fire is Shakti—the means of getting what we want.

The Two of Wands signifies the harnessing of one's personal power —learning how to use the fire that was born in the Ace. The receiving part of the personality is open to learning; she watches and listens carefully as the older spirit shows her how to create the fire by friction. The active part of the personality is demonstrative, patiently teaching a skill that will be useful throughout life. The dream-vision shown in the Motherpeace image signifies that the intuition is awakening—a form of fire that precedes verbal communication. The personality may have flashes of insight or understanding of what it is capable of doing.

Two of Cups

Two of Discs

Two of Cups

The Two of Cups represents another polarity, this time within the feeling realm. Watery and deep, the connection taking place is probably sexual in nature—the pull of the attraction force on the unconscious level of the emotions. The two people (or two parts of the personality) come together in a toast to love. The snake wraps itself around their cups and bites its own tail, sealing the connection, completing the circle. As the two figures experience harmony and interrelatedness, their joyful play is repeated in the frolic of dolphins in the background.

Overhead the waxing moon rises in the sky near the evening star and both shine blessings on this new love. Joining are the energies of Artemis and Aphrodite, the wildness of the night with the sweetness of the heart. As unconscious desires merge with the conscious love of the heart, the outcome will be union.

Two of Discs

The Two of Discs depicts the juggling required by a new mother of twins who stands in the center of her busy life and wonders whether she can hold the whole thing together. So far, she's doing pretty well and the babies are happy. But her hands are full, and the film runs on. Sometimes she feels like a two-headed snake writhing in opposite directions, as one baby wants to eat while the other wants to sleep. In the Motherpeace image, the film reels that carry her mental pictures also represent the Celtic wheels and symbols of earth that ground her in ancient power.

She gets her support from the earth, her feet planted firmly like the roots of tall trees drawing nourishment from the soil. She knows she has the means in her body to take care of the needs of her children. The waxing crescent moon in the twilight sky promises her strength and renewal in the difficult work of managing the twin aspects of her creativity. A person is like this young mother if she is trying to balance more than one project at a time, or handling both inner growth and outer achievement at once.

Threes: Synthesis

Synthesizing the active and passive presences, Three is more stable than the first two numbers, a triangle that signifies harmony and flow. Threes usually indicate some form of group activity, a coming together of more than two.

Three of Swords

The Three of Swords represents the way mental energies merge— through struggle. In a dance of power, difficulty precedes harmony. Three parts of the personality, or three personalities, are engaged in thrusting and guarding, a dance of defense that can only be painful. Either the mind is caught up in worrying about relationships and their dynamics, or several people are involved in what looks like "soap opera." They want to relate, but separate egos won't let them get close. The Swords of thought are piercing and pointing, leaving no choice but to shield.

In the Motherpeace image, the women have put on bird costumes to enhance their powerful repartee. The costumes are their *personae*, the masks they wear in order to escape being vulnerable to each other. They wish to be like Bird Priestesses of old, dancing the ego out of sight, but

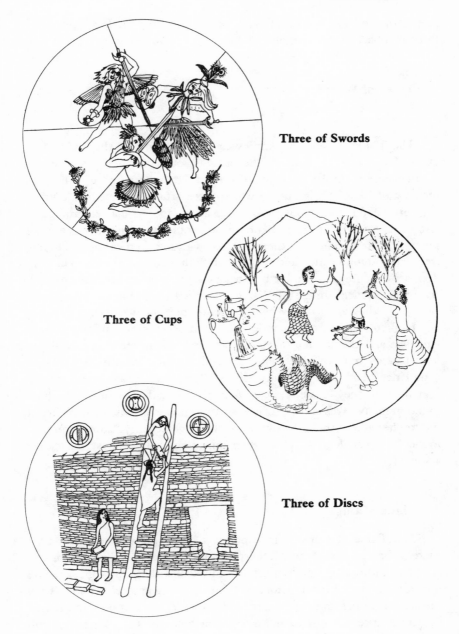

Three of Swords

Three of Cups

Three of Discs

they are still in touch with thought. The daisy-chain reflects the ways they are linked to each other, yet feel trapped by that. If this is a dance of love, then each party needs to get in touch with feelings of the heart, or else the end will not bring happiness or harmony. At least one of the three involved in this romantic triangle expects to lose a lover.

Three of Wands

See color illustration on Plate 14.

The Three of Wands signifies communication and the joy of self-expression. On rock walls in the Sahara, some of our early ancestors painted figures similar to the ones in the Motherpeace image. What was the way of life of the group to which these artists belonged? We know very little about them, but we do have access to a similar environment, also in Africa. I refer to the !Kung bush people, as egalitarian as any we know of. The !Kung raise their children with love and caring, including frequent communication and touch from both men and women. The children are encouraged from birth to be open, creative, and sexually expressive. Since ancient times, the !Kung have lived a life in harmony with the earth, and they are a happy people who do not practice war.

Human culture grew up around mothers and their offspring, through language and the sharing of experience. In this image, a mother shows her children how to paint and allows them the freedom necessary to experience their own creativity without fear. Notice the joyful sounds they make as they create replicas of their tiny hands—pictures like those found in many caves and on rock walls from prehistoric times. The fire of the torches allows them the light to make art, like early "stone lanterns" found by archeologists. Through manifesting their visions, they learn about life.

Three of Cups

The Three of Cups is an expression of happiness and joyful time shared. The group in the Motherpeace image feels no threat from one another, and openly revels together. The dance they do is musical and mystical, involving inner visions and fantasy, song and celebration. They meditate together, practice magic and mystery, use symbols and sacred objects to make their dance more real. One holds snakes, as the Hopi still do in order to make rain; another plays Pan's pipes or the double flute of Krishna; a third holds the ancient *thyrsus* made of the branches of three sacred trees belonging to the Moon Goddess. The image represents sharing pleasure together, having fun with others. The women celebrate "orgiastically," letting the spirits come through their feelings and emotions.

The magical creature floating in the crescent spring is a form of Pegasus, winged horse-child of Medusa. Legend tells that Pegasus touched his hoof down and created the sacred "Horse Well," where poets drank for inspiration. In the same spirit, the three celebrants represent the Muses and the powers of the imagination, the Three Graces, and the infinite possibilities of love. The Three Cups pour endlessly into the magical spring, and the willow trees dance in the background in honor of the ancient Willow Goddess, who brings wisdom and inner knowledge.

Three of Discs

The Three of Discs signifies work done together—a communal act of building. Z. Budapest calls this "building the church of the Goddess," which these early Native Americans might certainly be doing. It is now clearly understood that prehistoric American pueblo cities, such as Chaco Canyon in New Mexico, were constructed by women masons, just as Hopi buildings are today. The women architects and builders used eclectic methods. Hundreds of years later, many of the walls still stand. The secret of their success probably lay in their ability to work together, the way women so often can, on behalf of a group project.

Handing the bricks up one at a time and laying them in place, the women know that on the physical plane work must be done step-by-step. They demonstrate craft and dexterity. Each woman regards her sisters as necessary to the work. Their thoughtful, practical application of concrete skill pays off in personal and group appreciation, as well as a physical structure that endures and that they can be proud of.

CHAPTER 26

FOURS, FIVES, AND SIXES

Fixity

The Fours, Fives, and Sixes of each suit correspond astrologically to the "fixed" sign of the element. This second series of three cards in Wands are ruled by Leo; in Swords, by Aquarius; in Cups, by Scorpio; and in Discs, by Taurus. Fixed signs are still and inward, drawing energy to themselves rather than thrusting outward. Like the Hindu *tamas*, they correspond elementally to water and geometrically to the in-drawing circle.

Fours: Stability

Representing the four directions, the Fours in Tarot form a square or a cross, figures that bring order along with a sense of limitation. Four signifies the weighty element of physical matter and encloses the personality. In the practice of magic or ritual, the four "corners" of the magic circle are saluted, and the four elements (air, fire, water, and earth) called in. This creates a separation between inner and outer, a space where something special can occur.

Four of Swords

The Four of Swords represents the creation of a protected mental space, somewhat like the "time-out" represented by the Two, but this time more strongly intended. The personality needs time to withdraw and be alone, think about things, to cleanse the environment of tension and anger. The four Swords mark the corners and create a pyramid, one of the strongest forms in existence. Within this magical shape, a person can heal and renew herself. Power is focused and drawn up towards the sky, in order to bring down cosmic force.

The rainbow discs behind the figure represent the seven *chakras* or energy centers, which are housed in the spine and connect to the human nervous system. To clean out the *chakras* is a powerful psychic meditation, helping to ground the personality and center the mind in positive thoughts. In this protective environment, one may gain the sense of nonattachment necessary if the personality is not to feel lonely or abandoned.

Four of Wands

The Four of Wands represents a rite of passage—the joyful celebration of a young girl's *menarche* (the onset of her first menstruation). These girls feel themselves passing from one stage of life to the next, from girlhood to adolescence. The work of learning is put aside for now and the biological and spiritual elements of growth are acknowledged. The central altar is a hearth, around which they joyously dance together in honor of the life energy itself. They are bedecked with flowers, representing springtime and their own "flowering" womanhood. A ring of flowers surrounds them, binding them together in tribal cooperation and love.

The flower Wands symbolize their "male" energy, soon to become integrated into their lives as they take on more adult power and responsibility. For now they play in the freedom of youthful exhuberance. The cut lilies near the altar represent their own sweet purity, which is offered to the Goddess along with their menstrual blood in thanks and appreciation for life. Known to be a healing "medicine," the first menstrual blood of a young girl will be used by the tribe in gratitude and recognition of the magic inherent in the female sex. The hummingbird overhead (an African sunbird) blesses them with messages from divine realms. All is well.

Four of Cups

The Four of Cups represents a time for getting clear, refining things down to simple truth. Feelings are hurt. Things don't feel quite right, so

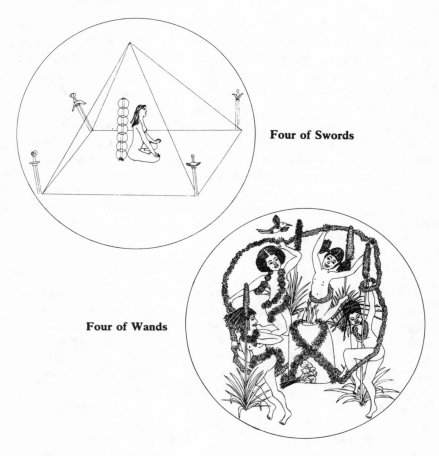

Four of Swords

Four of Wands

it's time to figure out what's wrong and change it. The personality needs to strip itself bare and undergo a cleansing. The figure has turned her back on us in a temporary rejection of help from others—her work must be done alone. The water from the river that flows into the ocean will be her helpmeet. Carefully, she steps into the cold stream and begins to wade across, letting the current wash her clean and revitalize her emotionally. Perhaps when the figure has completed her ritual, she will lie on the warm sand and imagine new opportunities.

She has entered a time of uncertainty, like the place where the river and the ocean meet, where the fresh waters swirl into the salt. This time can be used for re-evaluation of life and relationships. If there are tears, they can fall unseen into the water, allowing a free flow of feelings that will heal all wounds. Given time and attention, confusion will sort itself out and clarity will return.

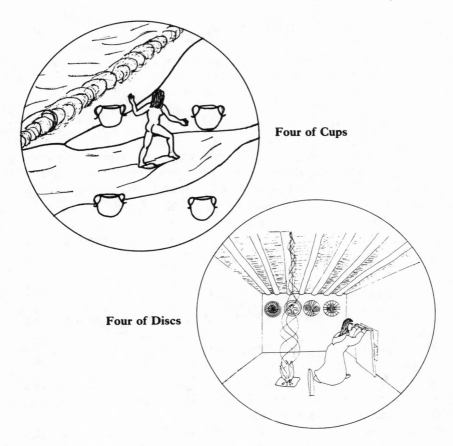

Four of Cups

Four of Discs

Four of Discs

The Four of Discs represents an inner sanctuary of some kind, perhaps a room or house, where a person can be alone and sheltered. The figure needs silence. Her personality wants a place as still as a monastery. In this private space, she is free to open or shut the door at will. A single fire burns for warmth, the smoke rising out through the fire-hole in the roof. The external trappings of social life drop away along with the rest of the nervous swirl of the world outside. The figure knows that she needs to say "no" to what others want right now, in order to figure out what she needs for herself.

The warm wood colors and spaciousness of the uncluttered environment allow the mind to be still and listen for inner voices. The Discs on the wall represent tasks she has set for herself, inner goals and ideals of spiritual growth. The first Disc suggests a spiral to the center of herself;

the second, a magical flight to heavenly realms. The third suggests that her going in and coming out will assume a rhythmic balance; and the fourth promises integration of the four elements in a cross-centered mandala. Gratefully, she shuts the door to the outside.

Fives: Struggle

Fives are traditionally the number of struggle and conflict, signifying change and some sort of break. Five is the sacred number of humanity, represented by the five-pointed star or "pentagram." Because change seems to frighten us, and a break doubly so, the fives have a fearful effect on us. What is important to remember is that destruction is necessary before we can change or be reborn. They are simply two parts of one process.

Five of Swords

The Five of Swords represents a powerful negative experience, such as a defeat, or at least a fight. Swords are mental, so the experience may be on the level of the mind, but it hurts. The wasp in the center of the pentagram signifies a "sting," or some kind of focused pain. The downward pointing pentagram means the energy is being directed not as a blessing or protection, or even a banishing spell, but as a hex or curse. The feeling of this card is something like, "Damn you!" or "I hate you!" Depending on the force behind it, the exclamation may or may not strike its victim in a conscious way. But it will certainly have repercussions on the psychic level.

Expecting to lose, or even secretly wanting to lose, reduces one's chances of winning—a situation the Five of Swords sometimes indicates. In this case, a person might ask: "Do I expect to get stung? Am I sure there has to be a winner and a loser to this? Am I willing to be cruel to get my way?" Inspired by the bright yellow mental energy surrounding the cursing pentagram, the personality may change her approach to the situation and give up power-tripping, anger, and victimization.

Five of Wands

The Five of Wands is a picture of struggle and strife without pain. Anger may bubble underneath, or some conflict remain in need of resolution, but there is an agreement—either within the personality or among

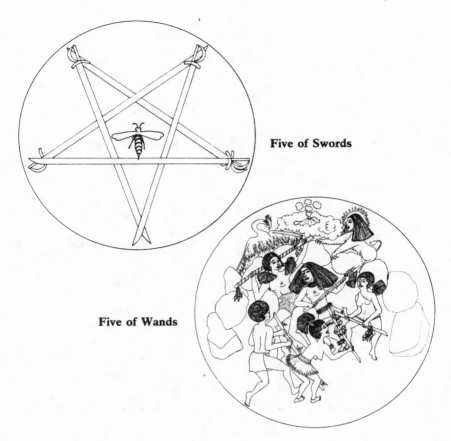

Five of Swords

Five of Wands

friends—that this struggle shall be fair, without curses or "stings." What remains is an effort to win a contest or game. Many different points of view are represented, various weapons and approaches are used. The "fighters" love and respect each other, because they are priestesses vying for the position of High Priestess, which rotates each year. "May the best woman win."

The red backdrop provides energy for a fair fight among equals. As a volcano puffs in the background, the Egyptian lioness-Goddess watches over them. Pressure released in small, contained explosions eliminates the need for huge, destructive ones. In conflict, each voice must be heard— each point of view expressed. Out of the flames a Griffin-Phoenix rises, a symbol of the rebirth of group harmony that awaits the outcome of this game that, in history, preceded the Olympics by centuries.

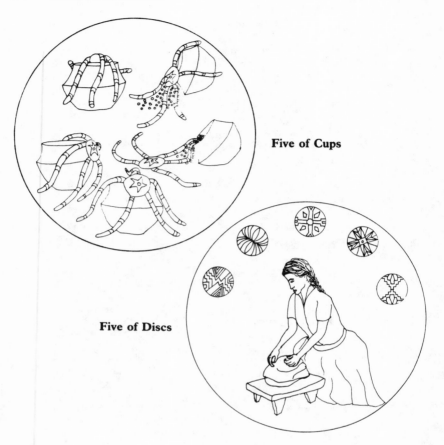

Five of Cups

Five of Discs

Five of Cups

The Five of Cups represents disappointment in love, being on the verge of despair, the blues. The feeling is like a long, sad sigh. Cups spill, pearls are cast to the depths, hope wanes. In the Motherpeace image, the tiny red starfish are able, collectively, to break down coral reefs, just as depression can break down the emotions.

Two cups have spilled, but three have not. On which should we focus? Despair offers nothing. Hope offers a chance. Perhaps everything is not really lost. Perhaps some pleasure waits just around the corner of the consciousness. Each of the creatures in the Motherpeace image wears at its center a five-pointed star of good fortune. Make a wish on the remaining cups and see what happens.

Five of Discs

The Five of Discs is a picture of tension held in the body, the kind of tightness that comes with worry. Probably the mind is focused on survival issues of some kind—money, housing, jobs, where the next meal is coming from. Change is taking place but on the inside, not yet manifest. Inertia threatens. It helps to keep the energy moving—maybe do something physical to keep from sinking into a dark state of consciousness (or unconsciousness). In the Motherpeace image, the woman works with her hands—kneading and rolling, pushing, touching—all these motions help keep her energy from getting stuck.

Worry never does any good anyway. Better to mobilize energy toward positive goals—use the hands to bake bread, make tortillas, sculpt something from clay, plant a garden, or give a massage. While the hands are busy, perhaps the mind can use the Discs in the background as centering devices for focusing calm, magical intentions toward the future.

Sixes: Exuberance

The Sixes are full and expressive, a peak number, always expansive and positive in some way. Six represents exuberance or triumph, being on top of things. Like the sun sitting at the center of the solar system, Six sits at the center of the Kabalistic Tree of Life and radiates out in every direction, saying "yes!" Six represents a moment of decisive action or a climax of some sort, a moment of glory.

Six of Swords

See color illustration on Plate 8.

The Six of Swords is probably the most spiritual of the Sword cards, after the Ace. The women—or the parts of the personality—come together at a central point, carrying red roses of passion for healing the heart, as well as their knives of truth. They float together above the sacred grove of thirteen evergreen trees—a grove of the Goddess. In the background, the golden-brown color of the mountains tells us it must be autumn, the season of the Death Goddess.

As the women join in flight, they think to themselves, "Something is dying, but at least we have a clear idea of what is really happening. It may not be pleasant, but the ability to see things as a whole always feels good in its own right. At least we're out of range of the pain and confusion." The card represents perspective, getting distance, and taking care of the hurt parts of the self.

Six of Wands
See color illustration on Plate 8.

The Six of Wands is a joyful card, expansive and warm, an emblem of personal creative power. This is the archetypal image of Shakti, a graphic illustration of pure radiant fire energy coming from the power center. A six-spoked wheel that represents the four elements plus head and body, the Shakti image takes its concept from Indian icons of many-armed deities. In her hand, she holds six Wands, each tipped with a different symbol: the four Tarot suits (air, water, fire, and earth) plus the sun and moon. The lion and salamander represent her fiery side, the octopus and snake her watery, receptive self. To be centered in fire, since it tends to radiate from that center, is a momentary victory.

The victory has taken place and Shakti is the winner; she radiates well-being. The personality takes command of the situation here and knows exactly how to handle it. Self-confidence is the main characteristic. Leadership emerges out of passion for life, and is sustained by perfect balance. As a result, this figure is centered in glory.

Six of Cups
See color illustration on Plate 9.

The Six of Cups represents an orgasmic rush of feelings, a wave of ecstasy. Riding the wave into shore, the horses and their riders experience joy and pleasure, a full-out expression of emotional intensity. Cups are held high. Snakes rise like *kundalini* spiraling up the spine. The riders are getting what they want, because they found the right spot and then caught the wave. Even if feelings are sad, the active expression of them provides a release that feels good.

There is a mythical, imaginative side to their pleasure—maybe it represents an especially nice dream, an orgasmic sexual experience, or a "high" of spirituality that feels like a leap into blissful *Nirvana*. Imagination unleashed, these figures easily ride the lavender sea-horses. Perhaps some memory of a distant past, like a wave, carries them into the future.

Six of Discs
See color illustration on Plate 9.

The Six of Discs signifies generosity, having more than enough, sharing health and good fortune. A healing is taking place. Someone gives a tender, careful touch, makes meaningful contact. Earth energy can be money or food, service or touch—it is physical and tangible. When a person gives the gift of healing, it circles back and heals the giver, too. This is a lesson that translates onto other planes, a basic law of the universe: what is given freely comes back two-fold.

The giving here takes place on several levels. One is the physical, the pure sense of loving touch. The next level is the "etheric" side of the physical, where energy passes unseen to most eyes, working invisibly to heal the body and balance the soul. The caring concentration pictured in the Motherpeace image demonstrates an ability to meditate successfully and bring results, to trust power and its use for good. Rather than hoarding, we pass this power from one body to another as a gift. This exchange of energy is the secret to success, which the Six of Discs traditionally represents.

CHAPTER 27

SEVENS, EIGHTS, AND NINES

Mutability

The Sevens, Eights, and Nines of each suit correlate astrologically with the "mutable" sign of whatever element they represent. This last series of three numbers in Wands are ruled by Sagittarius, in Swords by Gemini, in Cups by Pisces, and in Discs by Virgo. Changeable and cyclic in nature, mutable signs are represented by *sattva* in the Hindu system. Geometrically, they are expressed by a spiral, which combines the inwardness of a circle and the thrust of a straight line.

Sevens: Inner Work

Sevens are about inner work, accomplishments on the inner planes, and self-reflection. After the outward action of the Sixes comes a time of evaluation and completion, a response to what has gone before. Usually, Sevens concern an inner process of some kind. Something is happening, but one may not be able to see it; one may be essentially unconscious.

Seven of Swords

The Seven of Swords represents mental strategy felt to be necessary after the detached clarity of the Six. Having seen how things really are, the mind creates a plan to get what it wants. The personality may feel at this time as though it isn't going to get enough, or as though it might suffer guilt over wanting more and taking sneaky steps to get it. In such a situation, one may act uneasily or attempt to "outsmart" someone or get "one up." Avoiding a direct talk with the other person face-to-face, one must imagine what they think and make plans based at least somewhat on illusion and fantasy.

The fox is a predator—he represents stealth. The chickens are penned and unaware, representing a kind of naivete and foolish trust. They wait passively for whatever will befall them, as the sneaky fox creeps closer and closer to their pen. The Seven Swords are stuck in the fence, perhaps providing a way up and over for the fox—his ideas, plans, maneuvers. The plan here is pretty unstable, a foxy adventure on one side of the fence, a passive victimization on the other. Assuming the worst, the personality goes after its "due."

Seven of Wands

The Seven of Wands is about responsibility—the priestess of the Six, who won the contest of the Five, is now standing completely on her own and must trust herself to know how to handle the most difficult of situations. She wears the horned headdress of the silver crescent moon, representing change and female balance. The peacock feathers on her head are a longtime symbol of wisdom, power, and initiation. She carries a torch of truth in her right hand to light the way for others, signifying active leadership and philosophical knowledge. Around her neck are amulets and power objects. Bare-breasted, she stands tall and speaks in tongues of fire. Holding her position, she tells the truth as she sees it.

The other personalities are not completely supportive of her; they challenge her to hold her own. One of them confronts her quite directly, holding her wand of power aloft. The others seem to have varying responses to what's happening—boredom, interest, reflection, anger, support. This is a debate, an open verbal exchange. The energy here makes for sexual exchange or heated dialogue. There is an underlying feeling of deep purpose—this is not light or superficial interchange, but significant communication.

Seven of Cups

The Seven of Cups is very spacey—it represents imagination and dreaminess, watery visions, fantasy. The cups signify choices, an abun-

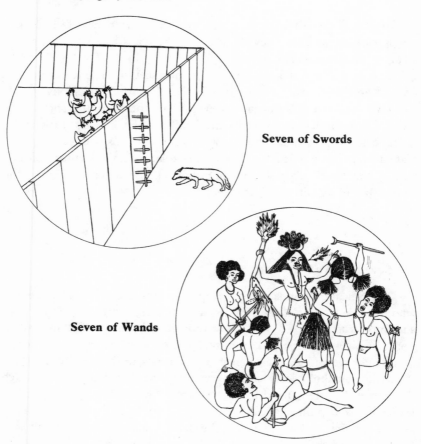

Seven of Swords

Seven of Wands

dance of them. They seem almost equal in their appeal—how shall the personality decide? It has difficulty, so much that it wants to fall asleep. The waters of the ocean behind the figure threaten to swallow her up completely, if she doesn't ground herself in some kind of reality. The net she carries may be for winnowing—separating what she will keep from what she will throw out.

There is a seductive sweetness to the Seven of Cups, a feeling of wanting everything at once, and a belief that one may have it. Sometimes this card signifies a "mystical vision" that would stand out from the other fantasies and probably correspond to the white dove settling into the cup on her head. Surely this one cup—this choice—calls more clearly than the others. The dove is Aphrodite's bird and symbolizes oracular power, the message of the mind spirit. An unrealistic desire to have all the cups at once can get in the way of actualizing the one higher vision of truth. But

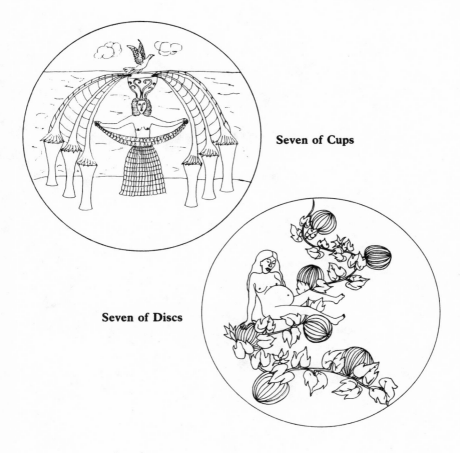

Seven of Cups

Seven of Discs

once she acknowledges the cup touched by Aphrodite, it pours blessings into all the other cups.

Seven of Discs

The Seven of Discs is a representation of growth and waiting. This woman—one of the "little people" of Irish mythology—is pregnant and will soon deliver. For now, as she feels the growth process taking place within, she waits. The message of the card is, "Be patient—there is nothing to do but wait. There is no way to hurry this birth, no way to see inside for certain." On the mental plane, a similar rule obtains: trusting that the idea is taking form, a thinker must wait, just as one would wait for pumpkins to ripen fully before picking them.

All inner processes of growth resemble pregnancy. Sometimes we

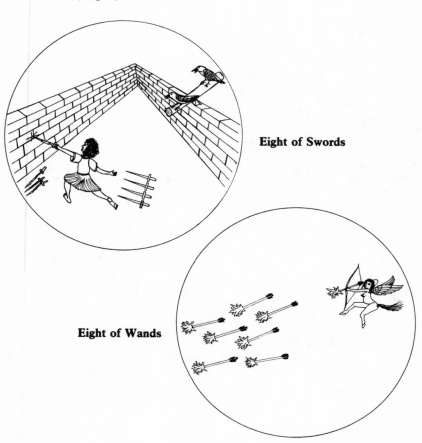

Eight of Swords

Eight of Wands

make the mistake of assuming that if nothing is born yet, if there is no physical manifestation, then nothing is really happening. We doubt our process. Or we become inordinately impatient, wanting to make the thing come before it is time. Aleister Crowley called this card "failure." It really is a failure of imagination if one cannot wait for what is to come. Gestation has its own schedule—if birth comes before gestation is complete, we call it "premature."

Eights: Change

Eight is a number of change and inspiration. The eights all represent a change of mood from what has gone before and an entering into some new phase that comes directly out of past experience. Ruled by Uranus,

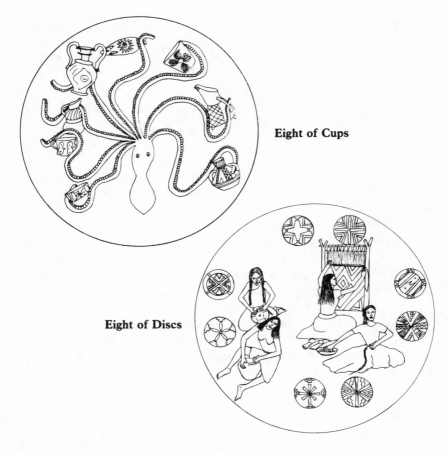

Eight of Cups

Eight of Discs

they signify movement and new direction. They are definite and external in quality.

Eight of Swords

The Eight of Swords represents the activity of fighting one's way out of a box created by the mind—a stuck place, an obstacle holding one back from success. Usually the card represents indecision and a feeling that things are working against one, ganging up somehow to foil one's best efforts. The plan made earlier in the Seven didn't work out, and the ego feels offended, tricked, blocked. The activity of smashing swords against the hard wall of resistance is a drama that momentarily captivates the attention of the swordsperson. Perhaps she has sought the protection of being "trapped" in order to avoid the larger world of possibilities outside the walls.

The image is very dreamlike and illusory—the wall against which the swords are breaking is a figment of the imagination. Freedom lies in understanding that what is needed is the more balanced perspective of the crows who see both sides of the situation with a sense of humor.

Eight of Wands

The Eight of Wands is about energy—fast-moving arrows of energy shot from a magical bow that belongs to an elf (or a partial centaur). This little winged creature has the nature of a Cupid, flinging its arrows who-knows-where and awakening the personality. Von Franz says "the bow and arrow have to do with the sudden directness of the unconscious libido." It is time to take a risk, try something new, let passions fly.

An arrow could signify a phone call, visitors, or any expression of life force. Someone may be bringing ideas or projects. Identifying with an arrow, a person might take a trip somewhere or move. This high energy is also psychic power, allowing one to tune in on people's thoughts or wishes, to hear the phone before it rings and know who's on the other end, to initiate a relationship that hasn't yet manifested on the physical plane.

Eight of Cups

The Eight of Cups represents an unconscious kind of change taking place—one happening on the very deep feeling level. The octopus has the ability to secrete "ink" that then shrouds its activities and protects it from harmful predators. Similarly, sommeone may feel the need to protect herself from the usual social interactions right now, as she dives deeper into the ocean of her unconscious mind to see what has led to a change of heart. She may not like what's happening, it may not be convenient or pleasant. Maybe she's changing in relation to someone she loves; maybe she wants something different and is afraid to say so, afraid of loss.

Perhaps the fantasies of the Seven of Cups didn't manifest quite as she expected. The Eight becomes a kind of "reality check" and may bring with it depression, gloom, a sense of sadness, and lethargy, even self-pity and morbid "existential *Angst*." If she swims with the feelings, however, allowing the emotions to dictate her direction, she will be fine. This change will take her deeper into her own spirituality. She will find meaning in the depths of her solitude and inward turning. There are, after all, Eight Cups, each uniquely styled with its own color, pattern, and shape. The feelings affecting the personality at this time are her jewels, treasures from the deep sea, a call from the high Self.

Eight of Discs

The Eight of Discs represents Craft—apprenticeship in a skill that will take one through life in a grounded way, and a sharing of skills between people. These women are serious in this work, and understand the "art" of meaningful occupation. Each character in the Motherpeace image is engaged in a particular, individual task, yet they work together toward common goals. One makes a pot from clay, another forms a basket from reeds. A woman sits at a loom and weaves a tapestry, another strings beads for a belt. All these objects are functional, yet made with care and a deep sense of love and beauty.

The underlying meaning of the Eight of Discs is "the Path," suggesting a spiritual undertaking, a movement of the personality onto the more spiritual road of the soul. Native American people embody this understanding of daily work that is infused with spirit—for them, the worlds of spirit and matter are not separate. What is utilitarian must also be beautiful, because it comes from the Mother and is made as an offering back to her. The Zen consciousness of work is similar. Every task is done with the simple understanding that it matters. Work is done for its own sake and not for personal gain or someone else's profit.

Nines: Completion

Nines, because they are the final single digits of our number system, represent completion and finality. They are the culmination, the summing up of the sequence of numbers. Nine is a magical number of the Moon Goddess and relates to the wisdom of the Crone (or Hermit) in the Tarot. There were Nine Muses in classical Greek mythology, and nine is a trinity of trinities, three threes.

Nine of Swords

The Nine of Swords represents a ghastly nightmare, the rising up from the unconscious of all the fears and projections the mind has made during its process of thought. Worry and anguish have become overwhelming terror, an experience of despair and even cruelty or physical

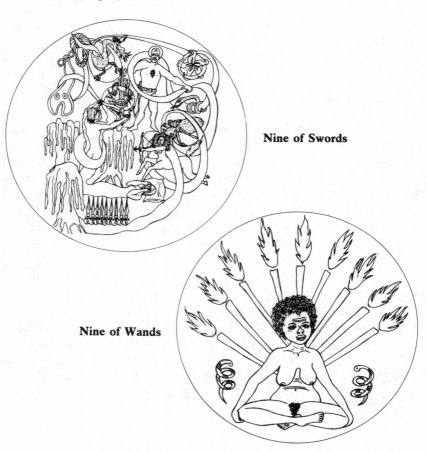

Nine of Swords

Nine of Wands

pain. All the unchecked fears and negative thoughts have accumulated to form what Jungians call "the Shadow." These fears may stem from childhood traumas, repressed hurts and wounds from anytime in life, or images projected by the culture one lives in. The twisting path shows the morass of confusion surrounding the issues that cause doubt and fear, the sense of difficulty as one awakens to this mess of anxiety and "demons." The rising up of this Shadow may keep a person from sleeping or give her physical symptoms of illness.

Although demons come from the unconscious, they can be fought by conscious intention. Part of the personality cowers in terror, hands covering her eyes, refusing to look at or deal with the problem, immobilized by fear. The other part of the self rises up in strength and confidence—ready to confront the Shadow. Power flames from the sword that appears in

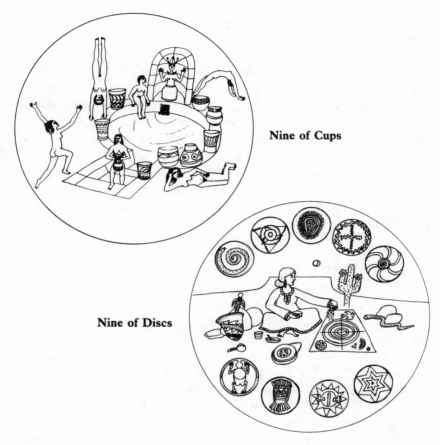

Nine of Cups

Nine of Discs

front of the heroic part of the personality, which reaches out with her right hand to grasp this tool of liberation. The only way out is through the pain and fear, through a confrontation with one's monsters.

Nine of Wands

The Nine of Wands represents an accumulation of energy—knowledge of energy retention leads to its wise storage and competent use. She knows not to waste her time or dissipate her energies, and represents the wise use of power. The flaming wands behind the wise old woman represent experience gained along the way. At the base of these torches of truth and light, she sits in a meditation posture, mastering the life force within the body and releasing it for use in healing and creative endeavor.

Her experiences have been "transmuted" into wisdom, she is ready for whatever action will be needed.

Since she has learned, like a shaman, to master the heat, she is surrounded by red energy. She sits within it without the difficulties of a younger or less-experienced personality. The two spiraling snakes on either side of her represent the dual forces of male and female, right and left, and signify that she has the sex force under her control and knows its inner mysteries. The snake energy is no longer latent, but awakened—she is very sensitive to its effects in her body and in the world. Her nervous system is alive, yet she is not overcome by the tremendous effects of this vitalization, for she has also learned mastery and self control. An illuminated personality, she represents the ability to respond creatively to all situations.

Nine of Cups

The Nine of Cups represents physical and mental enjoyment and well-being. Eden Gray has called this card the "wishing card," suggesting that when it appears in a Tarot reading, a wish will come true. These priestesses have come to visit the sacred wishing well, where a statue of the Goddess presides with her arms upraised in traditional Moon Priestess style. They bring offerings to the well—maybe they throw pennies, since copper is sacred to Venus-Aphrodite. Then they drink of the holy nectar represented by the deep blue water, becoming ecstatic and energized by the love and inspiration of the Mother.

This is a visionary card. The priestesses open themselves to the inner ability to envision future events—they "creatively visualize" what they want the world to be. Because they are open in their hearts and minds and senses, they are able to wish for what they want without doubts, without putting a "no" on their wishes as soon as they experience them. The willow trees behind them weep for joy, and the priestesses themselves turn handsprings and cartwheels in their ecstatic experience of the divine energy of feelings and desire. A card of optimism and trust in the future, it indicates a time of letting oneself wish for whatever one wants and trusting that one deserves to get it.

Nine of Discs
See color illustration on front cover.

The Nine of Discs is a picture of the archetypal New Age solitary witch or shaman. Although many people these days work in circles or "covens" to do their healing magic, others work alone. These creative "solitaries" are learning the work through art, meditation, dreams, direction from spirit guides, perhaps even through books. Such people are not necessarily isolated, lonely individuals, but simply regular folks who take a little time out to do what they have come to understand as "the Work."

This personality has transported herself to the desert in order to accomplish a healing through the disciplines of the Navaho sand-painter. Her tool kit includes a shaman drum, a wand, a rattle, and the grains and sands necessary to make her healing work of art. Like all sand-paintings, this work will be temporary art, lasting only until she destroys it or until the rains and winds come to erase it. Still, she does not doubt the absolute efficacy of this work of magic. She understands that through meditation and intent, she sets in motion the forces of the universe to do her bidding. She makes this image for the purpose of healing herself, someone else or even humanity at large.

One important quality of this Nine is the development of strength and courage. Grounding herself in Source energy, she does not fear going alone or facing her work. The moon rises over the mesa to light her way. The snake comes as a friend and guide. She feels herself in harmony with the elements. Like the blooming cactus flower, she embodies beauty and freshness, even in the ancient wisdom that she represents in this activity. She has overcome her survival fears and mastered her Craft. Like all medicine-women, she trusts the universe to take care of her and provide her with whatever she needs.

CHAPTER 28

TENS

Transformation

The Tens in the Tarot constitute a special astrological condition—they represent an overview or composite of the three signs of each element. Like an "oversoul," they take in aspects of each, organizing, synthesizing, and expressing them.

Thus the Ten of Wands represents aspects of Cardinal Aries, Fixed Leo, and Mutable Sagittarius, and is represented by a collective experience of energy generation and fire. The Ten of Swords, similarly, includes Cardinal Libra, Fixed Aquarius, and Mutable Gemini, and simultaneously transcends them all. The Ten of Cups embodies Cardinal Cancer, Fixed Scorpio, and Mutable Pisces as an overflowing group experience of feeling energy. The Ten of Discs partakes of all the earth signs—Cardinal Capricorn, Fixed Taurus, and Mutable Virgo in a dynamic community event.

Ten represents an overabundance of the element of the particular suit. Having reached completion in the Nine, development overflows into a cycle of return in the Ten. Ten marks a transition to something new, a transforming event. Ten seems to take the personality beyond itself into the universal realms, and in the Motherpeace images, Ten always represents a group event or experience of community.

Ten of Swords
See color illustration on Plate 10.

The Ten of Swords represents the final letting go of some idea to which the ego has been attached. In the picture, the idea is the ultimate one of life itself. Robert Graves tells a story of the priestesses of Athena, who leaped off a promontory into the ocean at the advance of patriarchal troops rather than submit to rape and patriarchal "wedlock." In this spirit, the card depicts the absolute abandonment of a cherished image, plan, or way of life.

There is a grace and spiritual joy in the bodies of the priestesses as they surrender to the inevitable end of life as they have known it. The card represents the dramatic end of a cycle, a sudden coming to terms with what really is, rather than with what one wanted or hoped would be the case. Traditionally a card of "ruin" and loss, this Ten represents a sacrifice that, once made, allows the personality to get on with its broader purpose in the world. In a certain sense, one may feel a relief in the certainty that the Ten of Swords symbolizes—the struggle has ended, the ego has no choice but to let go. But the dive into deep waters below may yield a new experience of feeling and emotional sensitivity.

Ten of Wands
See color illustration on Plate 10.

The Ten of Wands represents a release of all the energies that have built up over time—anxieties, tensions and strains, hopes and fears, all the contracts and commitments of everyday life that now and then overwhelm the personality. The women in the Motherpeace image are participating in a "trance dance" in order to express some of the monumental energy they feel passing through them. When *kundalini* power gets raised, it is very important to channel and release it—otherwise it gets stuck in the body and runs amok. The three people in the foreground of the Motherpeace image are working to bring focus and positive guidance to the energy being freed up in the dance. One character keeps a rhythm on a drum, a common shaman technique of gently guiding trance work and psychic opening. Under conditions such as these, creativity may be harnessed and spontaneity come into play. The adolescent girl in the center comes forth with oracular power, speaking in tongues, giving herself over to the cosmic powers in this safe environment of community. What she speaks, another member of her community translates and captures with stylus and clay tablet. Thus the sacred inspiration is recorded for the future.

What led up to this scene? Probably the girl had overcommitted herself and was feeling the demandingness of her life. Tension had built up. Her nerves were strained. Perhaps she had experienced some anger— diffuse and unfocused, because it was really anger at herself for taking on too much. Maybe she was about to get her period and felt particularly sensitive to everything. Instead of blocking the energy, she is now enabled, with the help of her community, to generate a great deal of power.

Ten of Cups

See color illustration on Plate 11.

The Ten of Cups represents communication with Source—the gratitude and contentment of a community after the rains have come and blessed it with certain harvest. Like the cups, the people are spilling over with happiness. Raising their arms in joyful reunion with the cosmos, they send their thanks to the miraculous double rainbow that blesses their endeavor. They know themselves to be in the presence of what is divine, and they partake of it. The underlying story of the card is that the community, through its harmonious work together, was able to call in the rains in the first place. Now they express their gratitude in a conscious way for the blessing that came because of their prayers and efforts.

Early American Pueblo communities were actually able to "control" the weather to a certain extent. They made deep cup-shaped holes at the top of canyons to catch the waters of a storm, and developed elaborate systems of canals at the foot of the cliffs where the water was quickly and efficiently spread over the entire ground and irrigated the plants. In this way, they could grow crops and feed thousands of people in areas where park rangers today feel mystified that there could have ever been enough rainfall to allow even a small tribe to exist. The rangers believe that "climatic changes" must account for this variance. However, the Hopi and other Native American people still claim the ability to attract rain, which they attribute to being in touch with the universe and its cyclic laws and seasons, and then working in harmony with this "plan."

Ten of Discs

See color illustration on Plate 11.

The Ten of Discs represents a circle of support in which manifestation takes place. This card symbolizes family and community, tribe, or group, the sense of being part of some larger organized body. Like all the Tens, it represents a transition, but this time particularly on the physical plane. Something is ending, and something else is being born, and all within some larger movement or expression. The women in the circle come from different cultural backgrounds—in this case, different tribes—yet they band together for the purpose of making this birth a joyful and healthy occasion. Young and old, they bring their sacred baskets to the circle and focus energy through them into the center where the birth takes place.

The central image is modeled after a relief sculpture from India, in which two women support the squatting birther who pushes down on her belly while another woman serves as "catcher" for the baby. In world mythology and religion, this emergence of the baby from the protective environment of the womb and out through the vaginal canal is a widespread symbol of "emergence" and "creation." It represents the emergence of humanity from the womb of Earth Mother, as well as the manifestation of everything else in the physical world, from money to health care. The Ten of Discs is a symbol of wealth—everything one needs for survival and more is contained within the power of the group energy.

CHAPTER 29

DAUGHTERS

Youthfulness

In traditional Tarot decks, the forty numbered cards just described are followed by sixteen cards depicting personalities. Originally, these were known as "court" cards, because they depicted a medieval court with its royalty and aristocrats. In the Motherpeace images, these hierarchical figures from a brief period of the vast human story are replaced by figures less parochial or time-bound. What were formerly "Kings" are now "Shamans" (a role filled, in fact, both by males and by females). The "Queens" of traditional Tarot have become "Priestesses," equal in status to the Shamans, but different in function. "Knights" are now "Sons," representing the archetypal male element; and "Pages" have become "Daughters," representing the young female force. These new titles do not change this inner meanings of the cards, but simply bring them up to date and into line with matriarchal concepts of power and development.

The Daughters are the young part of the personality, full of life and enthusiasm, waxing like the new moon. In addition to whichever suit they represent, Daughters reflect primarily the element of earth. The Daughter is what Starhawk calls the "Younger Self," symbolizing the unconscious part of a being, the child within, who "directly experiences the world, through the holistic awareness of the right hemisphere." Her functions, says Starhawk, are "sensations, emotions, basic drives, image memory, intuition and diffuse perception."

Daughter of Swords

Determined to make something happen, the Daughter of Swords represents the urge to action, impulsive and rash. She is the part of the

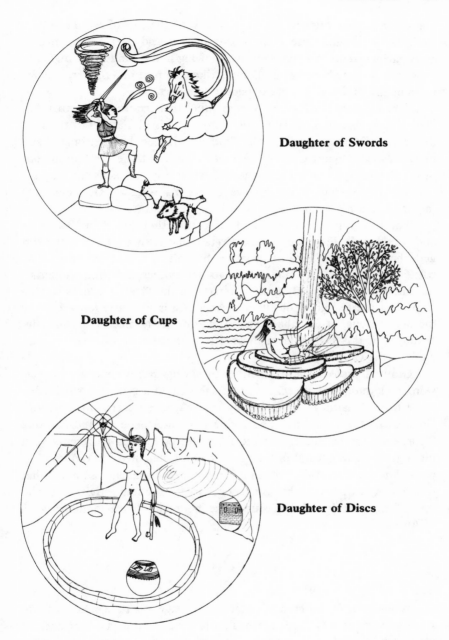

Daughter of Swords

Daughter of Cups

Daughter of Discs

self that wants ideas to manifest, yet feels young and innocent, inexperienced in the ways of the world. She's impatient and probably a rebel. Swords represent air, which is constantly changing and shifting. This

Daughter is the youngest, most energetic of the Sword family—like a Valkyrie, she would raise a storm or wake the dead. Her dress is that of an Amazon warrior maiden. Her hair blowing in the winds of change, she raises her Sword above her head and strikes the pose of a fighter. Yet she remains grounded on the rocks beneath her feet.

When a person wants to do something that requires more than her own power, she traditionally calls in the Winds of Fate from the four directions. Of these, the North Wind is considered the strongest and most magical. Robert Graves says that "whistling three times in honour of the White Goddess is the traditional witch way of raising the winds," and the horse-wind in the picture is the mare-headed Goddess, who might be the mother of this zealous Daughter.

The boar represents valor and *rajas,* the Hindu word for fierceness and passions. In Egyptian, Greek, Cretan, and Irish mythology, the sun god changes himself into or disguises himself as a boar in order to do battle with a rival. The mountain goats are mother and child, Amalthea the She-goat and her kid, another version of the White Goddess serving to protect the Daughter of Swords. Amalthea is variously known as the mother of Zeus, of Pan the goat-god, and of the horned Dionysus, suggesting that this Daughter of Swords is connected with an early "goat-cult" of the Goddess.

Graves links Athene to Amalthea by saying that Athene wore a goat-skin as clothing and alternately, that she carried a goat-skin shield that came from Amalthea's hide. In any case, Athene is certainly a warrior Goddess of the Amazons. The connection to Athene reminds us that Swords are of the mind, and the Daughter of Swords represents keen intelligence, a whirlwind of thought moving faster than she can keep up with. The stone with the hole in it represents the shamanic source of her wisdom. A powerful thinker, she is likewise a crusading activist, one who fights for her ideals and "rages upon the mountain" like a young priestess of Athene.

When you get this card in a reading, it suggests a time of activity and starting new projects. Your personality is impatient, maybe overeager. It may even be reckless. What you want you want right now! Your mind is a whirlwind of bright ideas. As long as the card is upright, you won't hurt others with your hasty decisions or spoil things for yourself. Take a deep breath and concentrate on the best possible expression of your boundless energies. Then proceed with caution to make your wishes come true.

Daughter of Wands
See color illustration on Plate 14 and on front cover.

The Daughter of Wands represents the young, fiery part of the personality that manifests through dance and movement, joyful change, and growth. She is verbal and uninhibited, propelled from within to express herself. She is a symbol of spring and the seasonal emergence of Persephone from the cave of the underworld, the darkness of winter. Persephone's return to earth is marked by new growth and sexual energy, the migration of animals and birds, and the dance of life energy felt in all of us.

The Daughter of Wands carries a sprig of witch hazel for healing. In her other hand she holds the Wheel of Nemesis, which all daughters of life carry with them through patriarchal culture. Nemesis is the Goddess of divine retribution for breaches of taboo, and her wheel, says Graves, "will one day come full circle and vengeance be exacted on the sinner."

Her white unicorn is a sacred, mythical beast who represents, as the five-pointed star does, not only the four quarters but the "zenith" or upper pole of spirit. In mythology, says Graves, the unicorn can be captured "only by a pure virgin—Wisdom herself." In this case, the virgin stands for "spiritual integrity." Like the unicorn, she dances the "wildness and untameability" of the free spirit who dwells in each of us.

The season of spring often touches the wild spirit within people who may not be consciously aware of it during the rest of the year. This is the magic of resurrection and rebirth, an awakening that lifts our spirits and sends us out in the world again, like the Daughter of Wands, after our winter rest. The ego gets a new burst of self-confidence—a sense of personal activity and possibility—as we scamper out of the dark cave and into the light.

When this card comes up for you in a reading, it represents the natural joy within you bursting free in some way. You may feel like running, dancing, or singing; your heart is on fire. This passionate movement from within demands expression, resulting in a transformation of your mood, a rushing toward some form of freedom, or an exciting life-transition. As long as the card is upright, you can trust that the free flow of your energies will carry you through any period of change or growth.

Daughter of Cups

The Daughter of Cups represents the playful, affectionate part of the personality, the part that has a wonderful sense of humor and knows how to feel good. This is an aspect easily lost in the modern-day rush of "business as usual" to which so many of us are committed. The Daughter of Cups symbolizes a necessary break from that kind of focused, stressful activity—a summer vacation—an opening into pleasure and the beauty within. She immerses herself in the beauty of the inner world and dreams new dreams of global peace and harmony.

Her supreme receptivity is reflected in her elemental qualities of earth and water. She is magnetic and inclusive, drawing to herself the warmth and life around her. What she desires she turns into creative visualizations—which helps her dreams come true. From within the pool of magical mineral waters, she sings softly, letting the waterfall caress her body, opening herself completely like a flower. In Starhawk's magical phrase, she represents "the Maiden who yields to all and yet is penetrated by none." Her senses and perceptions take in the world of nature, and she merges with it in a divine union of self and other. She celebrates her body, her desires, physical pleasure, and the joy of knowing deep relaxation and psychic awareness.

When the personality can touch the depths of its own being, desire and love spill over, like the spring waters overflowing and creating other pools. Feelings of pleasure radiate from her and touch other people. A young tree reaches out toward her presence, life touching life. Rock walls enclose her in love like a cave, yet the waters stream in like cosmic light entering through the crown *chakra* (energy center). Out of her communion with nature come fantasy and astral images. The Daughter of Cups represents the opening of the inner voice after a fearless dive into deep realms of self. She searches within for answers and ideas, hidden motives, and human needs that release as they surface.

The turtle represents the ability to come out of and go back into, the protected space within. Native Americans regard the turtle as sacred and call America "Turtle Island," believing it to be the oldest part of the world inhabited by humanity. According to Evelyn Eaton, the Cheyenne believe they emerged out of the "River of Turtle," and Indian sweat lodges are built in the shape of a turtle. Mythologically, the tortoise carries the world on its back. In the Motherpeace image, it bears the sacred water jar. The Hopi carry their sacred water jar with them and plant it in the earth wherever they decide to settle. They believe, says Broder, that if they are in a state of purity when they plant the jar, and follow certain rituals, then water will flow from the ground for their use.

When you get this card in a reading, chances are that you are experiencing your feelings very strongly. The little child inside you calls out for attention, and whether the feelings are sad or happy, the process of experiencing them is what counts. This is not a time for hard work or seriousness. Take a break—respect your feelings and your senses. The immersion in your private pool of emotion will pay off in self-revelation. When the card is upright, you know you are enjoying the flow.

Daughter of Discs

Signifying pure elemental earth energy, the Daughter of Discs depicts a young virgin on a vision quest—the personality seeking its own name through solitary prayer and fasting. She is the archetypal young female, the nymph or maiden, the Greek Kore, Persephone in her underworld aspect. Her horned headdress links her to Artemis and the High Priestess, yet she seeks the solitude and wisdom of Hekate the Crone.

Like many young Native Americans, the Daughter of Discs has come away from the tribal home and into the mountains or desert where she will survive on her own for at least a few days. She asks protection from the earth and nature. Her stone circle is a magical disc of safety. Standing within it, she holds up another disc in the form of an obsidian mirror, which reflects both the setting sun and the rising full moon. She asks them to awaken her knowledge and the ability to see into invisible worlds. Inside the cave, her stone house waits for the time she chooses to retire within the earth for sleep and a visionary dream.

Meanwhile, she holds the sacred pipe that the Lakota Sioux say was given by Wakan-Tanka, the sacred White Buffalo Woman who advised: "With this sacred Pipe, you will walk upon the Earth, for the Earth is sacred. Every step taken on her should be a prayer. . . . When you pray with this pipe, you pray for and with everything created." While the obsidian mirror reaches into the cosmos for information and inspiration, the Pipe becomes a universal channel between the Daughter and the

Earth Mother. The young Daughter, then, is studying to be a shaman. When she takes her Pipe and, in the words of Eaton, "goes into the desert or upon the mountain, or along a stream in the foothills, somewhere quiet and perhaps still unpolluted, to sit in a sacred manner and smoke in the ancient way, there is set up . . . a pipeline through which messages and signals ascend and descend."

When the Daughter returns from her virgin stay in the mountains, she will be transformed. She will have learned what her life task will be, she will have opened her psychic channels allowing for a sensitivity to the world unknown to her before. Her power is on the rise, she is pregnant with herself.

When you get this card in a reading, it signals a period of solitude and learning to trust the wisdom of the body. You are required now to rely on your instincts. New experiences may make you feel vulnerable and exposed, reminding you that you don't have all the answers. But as you seek truth, you learn courage. In asking Mother Earth for guidance, you open yourself to all the positive powers of the universe. When the card is upright, your awareness grows and you may experience new abilities, secret gifts from within.

CHAPTER 30

SONS

Male Polarity

The male polarity that lives within the Goddess, the Son represents her child and lover, the gift of her womb and the opposite force of energy. As Starhawk says, the Son is "Her mirror image, Her other pole." Early humanity worshiped a Mother Goddess who was whole and reproduced without sexual intercourse—a theme we still encounter in Mary's "immaculate conception" and the "virgin birth" of Christ. The resplendent Mother Goddess thus symbolizes the origins of life on earth and, in human terms, the long-time pattern of matrilineal descent, prior to the institution of "fatherhood." Traditionally, within the Goddess religion, the Son embodies a light, playful quality, a key element of the positive "male archetype." In the Motherpeace images, too, most of the Sons represent positive male energy, rather different from the usual roles for men in modern society. Meditation on these cards will help a person imagine positive ways of being male in a culture where "male supremacy" has all but destroyed manhood.

Sons, ruled by Mercury, also represent what Starhawk calls "Talking Self," which "functions through the verbal, analytic awareness of the left hemisphere" and which "speaks through words, abstract concepts, and numbers."

Son of Swords

The Son of Swords is the least promising positive male image—elementally all air, he tends to be overly mental and out of touch with emotions. Jumping from one thing to the next, he represents the active mind forgetting what it wanted five minutes before. In terms of human

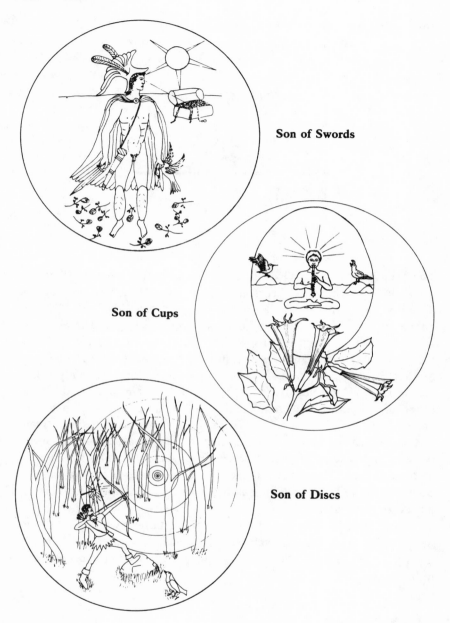

Son of Swords

Son of Cups

Son of Discs

interactions, this Son is fickle in the extreme. His gold helmet, sword, sheath and leg armor mark him as the archetypal "hero" of mythology, whose tasks generally included slaying the Goddess in one form or another. He signifies the Son who has rejected the Mother. In this case, the white dove represents Aphrodite. Our hero grasps her by the throat. What he will do with her is not clear, since already his roving eye has caught sight of the treasure chest behind him. The gemstones and flashy trinkets beckon to him, threatening to cause him to forget what he had in mind for the white bird.

His exploits concerning mortal women are another important part of heroic mythology. He frequently rapes them. Theseus, Achilles, Perseus, Hercules—they are always raping and abducting women, especially Amazons, and eventually abandoning or killing them. In terms of the Son of Swords, this means, "watch out, this mind may hurt another." The power of the human mind to project thoughts into others, and to control through manipulation is very great. One can be invaded by this mental power, raped psychically by this intellect, as the flowers in this image were cut and left on the ground at his feet.

Initially, this Son may seem very attractive, with his shiny armaments and the light of his mind; but until he gains spiritual control of his urges, he signifies trouble. In any case, he is disconnected from feeling, except, perhaps, a feeling for conquest and loot. In the image we find no water, only a barren landscape and a sun whose rays form a downward-pointing pentagram, the sign of cursing magic. In such a cut-off male, the ego is detached from the feminine. He has come to believe his own written mythology—that light is good and dark is bad; that male is right and female wrong. Afraid to feel his own woman-self, the hero thinks he needs to dominate women and the world around him in order to remain "strong." He represents the romantic male self-image, a dominance-submission script in which he is on top.

An intellect such as this, whether it belongs to a man or a woman, cuts deeply through the culture around it. To the extent that intellect can be united with the force of love, it can bring positive effects in the world; but the mind on its own, cut off from nature, leads us toward doom, as in the case of the nuclear arms race, a magnificent display of technical ingenuity. If the Son in this image can identify once again with the dove and the roses, he may have time to save himself and us from disaster.

When this card comes up in a reading, it implies that you are approaching your goals in an overly rational way. The thoughts that determine your movements are like swords cutting you off from the nourishment you need to sustain life. The cold logic of your ego is about to strangle the dove of your heart. You need to soften and remember that you are not functioning in a vacuum. Let go of the false sense of isolation you feel and connect to the rest of life. When the card is upright, you need to stop thinking and get down to feeling.

Son of Wands

See color illustration on Plate 14.

The Son of Wands represents the Horned God of ancient shamanistic religion and contemporary witchcraft. Unlike the Son of Swords, this Son is not cut off from the Mother or the group, but dancing at the center of it. He represents "pre-macho" masculinity, the archetypal positive male principle whose elements are light and fire. "He is untamed," as Starhawk says of the Horned God. "But untamed feelings are very different from enacted violence." Instead of going off to seek individual glory, "he remains within the orbit of the Goddess; his power is always directed toward the service of life." His sexuality, though wild, is also "gentle and tender." Traditionally the lover of the Great Mother, the Son delights, amuses, and entertains. He celebrates life in much the same way as his sister, the Daughter of Wands.

The Son, like the sun glowing behind him, represents the directed warmth of summer sunshine, ego expressing itself through a dance of life. The *I Ching* describes the sun as "the Gentle, the Penetrating," and in this way this Son represents the initiating force. In his hands, he holds a rattle and a prayer stick, Wands that will focus his energy in sacred ways and keep it clean and light.

Ruled by Mercury, the Son also represents thought and the positive power of the mind fired by intuition and joy. Not only Eros, he also represents *Logos,* the power of the mind. In witchcraft, there is "no opposition between the two." The God of the Witches is the untamed male presence in a world that predates patriarchal sex roles and control by males. He represents for all of us—women as well as men—the untamed part of us that will, says Starhawk, "never be domesticated, that refuses to be compromised, diluted, made safe, molded, or tampered with."

In this way, and archetypally, the Son of Wands resembles the Fool. He has painted his body like a Zia clown (who is also a shaman), and he dances to the drumming of a brother, for the pleasure of mother and siblings. "Out of foolishness and play, creativity is born." Like the cranes in the background, he breaks into a mating dance. "A model of male power that is free from father-son rivalry or oedipal conflicts," the

Horned God, as Starhawk says, "has no father; He is his own father." He represents, significantly, a time when fatherhood was an act of fertilization and community involvement, not yet a mode of "ownership."

The Son of Wands represents the contrast of male energy to that of the Emperor, who represents Father as Ruler. Light, like the bright yellow background, and connected to Goddess-space, like the light sky-blue behind him, he represents high energy, a penetrating mind, and cheerful success in the world.

When you get this card in a reading, it suggests a bouyant, energetic way of being in the world. Your personality is alive and delights in amusing, entertaining and attracting others. You are "turned on" and enjoy being the center of attention, charming those around you with your wit. Refusing to take things too seriously, you enjoy the effect you have on others. When the card is upright, it signals a lot of sexual energy or a period of easy creativity, a distinctly playful experience of the life force energies.

Son of Cups

The Son of Cups represents the quiet, inner aspect of the male principle—Shiva of the Hindu religion, who represents the High Self. Reflective like the moon, he signifies the stilled mind of meditation. Like the Egyptian Harpocrates, he is "Lord of Silence," communicating with the unconscious mind. The egg within which he is contained is the World Egg of the Great Mother, the cosmic circle of the feminine—he is her child. He represents the God of Autumn Equinox who, as Starhawk says, "sleeps in the womb of the Goddess, sailing over the sunless sea that is her womb." In this view, he combines, in a manner rare in modern men, light and dark, air and watery depths, mind and feelings. He practices two ways of knowing, analytic and synthetic. In Starhawk's words, he can "take things apart and look at differences, or form a pattern from unintegrated parts and see the whole."

Like the Hanged One, the Son of Cups has surrendered to the world of the feminine. Light radiates from his head as he communes with cosmic life, represented by the birds who seem to talk to him intelligibly. The flute he plays and the blue water he seems to float upon without effort both signify Krishna, the flute-playing god of play and sexuality.

Traditionally this card (the "Knight of Cups") is the "lover" and brings gifts of self to another. Along with the power of focused desire, the gifts he brings are music, flowers, perhaps a message.

Male water gods usually carry a trident, symbol of Neptune (and earlier of Poseidon). In the Motherpeace Son of Cups, the flower is the trident, a living symbol of beauty. In this case the flower also promises visions, since it is a form of Sacred Datura. Poisonous unless used with knowledge, this plant is taken by many "primitives" for its hallucinogenic properties. In the Motherpeace image, the Son of Cups sits in a trance state, spiritualized by the forces of the planet Neptune and the violet light around him. Yoga means "yoking" or "union," reflected here in the air and water he joins through his body.

Bridging the mind and the feelings, the Son of Cups works toward unbroken continuity between the vast ocean of creation (his Mother) and the airy realm of intellect in which his spirit might take flight and, like a shaman, bring back information. He brings to the surface of consciousness things that are usually hidden and makes them "objective" in some way. He may write poetry, hear voices or songs of the heart. He symbolizes the archetypal artist, bringing visions to the world as a gift from the deepest part of oneself.

When this card comes up in your reading, it points to self-reflection and peaceful, meditative awareness. Your mind turns to artistic visions or recognizes deep feelings; you sense your innermost desires and allow them to emerge. Your unconscious may reveal something to you now, as you prepare to act on inner knowledge. Your heart may open, letting you experience the gift of your own sensitivity. You may fall in love. As long as the card is upright, you may trust your ability to tap unconscious depths of pleasure.

Son of Discs

Traditionally, the Son of Discs represents the "Pan" energy of the Horned God, life force expressed through the body and the senses. In mythology he is the goat of Capricorn, son of the she-goat Amalthea, an aspect of the Great Mother. In Christian iconography, however, the goat was pressed into service as the Devil, yet another instance of reversing ancient symbols. In the Motherpeace image, the Son of Discs is the archetypal hunter, the male principle embodied in a seeker. As hunter, he is related to the Goddess Artemis, perhaps as her twin brother, Apollo. The two came to Greece from Asia Minor along with shamanism and the power of religious ecstasy. The Hunter, says Starhawk, "embodies all quests, whether physical, spiritual, artistic, scientific, or social."

The Motherpeace Son of Discs takes aim at a target that seems more ethereal than real, which he carries with him wherever he goes, and which changes shape as he, himself, transforms. Meanwhile, his feet are on the ground. He is earthy and sensual. He knows about his body and likes to be in it. He enjoys the opportunity to do something physical, but knows that animals must never be killed needlessly—he is in touch with his mother, the earth.

The Son of Discs is the Son of Earth—the Green Man, Robin Hood, Peter Pan, a leprechaun. In British folklore, green is associated with fairies' clothes. Graves explains that, "in so far as the fairies may be regarded as survivors of dispossessed early tribes, forced to take to hills and woods, the green of the clothes is explainable as protective colouring: foresters and outlaws also adopted it in mediaeval times." During the Middle Ages, when the old pagan religion of the Goddess was persecuted and witches were burned, ancient divinities had to don disguises, especially in the case of a powerful God such as Pan, who represented sexuality and the natural instincts of the forest. Margaret Murray has identified Robin Hood as a High Priest of the Witches, representative of the Horned God, consort and partner of the Maiden, the coven High Priestess.

In the Motherpeace image, a dragonfly above the archer's head represents focus that allows him to succeed in hitting the target. With a certain amount of concentration, a person doing yoga may begin hearing a gentle humming that recalls the sound of dragonfly wings. Buddhists make the point that in shooting, an archer should achieve total union with his bow, arrow, and target. The robin, traditional harbinger of spring, reflects the archer's more playful aspect, the light airy touch he brings to physical work and sexuality.

The Son of Discs represents a builder—someone who works with his hands to create beautiful, functional objects. He might be a woodcarver, sculptor, or carpenter, a gymnast, dancer, tumbler, or a terrific masseur. Comfortable with the physical plane and therefore able to earn money and meet his survival needs, he represents a faithful, reliable worker—dogged at times—a personality that rarely loses sight of goals once they are set.

When you get this card in a reading, it suggests you are working steadily toward your goals. You know what it is you want, and you hold a one-pointed focus on getting it. You probably ground yourself through some regular physical discipline, such as yoga or jogging, and you bring a light concentration to all acts of the body, including physical sexuality, which you instinctively enjoy. When the card is upright, it signals a good time to seek work or accomplish some task you've set for yourself, since you see the target so clearly.

CHAPTER 31

PRIESTESSES

Sacredness

The word "Priestess" frequently occurs in discussing witchcraft or New Age religions, whether or not the particular practice involves worship of the Goddess. "Priestess" seems to mean different things to different people, but essentially her function is to become a "channel" for energies and forces—a vessel for power to enter. A Priestess of the Goddess is a woman who opens herself and, for a period of time, "incarnates" the divine female presence in her body. During this time, she manifests the Goddess through her words and actions. When the time passes, she is once more "mortal" and normally human, but keeps within her a knowledge of the mystery.

The Priestesses in the Motherpeace images were Queens in the traditional Tarot. Ruled by Venus and the Moon, they represent administrative abilities, a sense of the sacred, and the authoritative presence of a Mother. In their own homes, mothers are Queens and Priestesses in their work. They rule from the heart. Venus represents Aphrodite, who is related to Ariadne, Astarte, Brigit, Ishtar, Isis. The Mother Goddess is the archetypal full moon, and a Priestess channels moon energies of water (emotions) and the inner fire (sexual feelings). A Priestess is any woman in her fullness of expression, and the "inner woman" of any man who identifies with her.

Priestess of Swords
See color illustration on Plate 12.

The Priestess of Swords represents the mind at work, a channeling of wisdom. The Snowy Owl she releases links her to the Goddess Athene,

209

Priestess of Cups

warrior queen and guardian of the cool female intellect. This priestess does her work in a stark environment of snow and ice—crystallized thought forms and ideas—but under the guiding light of the full moon. She is an Amazon administrator, a ruler through the power of her mind and her sharp tongue. Representing the critical mind, she is at once detached and stern, reasonable, clear-headed. She could be a judge or arbiter. However, she is now taking time out to think and reflect, to belong, as a Virgin does, to herself alone. In Tarot tradition, she is interpreted as a widow or separated woman.

The gold axe at her side is planted in the snow and grounds her thoughts, keeps her in touch with earth. It provides a vertical axis around which her mental energies can gather, and it is clearly a sign of administrative power. Her white fur coat is warm, probably polar bear skin. It links her to Artemis and the constellation of Ursa Major (the Great Bear), and it signifies the ancient power of the female group who knew the stars and the turning wheel of the zodiac. Thus she represents astrology and intuitive knowledge. On another level, she represents science—the systematized knowledge of our Ice Age ancestors who observed the movements of stars and planets, seasonal cycles, and other natural phenomena and recorded these in notational systems on bones and horns found at ancient cave sites. These notational and calendar systems are probably precursors of the first writing, as well as mathematics.

The Priestess of Swords might be a writer; she is certainly a thinker. She channels thought, letting it flow through her like water or light. It is through words and ideas that she channels, opening herself as a "medium" so that spirits may speak through her. In this way, she represents modern psychics like Jane Roberts, who channels the "Seth" material, or Alice Bailey, who earlier channeled material from "the Tibetan."

The owl can be seen as her thoughts taking flight. On a higher level, the owl represents the secret of shamanic flight and the potential for the soul to leave the body and take the form of an animal to travel to other realms. The nocturnal owl suggests the wisdom of the dream world and the collective unconscious. Being the bird of Athene and also Medusa, the owl symbolizes healing power as well as the ability to fight for one's life when necessary.

The Priestess of Swords is an austere personality, uncompromising and somewhat formidable. She may represent a strict teacher or older woman role-model, a disciplinarian or authority figure of some kind. But the pink light reflected off the snow and ice speaks of the subtle warmth of her heart, and the snowflakes swirling around like stars reflect the silver light of the Moon into her aura. Distant from the emotions, she is not cut off but simply reserved. The cool, clear light of the full moon allows for the release of ideas into form, the opening out of the mind from narrow interests to broader, more inclusive concerns. She has a quiet psychic sense that allows her to know the thoughts of everyone around her, even on a global level. Therefore she is able to imagine solutions to world problems. With her poetry and philosophy, she combines a political consciousness and an ability to speak on behalf of others as well as herself.

When you get this card in a reading, it suggests a journey to the cool realms of intellect, a time-out from the emotions in favor of a thoughtful, introspective period. You may be experiencing a separation from your lover, feeling somewhat "out in the cold" emotionally. Your mind is strong and open to cosmic wisdom; it's a good time to write and study, to think and "channel" ideas. When the card is upright, you can trust that your critical judgments are sound.

Priestess of Wands

See color illustration on Plate 15.

The Priestess of Wands represents the energetic archetypal witch—a symbol of personal female power in action. Chronologically, she is the

Mother of the ancestor group, the heart of the community. She enjoys the lively intelligence of a natural *yogini* or Mistress of Fire, and reflects a sense of satisfaction and well-being that go into her work of generating power on behalf of the group. Like ancient stone circles, this Priestess collects energy and holds it, becoming a powerful reservoir as time goes by. As Priestess of the Egyptian Goddess Sekhmet, "the Powerful" (one of Hathor's titles), she has the knowledge of *kundalini*, the serpent fire, which she "raises" in order to accomplish tasks and work magic for her community. She can stand in the center of a circle of people and, like the magical cauldron of Cerridwen, draw in life-force energy from the cosmos and store it for others to draw on. A font of inspiration, she is personally warm and kind, friendly and connected to others. She radiates the heat that heals, blessing anyone who comes into contact with her with a healing touch. Both the tiny red salamander and the Bloodroot flower symbolize this regenerative healing power of fire.

The lioness who walks by her side is her friend and "familiar," her "power animal" and a representation of her own regal simplicity, aligning her with the Lioness-Goddess, Mihit. She is fierce enough to defend her children and protect her close friends, and she is also alive with animal passion and untamed instincts. She channels these into magical work, such as the rainmaking that she has just completed. Notice the signs of her success, as the rain begins to fall from the clouds she attracted through her magic spell.

The Wand she carries in her left hand is a perforated bone, one of the oldest artifacts we have from prehistoric humanity. Archeologists call it a Baton of Commandment, but find themselves at a loss to decode its meaning. Because of the lines inscribed on it, and the absence of marks that would show if it had been used as a tool, they call it a ceremonial instrument of some kind, almost certainly connected with "fertility." The two sides of the T-shaped instrument make it balanced and "androgynous," which leads at least one writer to wonder whether the baton doesn't have something to do with shaman work. Siegfried Giedion notes that a Laplander shaman uses an instrument similar to the one held by the Priestess of Wands. In Lapp culture, it functions as a drumstick used to induce trance states, cure illness, bring success, or cause an enemy to suffer disaster. Together with singing, the drumming puts the whole community into a collective trance state, in order that the specific work be accomplished.

The Wand carried by the Priestess could also be a "dowsing rod" for "water divining," which still goes on today in many parts of the world. Underground channels of water flowing through the earth carry power and "magnetism." Their crossing points are the oracular centers of the planet. Certainly the Priestess of Wands represents the kind of sensitivity that would allow her to find such "hot spots" and use them for magical energy work.

When you get this card in a reading, it suggests a warm self-assurance and a fierce intensity of purpose. You are a charismatic personality, passionate and generally glad to be alive. Maybe you know the techniques of magic and natural healing; perhaps you use trance techniques in your work. Even in play you have a strong, fiery will; you are probably a wonderful lover. This is a time of power and energy. When the card is upright, it means you know how to channel this force in the right ways.

Priestess of Cups

The Priestess of Cups is all water—she channels feelings and emotions, desires, dreams, and inner visions. She is the archetypal Muse, one who inspires from within, the "anima" or inner female guide and Goddess. Her form as mermaid is amphibious—she can swim through the deep waters of the unconscious like a fish, and she can breathe air into her lungs and engage in human thought. Furthermore, "mermaid" is a shortened version of "Merry Maid," which is the witch name for a coven's High Priestess. Although this Priestess may inspire poetry and verse, she does not rely on verbal communication. In her left hand, she holds a lyre, one of the oldest stringed instruments in the world. Its seven strings make some of the most beautiful sounds known to human ears. The sounds made by the Priestess of Cups are heard by the whale who circles below her, communing with her on psychic and musical levels.

She represents the Soul—the inner part of the being, which mediates between the spirit world and daily events, the sky and the earth. As in the Zen *koan* of the pot in the ocean, the Priestess of Cups represents a vessel where what's outside merges with what's inside.

The Priestess of Cups is an enchantress, who, like the Goddess and her priestesses, fled from patriarchal invaders to sacred, secret islands. There, behind thickets and brambles, they continued to practice the religion of the Goddess. Her fish-tail signifies escape by sea, a theme that also arises in the image of the Tower. In mythology, "bewitching" priestesses of the Old Religion again come to notice when various heroes are drawn to their sacred islands. Drawn to the inner metaphorical island of Mother-love, the hero seeks out actual islands in the Mediterranean and Adriatic seas, among others.

Thus Odysseus is drawn by the enchantress Calypso to the island of Ogygia (which Robert Graves says was another name for Egypt, where Osiris was called by the same "siren"). Ulysses is similarly seduced by the "wailing" Circe, daughter of Hekate, and stays on her island for seven years. All stories on this pattern imply a lapse in the hero's rigidity, a falling back into the loving net of the Mother in her form as Sea Goddess. In the Motherpeace image, the tower behind the Priestess of Cups represents what Graves would call the "oracular island shrine" of her "sepulcral" island.

The message of the Priestess of Cups is that the "anima" calls, the unconscious draws one down into itself, the power of the feminine seduces even after it has been consciously rejected and supposedly overcome. The Priestess of Cups represents Aphrodite, "foam-born" Sea Goddess who not only communicates with the whale, but takes the shape of the Whale Goddess who swallows Jonah and every other hero who thinks of escaping the feminine force.

When you get this card in a reading, it suggests an inner musing, the gestating consciousness of a mother, the nourishment of the womb. Your thoughts are focused within, your mind engulfed by the power of the imagination. Your emotions are important now, your feelings and desires central. You may feel "spaced out" and find it hard to function on the physical plane. Upright, this is a card of mother-love and divine inspiration; you are asked to yield to the ocean of collective memory and experience represented by the unconscious where something new will soon be conceived.

Priestess of Discs

See color illustration on Plate 13.

Like the Aztec Goddess Tonantzin, the Priestess of Discs represents the procreative and nurturing aspects of physical mothering. She feeds her child from her breasts, and sustains new life with the loving touch of her hands. She respects her body as a vehicle for what is sacred on earth and keeps it well through the practice of yoga, as well as cooking and eating the right foods. Staying in touch with the Mother through planting and harvesting what she needs for herself and her family, she represents agriculture and the ability of the Earth to provide. As the Corn Mother, she is an aspect of the Empress, and a Priestess of the prehistoric Mexican Earth Mother, Tlazolteotl.

The Priestess sits on a yoga blanket—perhaps an antelope skin—and assumes the various postures designed to refine her glandular system and open her psychic centers. Psychically attuned to what is happening around her as well as within herself, she knows what her baby feels even without looking at it, her consciousness flowing in and out of the other at will. The Hopi shield she sees in her meditation depicts two serpents biting each other's tails, a symbol of the circuit of *kundalini* energy. As lover, the Priestess of Discs knows the mysteries of the body and is capable of ecstatic sexual union with her beloved. The hand in the center of the shield with an open eye in its palm represents psychic evolution and reminds us of Tara, Tibetan Goddess of Compassion.

The parrot sitting in the tree is a powerful fertility symbol, much loved by the Toltec people of the past and by Native Americans today. It stands not only for procreative abilities, but for artistic creativity. The inner visions of this Priestess can be painted or sculpted into objects of beauty and interest. Through such manifestation, she teaches what she understands about earth energy. The marijuana bush further enhances her visionary capabilities and opens her senses, as she burns a leaf in her incense pot for inspiration. Her brightly colored shirt was woven on a loom of her own making—she is a Mistress of Craft.

The green earth around the Priestess reflects the emerald essence of her heart. As the color of manifestation, the green also means money. The Priestess of Discs is the money queen—she can attract cash to herself as easily as any other commodity or physical need. Knowing that money is just a form of energy, she lets it flow through her without greed or grabbing. She counts on the Earth Mother for her survival. Like gravity, she holds to the planet and channels the energy of earth with love.

When you get this card in a reading, it indicates a personality grounded in the physical world, in harmony with the slowed-down energies of Mother Nature. Your inner calm functions as a sixth sense, allowing you to perceive reality in a more "holistic" way, your body and mind attuned and balanced, every pore open to experience. The well-being you are feeling may be expressed through cooking or gardening, sculpting or changing a baby's diapers. Through the gift of loving touch, you stay in contact with life. Upright, the card represents health.

CHAPTER 32

SHAMANS

Experience

The Motherpeace Shamans represent power and experience. In a traditional Tarot deck, they would have been "Kings," with all the authority and status that implies. A Shaman works with tremendous powers, but does not seek power over others. Primarily, a Shaman represents power over self, the conquest of fear and doubt, as well as mastery of the spirit realm. Lack of fear is obvious in the faces of the four Motherpeace Shamans, each propelled by the force of fire.

Their fire is mainly influenced by the planet Mars, which activates work energy and sex force. But they partake of the energies of Jupiter, as well—the fire of expansion and benevolent warmth—and they no doubt invoke the lightning fire of Uranus. Finally, they incorporate the fire of the sun, radiating confidence and well-being in all directions.

The Shamans go out into the universe to work—flying, healing, projecting their energies outside of themselves. Because they have overcome fear, including fear of death, they are not limited by ordinary boundaries of body and mind. They reach into the farthest heavens to communicate with stars, or into the deepest underworld to save souls. Confronting danger and healing illness, they drive out evil and mediate between the human community and the sacred realms. Priestesses work mainly from the heart, Shamans from the head—specifically the crown chakra. They may also use their hands and hearts, but it is their movement into formless realms that distinguishes them from the other character cards.

Shamans imply competence and ability, authentic know-how. Whatever the suit, the Shaman has control of that element and knows how to

Shaman of Cups

use it for personal gain as well as world problem-solving. Shamans are frequently spiritual teachers—the "elders" of a tribe, the old wise ones. Shamans are generally called to their vocation, although in some cultures the position is hereditary; occasionally someone becomes a Shaman because they want to, rather than because they must. The call to Shamanism is usually frightening, because it demands a different existence from the norm—more power and increased social responsibility, as well as unusual social roles and expectations. Shamans are expected to become androgynous—balancing male and female elements within themselves. This may mean, in different cultures, taking on the dress of the opposite sex, becoming homosexual, or remaining celibate, except for "spirit lovers."

Shaman callings have been rare in the modern world, but they are presently on the increase. The current level of world problems, especially the very recent practice of threatening one's enemy constantly with holocaust and living under a similar threat, requires more healers and wise teachers. The New Age brings a particularly forceful energy to us, bathing the globe in healing light and "tapping" certain human beings with healing power. When this happens, the modern Shaman finds that she (or he) has no role models, no real cultural context in which to function as a healer or teacher. The Motherpeace Shamans are four imaginative images of what Shaman-power might mean today and how it might be used for good.

Shaman of Swords

See color illustration on Plate 12.

The Shaman of Swords represents the higher power of air—intellect, intelligence, and abstract thought. The image represents a moving force so quick and changing, and so powerful, that it has become the Wind itself. Unlike the rigid old King of Swords in traditional Tarot, this Shaman presents a positive picture of unloosened mind—an emblem of Free Will. The Shaman of Swords creates her own reality and takes responsibility for her thought forms and the power of the mind. She symbolizes the spirit of all Shamans which, as I. M. Lewis says, "becomes very small and light and is able to detach itself from (her) body and fly with the aid of 'ladder spirits' into the skies." The ladder in the picture represents the ascent and descent that are possible to all Shamans, although the Shaman of Swords will naturally be most at home in the air.

The bird at the top of the ladder is a kite, sacred to Boreas the North Wind. In Thracian magic, Shamans were able to transform themselves into kites, which, says Graves, are linked with the hawk, bird of the Egyptian Horus and his mother Isis. Native Americans call the kite "the Clairvoyant Woman," referring to the Shaman's intellectual power to pierce space and know everything. Thus the Shaman of Swords represents "genius" and universal mind.

The four-petaled flower below her head marks the four cardinal directions, the four winds, the elements. The point of union at the center usually hides the fifth element, which is "ether" or spirit. In this card, the spirit or "quintessence" is released into manifestation, probably through the voice. The red of the flower symbolizes passion and female power, the force of inner knowing that pushes one out into the larger world to act. Writing on how the force of desire releases us, Susan Griffin asks:

> Do you know how . . . wanting lets your eyes pierce space? How a resolve to act can traverse this atmosphere as quick as light? . . . despite the threat of fire and our fear of the flames, we burst out through the roofs of our houses. Desire is a force inside us. Our mouths drop open in the rushing air. Our bodies float among stars. And we laugh in ecstasy to know the air has wishes. . . . "Yes," we call out, full of ourselves and delight, "Yes," we sing, "We fly through the night."

The Shaman of Swords speaks out of necessity. Her words come bursting from her heart and throat. She could be a speaker against war.

The blue stream of thought rushing from her mouth represents the voice of the higher mind—words from the source of wisdom. The speaking of this spiritual truth is the means to her ascent. It takes her up the ladder, into free space. She is a symbol of the active "animus" of a woman expressed in action.

When you get this card in a reading, it suggests a strong blend of fiery ("female") emotions and powerful ("male") thought. Let what you see and feel be said; don't hold back what you know to be true. Through the emergence of your insights, fired by the passion of your heart, you have the power to transform reality. Share your visions and thoughts, your hopes and dreams. The force of your ideas demands that you speak out. As long as the card is upright, you won't be overbearing in your assertions.

Shaman of Wands
See color illustration on Plate 15.

The Shaman of Wands represents positive male power. In a notably complex situation, he knows how to act. Behind him are symbols of kingship and patriarchal power—the throne of the Pharoah, the falcon of the Sun-god, Horus. However, in his left or maternal hand he holds a staff that rests on the waning crescent of the Moon Goddess and signifies matrilineal descent. His right hand forms an open gesture of welcome, invitation, gift-giving. He clothes himself in garments woven by the women of his tribe, and wears a matching beaded collar around his neck. Ready to explain himself, he is also ready to listen to others and to interact.

Chronologically, the Shaman of Wands represents the transition period between pre-Dynastic Egyptian culture and the new "unification" period of the first Dynasties. This places him at around 3000 B.C. Horus, the falcon-god, was made deity of all Egypt, and the "followers of Horus," who were mainly an influx of invaders from the East, formed a "civilized autocracy or master race" that was to rule over the entire African continent. The "Royal Burials" were destroyed by fire; the religion was changed from female to male-centered; and "wars of unification" were fought—supposedly to bring the country together, actually to wipe out the old traditions of the matriarchal culture. According to Margaret

Murray, early inscriptions mention "many priesthoods of women," but in later inscriptions women are "only singers in the temple."

The Shaman of Wands represents the old matriarchal traditions. He might be the mother's brother or uncle, a liaison between the female-centered culture and the new monarchy. In the midst of the chaos and confusion of the new patriarchy or "reign of the fathers," this type of male presence would have been very helpful to followers of the Goddess, and his descendents remain helpful in the modern world. He represents a personality able to respect women and the feminine principle, yet by virtue of his sex, as well as ability, has acquired a certain amount of personal power in the world. A strong liberal presence, he becomes what Sally Gearhart calls a "feminist friend." The round basket to his left signifies his appreciation of the female, as does the large Protea flower to his right.

Elementally, the Shaman of Wands is all fire. Ruled by Mars and Jupiter, he represents force and healing power. His open hand no doubt channels the heat that heals, and he represents a positive, nurturing image of fatherhood. On the falcon's head the solar disc represents authority, strength, clarity, and nonprejudicial intelligence. In its talons, the bird holds the *ankh* of life-force, sign of Isis. In the midst of all these symbols, the Shaman of Wands attempts to deal with the crown of power and the throne of authority with conscience and goodwill. He may be a philosopher or teacher, verbally skilled and warmly human. A symbol of thoughtful political power, he is a good male role model for either women or men.

When you get this card in a reading, it suggests a powerful personality capable of accomplishing long-term goals and handling extremely complex situations. Whatever task you have set for yourself, you have the intuition to understand what's required and the will to carry through. Your warm, friendly approach is disarming and assures you the cooperation of others, making you a good administrator or co-worker. As long as the card is upright, it indicates no abuse of power.

Shaman of Cups

The Shaman of Cups stands at the doorway to the West and personifies Hekate, the force of dark power of the moon. The presence of the dark Goddess is reflected in the black cauldron that places this scene in the early Iron Age. The dispassionate Shaman has painted her face with white gypsum, which the priestesses of Artemis used to mask themselves for spiritual or ritual work. The Shaman of Cups represents feelings under control, passion transmuted into detached and focused awareness. As the fire under her cauldron transforms the liquid she brews, she represents the archetypal alchemist, directing the will in such a way as to change elements from one form to another.

Bent on magically controlling her environment, this Shaman works a spell or a ritual that will benefit her community and the religion of the Mother. She probably lives in the hills of Crete with other native "peasants" and has come into the Palace at Knossos to perform this ritual event. The rich turquoise and rust colors painted on the interior of the palace are similar to certain favorite Hopi tones, and reflect the many similarities between the Mediterranean island of Crete and the American Southwestern cultures.

The Shaman of Cups is a stern judge of character and situations. Having confronted and conquered death, she knows it to be nothing more than change, which she accepts without comment. She represents moral courage and the willingness to do what one must. She has both the calm power of a religious leader, and the controlled passion of someone firmly committed to social change. As a counselor, she tells it exactly as she sees it. Embodying the Hekate consciousness, she gets straight to the point. Her wisdom is sometimes painful to hear, but deeply truthful and ultimately welcome.

The cauldron always represents the female vessel of fertility or transformation. In the *I Ching,* the Cauldron is called *Ting* and represents deep, feminine wisdom that can be drawn upon endlessly. An Aztec codex pictured in Neumann's *The Great Mother* is called "the Underworld Vessel of Death and Transformation." Comparing the cauldron to the female body, Neumann says that "the magical caldron or pot is always in the hand of the female mana figure," and gives as an example of such a figure the Greek Medea. He goes on to stress that transformation cannot take place until one surrenders totally to the Mother Vessel, for "renewal is possible only through the death of the old personality." The Shaman of Cups represents one who has been through this process and come out on the other side. No longer swayed by the desires and urges of the "lower self" or unconscious personality, this Shaman has become one with her own "high Self."

When you get this card in a reading, the message is focus. You know how to pull all your energies into facing the task at hand. You temporarily "sacrifice" the fleeting desires of the personality for the "higher" goals of group work or spiritual purpose. The mask you wear hides your emotions; you keep your feelings to yourself, maintaining the equilibrium necessary for completion of your transformation. You are better in emergencies than you are in intimate relationships, where you sometimes fail to communicate your personal needs and desires. As long as the card is upright, you'll never be overwhelmed by your feelings.

Shaman of Discs

See color illustration on Plate 13.

The Shaman of Discs represents a human being who has learned to work on the physical plane in such a way as to succeed at whatever she does. Firmly committed to "the Path," she is not distracted by events along the way or deluded by glamourous images of fame or fortune. She keeps to the road and always knows where she's going by her internal sense of direction. Purposeful and self-directed, she represents an understanding of what Buddhists call *Dharma*—the task that must be faced in order to allow a further evolution. Knowing what is important, she is free to enjoy the journey, paying sensual attention to what happens along the way and interacting with others as easily as she is able to be alone.

The mule on which the Shaman of Discs sits represents her steadfastness and the sure-footed way she rides the canyon trail. In an esoteric way, the mule may also represent the androgyny of the Shaman—her almost "hybrid" form, which prevents her from reproducing herself. Physical motherhood is behind her now. Thus she could be the menopausal woman, freed up to work on her spiritual task—no longer tied to biological or domestic work. The shield she carries bears the image of a little monkey ready to bite its own tail—a primate, who, like herself, is closing the circle.

The bald eagle on her right symbolizes the power of flight and clear, long-distance vision. This Medicine-woman, like all Shamans, has the power of future vision. The eagle is one of her spirit guides, helping her along the way, gathering information and knowledge for her. The eagle makes its nest in cliffs and high places, and this Shaman may be one of the pueblo people (the *Anasazi* or ancient ones) who built their incredible cities on the sides of cliffs and in canyon floors of the Southwestern United States.

The setting sun behind the Shaman of Discs represents a lifetime of work—and portrays her "elder" status. She has reached a high degree of success and power over the years and is well-paid for her work. If her personality were dominant, she might be materialistic or greedy, but she is guided by her high Self and does not yield to the impulse to hoard objects or cash. She is grounded in work and service, a traveling healer who knows the natural cycles. Her closeness to the earth is reflected in a knowledge of herbs and medicinal plants, which she uses in her healing work. The soft buckskins she wears against her skin are of her own making—she tanned the hide herself. Because of her skills and a well-developed sense of equanimity, she is welcomed wherever she goes.

The Shaman of Discs is a symbol of self-discipline and perseverence, congenial strength and patience. Her humanitarian consciousness works toward development of a highly evolved spiritual presence as well as a lively human being who can get along with almost everyone. She is occasionally stubborn, but like Spider Grandmother of the Hopi, she has spun a lifetime of creativity and knows why she is still on the path.

When you get this card in a reading, it suggests you know where you're going and how to get there. In matters of money and work, you understand the necessary steps to be taken, the right path to success. You have a sharp eye for details and your calm sense of direction makes you a trustworthy co-worker or a capable free-lancer. You have a great deal of experience in the world, which has taught you wisdom. As long as the card is upright, you won't take any wrong turns or become materialistic.

THREE

The Spirit of Motherpeace

CHAPTER 33

Reading the Cards

As the New Age dawns, in the midst of terrible world danger, many people are opening to the "good news" of healing and, like the Navaho described in Chapter 1, are seeking a "restoration of the universe." In this process of psychic transformation, the Tarot is a fundamental tool that can be used by anyone, in any walk of life. The practice of the Tarot is less forbidding than some of the more obscure or esoteric forms of psychic practice. Richly evocative, the images elicit an immediate response, even from users who possess none of the background provided in this book, and who simply imagine themselves in the scenes.

Now that we have journeyed through the entire cycle of Motherpeace images, including both the Major and Minor Arcana, some readers may wish to learn to use this set of images as a Tarot deck. The Motherpeace images illustrated in this book are also available in the form of round Tarot cards about 4½ inches in diameter, all of them in full color.

In the Tarot community, there is a story that when the ancient sages were trying to decide the form in which to pass on secret knowledge of the Initiation Mysteries, they considered both a book and a game. In dealing with a society that regarded books as a "virtue" and games as a "vice," they chose the latter, figuring it would last longer, since people gravitate to it for fun. Whether or not the story is true, certainly it holds a message of symbolic wisdom. The cards work for us, partly because they are serious and contain profound secrets, but mainly because they allow the child within us to come out and play.

Psychologists among us are aware of the need for "play" in the lives of human beings, but what kind of play do we really need? People play sports. They dress up in costumes and pretend to be someone else. They adopt new social roles. They play music. They play table games. The main idea seems to be to suspend ordinary rules and seriousness, in order to become temporarily light and "young" again. But table games often require close attention and prowess, as in the case of bridge or chess. Success at sports such as baseball, football, or basketball calls for strength and agility, plus a good deal of active drive and competition. Sexual role-playing, which may begin in fun, frequently leads away from true intimacy. It seems we haven't quite captured what is meant when we think of play in relation to the human heart.

When you "play" with Tarot cards, something broader opens out—consciousness expands into a realm rarely traveled by most of us. It happens, not when you are willing something to happen, but at that moment when you forget yourself and discover something larger than ego and daily reality. This "space" has been called "magic" and "sacred." Sometimes experience within it is beyond the reach of words to describe, although language can help us to reach the magic space. In order to enter this world beyond the ordinary, one must take up the consciousness of the Fool—the childlike innocence that allows one to come to an event or situation unrehearsed. For the Fool, each moment is new, requiring psychic improvisation.

Most of us, by the time we reach adulthood, have an investment in how much we know. We think we need to know almost everything in order to be successful at our work, and in larger terms, our lives. But in order to enter the psychic realm, we must act as if we know nothing and be open. Techniques exist to help open the mind and carry a person into the unknown safely and without fear. One important skill is "grounding," a process that occurs in many of the Motherpeace images. Whenever I am working with other people, whether in a yoga class, a healing session, or a Tarot workshop, I begin by helping us all get grounded. One way to do this is to sit in a chair or cross-legged on the floor and be aware of your spine. Feel how straight it can be, how long it is, and how it connects your coccyx (tailbone) with your head. When you can remain aware of your spine all the way from one end to the other, begin to imagine a tail growing out from your tailbone, down through the floor and into the earth, curling down through layers and layers until it reaches the very center. To some people this image at first seems absurd. Its only advantage is that, after a while and often right away, it works.

Once your tail has grown, begin to imagine that the center of the earth is made of fire, like lava, which you can "breathe" into yourself through the channel of your tail. You are now taking in "earth energy," which comes up through your legs and your spine into your torso and head, filling you with life-force and a marvelous sense of security and well-being. Let it flow all the way to the top of your head and your fingertips. When you are full of "earth," begin to imagine the top of your head opening like a flower or a cup, into which you invite Cosmic energies from above—light and love. Imagine the energy pouring down into your head and flowing through your body in a downward direction, filling you once more to your fingertips as well as the tips of your toes.

Now you are ready to "open your heart." In the world of psychic healing, people talk a lot about opening the heart—how everybody needs to do it and so forth. But what does it mean? In yoga, the "heart *chakra*" is the love center in the body, located in the center of the chest, encompassing the lungs and heart. It is not "physical" in the sense of organs or blood vessels; rather, it represents an "energy center" or a place where energies come together in a certain way and create a particular force. Opening or "activating" a *chakra* will also influence the physical body. The heart center is related to the "right brain," which controls intuitive, nonrational thinking. When you "open the heart," you stimulate your intuitive side—in effect, you cause the "feminine" in yourself to come into activity.

To begin to open the heart center, just breathe and be aware of your breathing. Earlier we focused on opening the vertical channel between the earth and the sky—and between the body and mind. Now you are breathing into the very center of balance in yourself, the middle of your chest. As the breath comes in, allow your chest to grow and accept it. As the breath goes out, allow your belly to push gently, expelling all the air. Keep breathing steadily, and each time the breath comes in, imagine the chest growing larger and taking in slightly more than the time before. Each time the breath goes out, expel all the air in the lungs and belly, until you are temporarily an empty vessel.

There is no need to use force when working in the heart—simple breathing will open and expand not only the physical cavity of your chest, but also your intuitive and "psychic" abilities. The breathing is gentle, with pauses between the in and out breaths. The only thing you need to do is to allow the opening to take place; you cannot make it happen. All of this is very subtle and you may not feel anything out of the ordinary. Just trust that something is going on, and proceed to working with the Tarot cards, keeping in mind the various things you have imaginatively set in motion: your root to the earth, your opening to the sky, and your expanded heart center. Place your awareness in the very center of your chest as if you were sitting there, and continue.

The first thing to do with the cards is to mix them up. If you like shuffling, try it. You may find at first that you have difficulty with the round Motherpeace cards, but after a while it will feel as if you've been working with them forever. You can mix then in any way you see fit. The idea is to exchange some energy with the cards—put a little of you into them, and get a little of their energy in you. Once that is done, they will more clearly "speak" to you concerning your personal needs and questions. As you shuffle or mix the cards, begin to focus on yourself and your concerns. Maybe you have a specific problem or question; maybe you want a "general reading." Just think about what you want the cards to show you, the way you would ask a therapist or teacher about something you are having trouble with or don't fully understand.

When you feel ready, hold the cards quietly for a moment and be aware of yourself again—your vertical channel, your open heart. At this point, I like to ask the Goddess to give me clarity and make me an open channel to universal wisdom—a prayer I also made while working on the Motherpeace cards and on this book. I ask her to help me transcend ordinary states of confusion, doubt, self-deprecation, fear, and powerlessness. You may do this part of the work in whatever way feels comfortable to you. If the Goddess has not become a living presence for you, you may want to imagine something more general—the universal spirit guiding you, cosmic light giving you the clarity you need. Perhaps you simply want to take a deep breath and set a calm intention of clarity.

Now cut the cards. I do this using the left hand, cutting twice. Use whatever method feels appropriate. Stacking the cards once more, turn the top card over and look at it. Notice which way it comes up, since "reversed" or "tilted" cards have a particular message in addition to the intrinsic meaning. Look at the card without any particular thoughts for a moment—get some impressions from it. How does it make you feel? Usually, a card has an initially "positive" or "negative" sense for the person looking at it. Just take that in, and feel yourself responding. This is a good opportunity to listen to your own mind at work, with the same kind of attention you earlier gave to your spine. Perhaps your skepticism will emerge at this point, and you'll wonder what on earth you are doing! Maybe you'll reject the image. On the other hand, perhaps you'll begin to feel slightly awed by what you see and feel.

Focus on the colors—how do they feel to you, what do they seem to evoke? Let the action in the picture tell a story—what is happening? If there are people, what are they doing? If there are more than one, which person do you particularly identify with? Imagine that you are gazing into a dream picture—a tiny astral scene where you can become part of the action. As you move into the image, ask how it applies to your own situation. In what way are you like the person or animal or symbol in the picture? What meaning does this particular card have for your life at this time? If you were reading this card for someone else, what advice would you give them, based on your feelings and impressions? How does this advice apply to you?

You may want to keep the card around for a while—put it somewhere in your house where you will see it as you go through the day, or before you get into bed. If at first you don't get a strong sense of what the card means, chances are it will hit you later. The cards never show you an image that doesn't apply in some way, so once you learn to trust the message to come—once you decide to open to the cards as a magical guide and allow them to reveal to you—at some point you will "get it."

For a while, you will probably want to choose only one card at a time, until you have a sense of how they work. But anytime you feel like it, you may begin to do more complex "readings," perhaps using three cards to stand for past, present and future. Lay them out, side by side, and read them one at a time and then in relation to each other. See whether the card for past seems truly to reflect what you have recently experienced. Check the present card to see whether you are in touch with the feelings or energies it suggests. Look at the future card, trying to intuit what it might mean. And finally, relate the three cards to one another. Generally speaking, in reading the future, you say something like: "Given that this happened, and I'm experiencing this right now, it looks as if the energy will move in this direction and I can expect. . . ." The future is always open to change; if you don't like how it looks, you can begin working to make it different by your present choices and decisions. If you like it, you can move into it gracefully, embracing it fully.

Another reading you might like to try is a "yes-no" question. Mix the cards and ask yourself a question that's on your mind and can be answered with either a yes or a no. Focus intently on your question, putting it in the clearest language possible. It can be anything, from "Shall I stay in this relationship?" to "Will I get the new job I want?" It doesn't have to be "serious" either—you could ask about tonight's party. But whatever energy you bring to the cards is the energy they will reflect back to you, so if you think your question is dumb, you probably won't get intelligent help in answering it. Take yourself seriously, even though you are "playing." Drop your ordinary way of relating to the world and assume for the moment that helping spirits exist—it is to them you put your question.

When the cards feel ready, cut them and begin to turn them face up in a single pile, counting to thirteen. If an Ace comes up, stop—that pile is done. Go on to the next, until you have three stacks of cards in front of you with either thirteen cards each or an Ace on top. Aces right-side-up mean "yes" and upside-down mean "no." The more Aces you get, the stronger the yes or no. (If you happen to get one Ace up and another down, you may read it as a "maybe," or as a sign that the situation may change, or that it's too early to know the outcome.) Often however, the reading of Aces is immediately clear and needs no further explanation—it is obviously yes or just as obviously no.

As you come to know the cards, you may want to try a general reading layout. The one I use takes the shape of the design on the back of the Motherpeace cards, which was painted by Cassandra Light. It depicts a circle or wheel with a central disc surrounded by eight smaller discs. Place three cards within the hub and eight in the numbered positions as the peripheral discs—a total of eleven cards. Each card is read according to its position in the diagram.

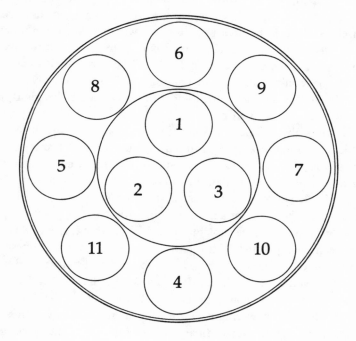

Key to Diagram

1. Significator: your essence, who you are, especially right now; the heart.

2. Atmosphere: the place from which the question emerges; what's going on for you now; the context.

3. Cross Current: the obstacle facing you, the central challenge; what needs to be integrated.

4. Root: the unconscious mindset; whatever lies at the foundation; the body.

5. Recent Past: what just happened, what is now passing away.

6. General Sky: what is conscious, what you think about it all; what is coming in; the mind.

7. Near Future: what will happen soon; what you can expect if things keep moving in this direction.

8. Self Concept: how you see yourself in relation to your significator; self-image.

9. Hopes and Fears—what you hope for, you also fear; your unconscious projections.

10. House: who is in your psychic space, your environment; who is close to you.

11. Outcome: resolution; integration. (If a Major Arcanum comes up in the outcome position, I stop with that. If no Major shows up, I draw at least two more cards, which I think of as "x-factors." If neither of these is a Major, I regard the outcome as uncertain at this time.)

At first the full reading will probably seem confusing, with so many different things to remember. But soon the positions will make sense, and you will learn to read the cards in terms of them. In the beginning, just read each card by itself for meaning, then attempt to put them all together in terms of the story they tell. I like to notice that the vertical axis through the "root" (4) and "sky" (6), like the spine in our earlier grounding exercise, provides a link to the mental-spiritual realms. The horizontal axis that runs through "past" (5) and "future" (7) positions reflects the physical plane and daily actions in the world. The inner circle of three cards moves counter-clockwise ("moon-wise") and represents the "heart" of the reading, its central meaning. The outer circle of eight cards moves in a clockwise ("sun-wise") direction and represents what is changeable.

In a full layout such as this, a particular card would have different meanings according to the position it occupied. A card that comes up as your significator (1) means this is who you are right now, period. But the same card falling in "self-concept" (8) would indicate that although you see yourself in this way, it may not be objectively "true." (If positive, keep it; if negative, you might wish to change it.) A card in "hopes and fears" (9) could be a projection that might eventually become "reality" but is now really just a thought form. The same card falling in the "past" (5) position refers to an event that has already happened. A card in the "near future" (7) represents something to be encountered very soon, whereas the same card in "outcome" (11) may indicate the final resolution after many other experiences and encounters are assimilated and integrated.

What about reversed cards? In traditional, rectangular Tarot decks, the cards come up one of two possible ways—either "up" or "down." But when you use round cards, the images may be slanted any which way. The best thing to do in any case is first of all to read the image as if it were upright. Figure out what it means, and then work with the additional complexity that a "tilt" or a "reversal" presents.

You can approach it in terms of polarity, using symbolic representations for right and left, such as "sun" and "moon." Traditional schools of symbology and therapy work with these ideas, and you may wish to use them, but you have to discriminate carefully, since they are so often formed within sexist constructs and reflect this bias. For instance, if right is "male" or "active," and left is "female" or "receptive," this may help you to interpret. But if right is "good" and left is "sinister," you may find your readings limited by these traditional and oppressive views. I generally approach cards that lean to the right as representing a slightly "forced" or pushing quality—the ego may be controlling the expression of energy represented by the card (not automatically bad in itself). When the image falls to the left, I tend to feel that the energy must be slightly "held back"—perhaps the person lacks self-confidence about the particular expression or quality of energy. When a card falls upside down (a full reversal) I generally take it to embody the "negative" or opposite aspect of whatever the image means in its upright form.

For instance, if the Daughter of Swords—a usually impatient, active, and energetic personality—is reversed, then her negative tendencies may surface. She might indicate recklessness or inappropriate behavior, poor judgement, or angry actions. Instead of brightly directed exuberance, she may express misdirected or misapplied energy. On the other hand, if the Five of Swords is reversed in a reading—a basically "negative" image to begin with—then I might feel a sense of relief, as if the negativity and hostility of the image were reduced, and the person had decided to withdraw from the negative mind-space ordinarily represented by the card. Righting the card's normally downward-pointing pentagram could mean an active choice to think more positively about one's situation, the setting of a new intention.

The main thing in reading the cards is not any of these technical meanings, but how you yourself feel about the cards and what they seem to say. Your intuition is more critical to reading the Tarot than all the books available on the subject, including this one. Most of us like to have some intellectual background when dealing with any tool of consciousness, so it doesn't hurt to read books—it calms and informs the rational mind. But irrational forces are what you must summon in order to move beyond ordinary understanding into the magical realms of "divination," in order really to be a "seer."

Intuition is not an inferior form of mind—it is, in fact, superior to ordinary intellect, more like a "super-mind" into which you plug during extra-ordinary states of consciousness. That is why meditation and grounding are important, along with opening the channels of inner communication. The more you open to these less familiar parts of your psychic terrain, the more healing energy will come your way. Your abilities to "read" the cards will grow, along with your general health and well-being. The simple effort of asking questions of your "high Self" or "the Goddess" will gradually strengthen your self-love and deepen your experience of reality. The "power of prayer" works—we just need the right context in which it can flourish, and for many of us the patriarchal forms have lost their meaning.

For some people, the Tarot cards will serve as a simple and satisfying "oracle" that will help them adjust to their real situation by knowing more of the picture and making choices grounded in this knowledge. In other words, the Tarot will work as a daily or weekly guide to life on the physical plane. We all need some form of this guidance, and the cards are one effective tool toward responsible living. For other people, however, a deeper process will begin to take place. Described in Chapters 1 through 23, this process pertains to the ancient mysteries of Initiation, and thus involves transformation on the level of the soul. This is the oldest "religious" undertaking of the human species.

CHAPTER 34

Group Work

So far we have discussed reading the Tarot cards by oneself, but reading them in groups is also very useful, allowing for collective focus and a chance to unite the group around a single issue or personality. This brings each member into touch with what psychics have called the "group mind," their central mental identity. For people who work together, this use of the cards can facilitate deeper understanding of each other, a method for reaching inside and expressing feelings that would otherwise remain unconscious, and a simple, positive way of working out conflict.

In my Tarot classes, after I have taught people to use the layout presented above (or some other), I ask a member of the class to "do a reading" for someone who volunteers to be "read." Usually there is at least one person with an immediate problem or need, and another who would like to try her skills at reading. The same preparatory grounding procedures are used as for an individual reading—breathing and centering in the heart chakra—only now the whole group works together to accomplish this.

The group might first like to hold hands and "channel" energy together, imagining a circle of "electricity" running through the joined hands and hearts, stimulating and harmonizing the group. Since one person is going to receive the reading, the group thinks about or focuses on that person—on his or her essence, the general self. If the person verbalizes a specific question, the group focuses or concentrates on that question in regard to the "client." Since everyone in the group will want to be able to see the reading layout, it works well to put the two people directly involved in the reading in the center of the circle, with everyone else watching from the outer ring. This allows the group continuously to "hold the focus" as they would in a "healing circle," and permits extra energy to come through. This will benefit the person doing the reading by increasing potential intuitive abilities.

The client mixes the cards up, allowing her energy to merge with them, and then passes the deck to the reader, who similarly mixes them, focusing on the question or the client. When the reader is ready (and while the group waits quietly and with concentration), she cuts the cards (or has the client cut the cards) and lays them out. It is important at this point for the reader to take some time and get a sense of the general nature of the reading, as she would for any other reading experience. When ready, the reader begins to tell a story to the client by reading the cards. During this part of the process, the group does not participate verbally or interfere in any way with the natural flow of the reader's intuition.

When the reader feels finished, the group may share their "hits" and thoughts about the reading. Sometimes a second reading is appropriate, if time permits and if the group is willing and the client receptive. A second person's reading will often pull in ideas and suggestions that, although not in disagreement with the first reader, might have an entirely different focus or perspective. In this way, the client gets the greatest possible variety of psychic or intuitive impressions. By the time two or three interpretations have been given for the same layout, things have usually progressed from the mundane into deeper levels of understanding and insight.

Obviously, the closer the group, the more harmoniously its members work together, the deeper and more effective this process will be. A group of people may decide to come together for the purpose of reading the Tarot cards each week, as a "self-help" or growth process. Something magical takes place on the group level with ongoing study and experience of psychic realities. A group that comes together regularly to read the cards will become unified in an invisible way, their energies harmonizing on the psychic planes. If there is a spiritual focus, as there is in the Motherpeace Tarot cards, the group will automatically grow in spiritual awareness and appreciation. This leads to a "raising up" of one's personal energy to "higher" levels of reality, less involved in ego.

Besides a group mind, there is what esoteric teachers refer to as a "group soul" or "oversoul," the prevailing spiritual ideal that brings the group together in the first place and gently guides it through one "initiation" after another. The group soul is a source of energy and healing "light" on which members draw in their daily lives. It is an invisible center of energy that radiates out through each individual life, bringing balance and growth through the process of gradual transformation.

In general, esoteric or psychic work tends to lift the personality out of "darkness" and confusion and onto a more conscious level. What the group does to facilitate this process is to help the individuals sustain the impulse to rise to the conscious level of reality. People differ in their strengths and weaknesses, their fallow periods and creative bursts. The group functioning together lets each person have highs and lows and gives support and recognition through the natural, normal changes that come in the transformational process. A sense of continuity is built, creating a feeling of acceptance and solidarity even through change.

Finally, the group soul functions as a center of universal, unconditional love. Healing energy pours into a person through the crown chakra, or enters into a circle of people meditating or reading the cards together. By asking the universe questions and seeking answers and guidance, each being opens to cosmic information and intuitive wisdom. The combined presence of the "high selves" of the members of the group makes a very strong light, which continues to take care of each individual even when an individual isn't strong enough to make contact with her own higher self.

This is the real meaning of "community," and it is this premise that underlies all religious organizations and psychic groups. In the modern world, such organizations are generally bureaucratic and ponderous in their workings, rarely reaching the individual on a heart level. But the potential for group support and "group work" is very great, especially at the end of the twentieth century. The world is going through a crisis unlike anything known to us from our history books, and most new age teachers agree that it is human separatism and isolation that have brought us to the present critical state.

With the activation of small groups attracted to a central spiritual form (such as the Motherpeace Tarot cards), the vast work of transforming the world can find ways to begin. There are many and varied prophecies of what might happen to us and our planetary home in the next twenty years, and it is difficult to know in advance which, if any, of these possibilities will become "reality." The only positive thing to do, as far as I can tell, is to work together toward understanding each situation as it presents itself (whether the focus is the economy, the church, the family, the workplace, or the ecological balance) and then transforming in ways that adapt to the changing situation. The spiritual focus of small groups working toward such change will allow wisdom and information to be channeled—guidance for the transition from the old forms to the innovative modes of the future.

In the recent movie *My Dinner with Andre*, the central character quotes Swedish physicist Gustav Björnstrand as saying that "probably we'll be going back to a very savage, lawless, terrifying period," which Andre suggests is a dark age to come. "But," he says, "the Findhorn people see it a little differently," and he explains to his companion what the new age community in Scotland sees lying ahead of us. "It's their feeling that there will be these pockets of light springing up in different parts of the world, and that these will be in a way invisible planets on *this* planet and that, as we or the world grow colder, we will be able to take invisible space journeys to these different planets, refuel for what it is we have to do on the planet itself, and come back."

This idea is not very far removed from what Alice Bailey called "The New Group of World Servers," who she predicted would form small groups around central lights of spirit or hope, working together to build the new world. This building necessarily begins from the invisible plane of psychic awareness and magic, eventually affecting the physical plane of manifestation. Shamans and magicians have always known this secret, but the time has come for "regular folks" to begin using these techniques to make changes in their own lives and in the world around them. In this spirit, the Motherpeace Tarot cards can successfully be used in group work as a way not only to the Goddess, but to what the Navaho call the "restoration of the universe."

CHAPTER 35

Creating a New Mythology

As a guide to telling stories about our lives together and as an illustration of these stories, the Motherpeace images can lead us toward the creation of a new mythology, a "creative visualization" for the future, as well as toward an account of our evolution that is no longer biased by the distortions of Patriarchy.

Creative visualization is the active, graphic imagining of possibilities —an attempt to "see," in some detail, events that have not yet taken place, and to make them as rich and healthy as possible. One can use the technique to prepare oneself for the simplest future occasion—a meeting, a class, a party, a date. Or, in the case of creating a mythos, we can imagine a world in which we would like to live.

Because of our benumbed existence within a virtual time-bomb of nuclear disaster, organizations such as Physicians for Social Responsibility have used "scare tactics" for the purpose of waking people up in a hurry to the almost unfathomable dangers of the nuclear arms race and a possible nuclear war. Details of holocaust are imagined, horrors elaborated, until people are shocked into realization that something must be done to stop the robotlike drive to disaster.

What then? Once we have declared, "No more nukes!" we are left with the problem of imagining what else is possible. This imagining comes best from the creative right brain—the intuitive mode of consciousness, which can be activated through use of Tarot images. These archetypal energies are living forms with the power to awaken creativity and the oracular power of past and future vision. Like our ancient ances-

tors, we allow the "other world" to speak to us through a magical intermediary—in this case the medium, seemingly so simple, is Tarot.

Creative visualization can thus provide us with a guide for the future,
a model, at least one possibility of existence that differs from the terrible
vision of global disaster that Patriarchy now blandly offers to us. In the
name of "national security," the U.S. and the Soviet Union seem to be
stumbling toward a joint global suicide. On our side, the slogan "better
dead than red" represents an idiotic reduction of our potential choices
and takes on new irony in light of the ancient connection between the
color red and women's natural power, so long suppressed.

I developed the following material when I was asked to give a slide
presentation at antiwar meetings and group ritual events. I offer it here as
a summary of my view of matriarchal peace, as well as an example of how
Motherpeace Tarot can be used to improvise stories from clusters of
cards. The appropriate Tarot image is listed beside the text, to allow
interested readers to refer to the inspiration for the story.

Empress	There was a time when life on earth reflected abundance and right relationship with all of nature —a time that lives still in the recesses of our racial memory as a golden age or paradise lost.
Shaman of Cups	From archeological evidence, it is possible to piece together this prehistoric time of peace and harmony when the Great Mother was worshiped and the female principle revered in all things.
Two of Wands	The discovery of fire, generally attributed to women, brought social grouping and the development of language and communication through sound and artistic expression.
Three of Wands	The mother-child bond was the original model for all other relationships, and the key innovation in the evolutionary leap from ape ancestor to human family.
Priestess of Wands	Religion developed hand in hand with an appreciation of sexuality and other natural phenomena, including the practice of magic, which remained peacefully and powerfully in the hands of the mothers for millennia. Still practiced by Na-

tive Americans, the art of rainmaking was an early form of magical prowess that made the reliable cultivation of crops possible and led to the early agricultural civilizations that represented the peak of matriarchal consciousness, as well as human artistic and cultural achievement. Cultural artifacts, like the carved bone Wand carried by this Priestess, are considered by archeologists to be early ceremonial implements used in "fertility cults."

Shaman of Wands

The male functioned within this loving mother-centered context, fully developing his powers and participating according to his gifts in the central mysteries of life and death, birth and rebirth.

Nine of Wands

In these early Stone Age cultures, from which our modern culture has ultimately evolved, aging was valued and respected.

Four of Wands

Life and all its passages were celebrated through ritual and dance, song and prayer.

Ten of Wands

Energy was raised in ways that were constructive and useful to the group, and its expression brought health to the entire community and even to the fertile earth herself. The power of the female was symbolized most strikingly in the *mana* of her menstrual blood, which is still recognized today in some cultures as a powerful sexual essence, an effective elixir for healing, and a magical fertilizer for whatever is growing in the fields.

Daughter of Wands and Son of Wands

Daughter and Son—Artemis and Apollo—were once twins and equals in the eyes of the Great Mother, as were all forms of female and male energy. Polarity was recognized as belonging to and reconciled within the Mother who contains and gives birth to both male and female elements. She ruled through love and respect for all, the life-giving principle of the cosmos. All females were her daughters; all males her loving sons. The parallel traditions of witchcraft and shamanism descend, in fragmented form, from these two archetypal expressions of the "sacred play" of our ancestors.

Tower

Almost overnight in terms of human evolution, this peaceful coexistence with the earth and its life-forms was forced to change radically. The ancient prophetess or "seer" received an Oracle of disaster— preparations were made to flee the homeland and transplant the religion and culture of the Mother to other, safer areas.

Emperor

Nomadic and patriarchal hordes swept into thriving but undefended areas of the matriarchal world, shattering the peace of centuries with thundering sky-gods, war and separation, kingship, hierarchy, and dictatorship. Now the concept of fatherhood-as-ownership developed with a vengeance, bringing rape, murder, slavery, racism, and violent domination of the earth and all life on it.

Son of Swords

Developing a "heroic" code of "honor," alienated from the ethics of the Mother, the patriarchal mind glorified light over dark, male over female, master over slave. Through elaborate written literature, which we call myth and scripture, the deliberate overthrow of the Goddess was documented and passed down through the ages.

Hierophant

We have internalized this worldview in our very cells as law, custom, and conventional morality. It functions to keep us in our place as individuals and to justify five millennia of mass violence in the name of religion and nationalism. Now, as one feminist writer put it, "Your five thousand years are up!"

Death

Either we can die—literally—as a people and possibly a planet, or we can, like the snake shedding its skin, consciously witness the death of the existing culture and identify with the bright new skin beginning to reveal itself from under the surface of the old.

Six of Swords At this precarious moment in history, we need to grasp that war is not caused by somebody "out there," leaving individuals free of responsibility and separate from it. We need to reach a broader perspective.

Nine of Swords We are each responsible, male and female, for the actions of our culture. The demons against whom we wage our constant wars are gnawing at our insides and screaming through our private nightmares.

Three of Swords We are hooked on the culture that is destroying us. We argue, compete, and engage in petty power struggles.

Devil We experience addictions and greed, rage, jealousy, possessiveness, egotism, and materialism. The healing we need is an exorcism of the mentality that holds us captive in a hierarchy of dominance and submission.

Wheel of Fortune Fortunately, the wheel of life turns to reveal a new face of the Goddess for every age.

Ace of Wands The Age we are now entering is one of healing and rebirth, a time of starting fresh, a release of spirit.

Ten of Swords To enter into the healing, we must die to the past and all we are used to, standing firm in our ideals like the priestesses of Athena who chose death rather than succumb to patriarchal rape and wed-lock.

Ace of Cups We must dive, now, into the deep well of feelings within and get in touch with our own passionate desire for peace and joy and love.

Fool Then we can become like the Fool—childlike and free of cultural regulations, secure in the world, guided by the light of spirit. We would know then that, between the Vulture of the heavens and the Crocodile of the underworld, every true child of the Goddess is protected from evil and led through lifetimes by an open eye of wisdom.

High Priestess

But how is it possible to throw off five thousand years of cultural conditioning? Both right and left brains must be involved, the female and male aspects of each one of us called into play. Like the High Priestess of the heart, we must become still and allow the divine female presence to enter and be felt in us; to open to the intuition once again; to reconnect ourselves with our bodies and the spirit of compassionate love and divine wisdom that they represent; to listen for guidance and direction from within.

Magician

Like the Magician, we need also to manifest our heart's desires physically, to mobilize and focus our energies into the external world around us in order to make it what we want it to be. We need once more to dance the shaman fire and channel the heat that heals. The Sphinx reveals the way.

Daughter of Swords

A challenge such as the one we face today requires that we call in all our powers and raise the storm of energies needed in the fight for life.

Strength

Matriarchal consciousness is spiritual strength, grounded in the earth and moving from the heart. The mysteries of Sumerian Ishtar, Tibetan Tara, and Irish Brigit all link the full moon to the oracular powers of the menstrual cycle and the unfettered sexual expression of the female. As Artemis, Lady of the Beasts, the Goddess represents the unbroken continuity of relationship between human and animal nature, a recognition of our roots and interdependence.

Priestess of Swords

We must reach into the background of our experience and draw on the irrational and unknown forces available to us. We must become shamans and visionaries—in short, empowered human beings.

Six of Wands   Individually, for women, this means mobilizing power (Shakti) and developing self-confidence,

Shaman of Swords   speaking out like the wind, overcoming fear and choosing to win.

Four of Discs   It may also mean closing the door to others' needs for a time, in order to listen in the stillness for the guiding voice within.

Son of Cups   For men, it means stopping the active flow of the mind and allowing a gentler energy to emerge, which will nourish and enlighten the generally overactive ego. The analytical mind can be used to unite feelings and thoughts, stimulating poetry, music, or visual forms of artistic creativity.

Star   The Goddess is reawakening and her energy can be felt by all of us as a guiding, healing light that feels like grace, a blessing, the touch of Aphrodite's love, Kuan Yin's compassion.

Priestess of Cups   As the Muse, the Goddess inspires us to dream new dreams and experience new visions of what is possible. From the mysteries of the collective unconscious, she communes with us through imagery and sacred sounds.

Moon   She takes us down into the depths of the unconscious, leading us through the labyrinthine way, where we face our darkness.

Sun   With her help, we return into daylight fresh from the chrysalis of transformation with new visions of group union and cooperation.

Eight of Discs   We manifest this vision by working and and building together,

Three of Discs   constructing the new forms that will replace the outworn dwellings of today.

Three of Cups

In addition to work, there will be enjoyment and pleasure, time spent together in the play and relaxation of magic and music.

Daughter of Discs

And each of us alone must become a seeker, innocent and cleansed of our cynicism and hopelessness, young and fresh in our hearts and open to new ideas and possibilities. Like an ancient horned priestess or a contemporary Native American, we must request a vision—perhaps a new name—and then open ourselves to the divine response.

Crone

At the same time, we must reach into the most ancient sources of wisdom and knowledge, following the movements of stars, waiting for the voice of the Oracle. A period of solitude may be required, a journey of the soul into its own realm. When energies are conserved, the personality can learn to ask for and receive advice from the high Self. The crossroads now facing humanity demands our undivided attention and calm, clear judgement about which way to go. Will we go ahead into nuclear suicide, or will we change our direction and learn to follow the advice of our spiritual guides?

Priestess of Discs

One step toward inner balance and right relationship to body and earth is the practice of yoga, which softens the personality and opens the spiritual centers.

Chariot

Equally important is the development of a spiritual warrior consciousness—the discipline of Athene to enable us to work actively in the world. With the protection of the Goddess, one rides unharmed through obstacles to moral victories and Amazon triumphs.

Shaman of Discs

When we travel with purpose toward the goal we know to be true for us, then we can be said to be "on the Path." Our journey through life will lead us to the experiences we need as evolving individuals, and our responses will pave the way for future understanding.

Nine of Discs

The earth is alive and forever revealing her secrets to those who are open and ready to receive from her. To learn one's craft to the best of one's ability—to conquer fear of the dark and of time spent alone—these are signs of the creative healers of the New Age.

Son of Discs

The trick is to learn to balance the inner and outer needs. At times one must know how to focus completely on the goal, concentrating all one's attention on the task at hand, if success is to be gained.

Six of Discs

And then success must be shared, energy freely given, a circle created between "I" and "the Other." Through meaningful contact with another human being, one comes to know the depth of love available in the universe. Through such loving, one learns to let the energies flow freely, healing and freeing the body of dis-ease.

Ten of Discs

And especially when we come together in circles of energy for sharing group experiences,

Ace of Discs

something new is born through our combined presence. When we express our experience of well-being, we are healed and we give back.

Ten of Cups

We learn to feel bliss, ecstasy, reverence for all life.

Justice

We come into touch with an earthly balance that is natural and real: the harmonious power that belongs to us by birth as children of the Earth Mother. Together we can set things right, change patterns, make amends.

Judgement

Through this means, and only through this means, we may be able to save from destruction our planet and ourselves. Blessed Be.

Notes

This section contains the sources of direct quotations and, in some cases, of art works that are reflected in the Motherpeace images. When an author is cited in the text, you will find the last name repeated in the notes, followed by a page number. If the bibliography includes more than one book by an author, the note shows the year of publication of the relevant book. When a single author is cited more than once in a chapter, the name in the notes is followed by a page number for each quotation.

Please bear in mind that, in their original contexts, very few of the quotations refer to Tarot. Instead, nearly all of them are drawn from mythology, history, or discussions of the Goddess, in which I have found striking parallels to Tarot themes. In order to recover the full context of the various quotations, readers are encouraged to consult the works from which they are taken. I have listed all of these works in the selected bibliography, together with others that were helpful to me in writing this book.

Prologue

The charge of the Goddess: Starhawk, p. 77.
Churchill: speech in the House of Commons, March 1, 1955.
Tanner, p. 267.
Durdin-Robertson, (1975), index.
Stone (1978) on women's power, p. 153; on castration, p. 148.
Ink drawings of Eight Goddess Figures: (1) Giedion (1962), p. 457; (2) ibid., p. 509; (3) Neumann, plate 1; (4) Giedion (1962), p. 440; (5) Hawkes, p. 34; (6) Neumann, plate 24; (7) Neumann, plate 26; (8) Neumann, plate 8. Ink-dot drawings of figures 1 and 2 are reproduced from Giedion by permission of Princeton University Press. The line drawings of figures 3–8 are by the author, after the sources indicated.
Mithila women: Vequaud, p. 27.
Malle film: Shawn and Gregory, p. 87.

Chapter 1

Blavatsky, quoted by Durdin-Robertson, p. 94.
Graves (1955), p. 145.
Durdin-Robertson on Nuah, pp. 93–4; on Isis, p. 296.
Neumann, p. 256.
Knight, Vol. I, p. 95; Vol. II, p. 237.
von Franz (1972), p. 17.
Sandler, p. 4.

Chapter 2

von Franz (1972) p. 147.
Eliade (1969), p. 272.
Newspaper for psychics: *Circle Network News,* Fall 1981.

Chapter 3

Ashe, p. 140.
Earliest evidence of human tool-making: findings announced in 1982 by an-
thropoligists at University of California, Berkeley.
"What comes from the egg": von Franz (1972), p. 146.
Giedion (1962) on the female, p. 503; on bird-headed women, p. 284; on
Pech-Merle, p. 506; on death, p. 285.
Daly (1979), p. 75.
Boardman (1973) on sphinx at Delphi, p. 63; on Attic sphinx, p. 76.
Graves (1966), on sphinx: Graves distinguishes between Egyptian sphinxes,
which became masculine with the rise of Patriarchy, and the Pelasgian sphinx,
which remained female and was linked to Athene.

Chapter 4

Hall (1980), p. 161.
Sjöö on dream-body, p. 11; on Mantics, p. 50; on abstract notation, p. 37.
Giedion (1962) on earliest female symbols, p. 173; on the natural protruber-
ance, p. 211.
Durdin-Robertson (1974), p. 22.
Sacred pebbles: Broderick, p. 23.
Ashe, p. 127.
Temple, p. 65.
Dames (1977), p. 194.

Chapter 5

Bladelets from Pyrenees: Hadingham, p. 84.
Gimbutas: in Spretnak (1982).
Neumann, p. 98.
Giedion (1962) on horn, p. 470; on La Magdeleine, p. 478.
Mees, p. 20.

Chapter 6

Neumann on seated Great Mother, p. 99.

von Franz (1972) on world as dead object and making a plan, p. 90; on fire and writing, p. 139; on number four, p. 169.

Occult tradition: Mess, p. 59.

Giedion (1962) on ordering ego, p. 519; on separation, p. 272.

Chapter 7

Godwin on Pontifex Maximus, p. 57; on chastity, p. 19; on veritable cruci-fixion, p. 29; on monk's path, p. 17; on thought, logos and teaching, p. 92; on precision of words, p. 9; on Mithraic text, p. 28.

Daly (1979) on perpetual war, p. 346; on cauldron, pp. 81–2; on patriarchy, p. 50.

Stone (1978) on *asherim,* scattered passages.

Chapter 8

Boardman (1973), p. 86.

Bailey (1950), p. 79.

Douglas and Slinger (1979a), scattered passages.

Chapter 9

Graves (1966) on Athene, p. 231; on Medusa, p. 230; on number seven, p. 378.

Chesler: on Spretnak (1982), p. 103.

Murray, A., on Ushas, p. 386; on Athene, pp. 96–8.

Downing, chapter 5.

Leek, p. 22.

Chapter 10

Roberts on key system and on subjective life, p. 98.

Neumann, p. 250.

Larousse on "old wise woman," p. 278.

Harrison, p. 487.

Broder, p. 87.

Forfreedom, p. 127.

Chapter 11

Hall on old woman, p. 213; on Hekate, p. 64; on midwife to psyche, p. 197; on initiate, p. 85; on introversion, p. 223; on spider-woman, pp. 147–8; on witch-craft, p. 204; on birth moment, p. 179; on loneliness, p. 147.

Murray, A., on Vestal Virgin, pp. 78–81; on Hekate, pp. 76–7.

Monahgan, p. 131.

Daly (1979) on separatism, pp. 365–6; on spinster as Witch, p. 378; on labyrinth, p. 390; on network, p. 397; on call of our wild, p. 407.

Chapter 12

Neumann (photo section) on Denderah, p. 93; on Isis and Horus, p. 38; on Aphrodite on goose, p. 137; on Gorgons, p. 70; on Winged Artemis, p. 132; on many-breasted Artemis, p. 35; on Tara, p. 184.

Hawkes on Mohenjo-Daro figurine, p. 109; on New Grange, p. 71.

Boardman (1967) on Cretan frescoes, p. 29; on Winged Artemis, p. 92.

Boardman (1973) on Aphrodite on goose, p. 167; on Gorgons, p. 53.

Stone (1976) on Winged Isis, photo 11; on tree cult, p. 214.

Dames (1976) on eye idols, p. 67; on clay figure holding breasts, p. 172; on Sumerian bird-headed Goddess, p. 70.

de Stasi on spiral eyes from Malta, p. 101; on Egyptian eye of Horus, p. 103.

Graves (1966) on "merry maid," p. 395; on Gorgons, pp. 227–232; on wheel of Arionhod, p. 98.

Fix on astrological observation, pp. 60–2.

Arguelles on Aztec Earth Mother, p. 7.

Emmerich on pre-Columbian figurine, p. 40.

Segy on squatting figures from Belgian Congo, scattered passages.

Mallowan on eye idols, p. 49.

Giedion: cave paintings and figures of dancers.

Patai on Hebrew idols, photo section and *passim*.

Blofeld on Kuan Yin (photo section between p. 80 and p. 81).

Beyer on Tara, frontispiece figure, 1; and p. 364.

Metropolitan Museum of Art (1975) on Scythian mermaid, color plate 11.

Fell on inscriptions, scattered passages.

Chapter 13

Beyer on potent protections, p. 237; on potent moon, p. 460; on posture of meditation, p. 182; on menstrual blood, p. 303.

Temple, p. 130.

Hall on hour of the wolf, p. 117; on Artemis, p. 112; on a sybil's ravings, p. 185; on the first flow, p. 173.

Harner on Shaman animals, whole book.

Chapter 14

Fix on soul leaving body, p. 115; on Ishtar, p. 134.

Moss on dissolving ego boundaries, p. 33; on energy, p. 51; on unconditional love, p. 28; on the yes, p. 44; on transparency, p. 47.

Rasmussen: in Eliade (1964), p. 61.

Blofeld (1978), p. 124.

Eliade (1964), p. 55.

Hall, p. 100.

Starhawk, pp. 25–6.

Chapter 15

Downing, p. 13.
Medicine Eagle: in Halifax, p. 86.
Sjöö on menstrual cycles and carved bones, p. 36.
Halifax, p. 4.

Chapter 16

Halifax, p. 55.
Moss on every cell alive, p. 53; on transformation, p. 35.
Crowley, "The Thoth Deck" of Tarot cards.
Ehrenreich and English on charge of possessing obstetrical skills, p. 10.
Lewis on possession cults, scattered passages.

Chapter 17

Murray, M. on witches; also Daly (1979) on witches.
Mallowan on the Standard of Ur, p. 90.
Schell, Chapter 1.

Chapter 18

Mookerjee (1977) on Kali, pp. 75–77; p. 182; and pp. 190–1.
Former Special Assistant McGeorge Bundy, in Griffiths.

Chapter 19

Turner: "Contemporary Feminist Rituals" in "Great Goddess" issue of *Heresies*.
Budapest (1976), p. 83.
Sandler on Navaho chant, p. 193.
Beyer on White Tara prayer, p. 216.
Halifax on night, p. 182; on water-babies, pp. 106–7.
Macy: I am reporting here on a workshop conducted by her, but see the bibliography for her article on despair.

Chapter 20

Neumann, p. 73 (photo section).
Bailey (1950) on "Dweller on the Threshold," p. 22.
Sjöö on double-spiral, p. 50; on shamanism, p. 41.
Durdin-Robertson (1975), index.
Patai on Lilith, pp. 180–225.
Hall, p. 9.

Chapter 21

Bailey (1976) on the New Group of World Servers, scattered passages.

Knight on the Kabalistic Tree of Life, scattered passages.
Hamlyn on Amaterasu, p. 15.

Chapter 22

Durdin-Robertson on the Female Aeon, index.
Gearhart on the Judgement card, p. 24.
Sun: radio appearance, KPFA, 1980.

Chapter 23

Avalon (1978) on union, p. 693; on expansive power of the Tao, p. 233; on immortal spirit, p. 291; on the Mother, p. 691; on throwing one's eyes, p. 461; on multiple masks, p. 299; on enjoyment, p. 701.
von Franz (1972), p. 241.
Hall, p. 232.
Starhawk on circles, pp. 196–7; on subtle current, p. 37; on layers of meaning, p. 58; on Goddess being not ruling, p. 9; on feeling our breath, p. 43.
Dames (1977), p. 36.

Chapter 24

Eaton, p. 19.

Chapter 25

A two-headed snake lives at the Steinhart Aquarium in San Francisco's Golden Gate Park.
Graves (1966) on the Pegasus-spring, p. 383.
Budapest (1976), p. 125.
Fried, chapters on Kung bushpeople.

Chapter 26

Lincoln on menarche rituals, p. 17.
Graves (1966) on pre-Olympic games, p. 132.

Chapter 27

von Franz (1980), p. 115.
Boardman (1967), p. 31, on Minoan octopus.
Gray on the Nine of Cups, p. 96.
Neumann on Cretan Mother Goddess statue, p. 27 (photos).
Villasenor on Navaho sand-painting, scattered passages.

Chapter 28

Graves on Ten of Swords (1966) priestesses of Athens, p. 321.
Rawson, illustrations.

Chapter 29

Starhawk on younger self, p. 21; on maiden, p. 166.

Graves (1966) on whistling, p. 435; on changing into boar, p. 210; on Athene, p. 437; on Nemesis, p. 255; on unicorn, pp. 411 and 255.

Eaton on "Turtle Island", p. 81; on Buffalo woman, pp. 100–3.

Broder, p. 44.

Chapter 30

Starhawk on mirror image, p. 95; talking self, p. 21; horned God, p. 97; untamed self, p. 100; God of Autumn Equinox, p. 99; taking things apart, pp. 97–8; on the Hunter, p. 99.

Bahti on Zia clown, p. 19.

Graves (1966), p. 171.

Murray, M. (1960), p. 35.

Chapter 31

Giedion (1962), p. 172.

Graves (1966), p. 107.

Bushnell on Tonantzin, p. 70.

Emmerich on Tlazolteotl, p. 110.

Chapter 32.

Lewis, p. 47.

Graves (1966), p. 209.

Griffin, p. 176.

Emery on Horus and Egypt, scattered passages.

Murray, M., p. 61.

Gearhart on King of Wands, p. 91.

Metropolitan Museum (1976) on Horus falcon, color plate 16, and p. 138.

Neumann on Aztec cauldron, p. 193; and on "mana figure," p. 287–88.

Part 3

Shawn, p. 94.

Bibliography

Adler, Margot. *Drawing Down the Moon: Witches, Druids, Goddess-Worshippers, & Other Pagans in America Today.* Boston: Beacon Press, 1981.

Arguelles, Miriam and Jose, *The Feminine—Spacious as the Sky.* Boulder, Colorado: Shambhala, 1977.

Ashe, Geoffrey. *Ancient Wisdom.* Tunbridge Wells, Kent, England: Abacus Books, 1979.

Avalon, Arthur (Sir John Woodroffe). *The Serpent Power: The Secrets of Tantric and Shaktic Yoga.* New York: Dover Publications, 1974.

_____. *Shakti and Shakta.* New York: Dover Publications, 1978.

Bachman, Louise, and Ake Hultkrantz. *Lapp Shamanism.* Stockholm: Almquist & Wiksell International, 1978.

Bahti, Tom. *Southwest Indian Ceremonials.* Las Vegas: KC Publications, 1979.

Bailey, Alice A. *A Treatise on Cosmic Fire.* New York: Lucis Publishing Co., 1962.

_____. *Esoteric Astrology, Volume III: A Treatise on the Seven Rays.* New York: Lucis Publishing Co., 1951.

_____. *Glamour: A World Problem.* New York: Lucis Publications, 1950.

_____. *The Rays and the Initiations.* New York: Lucis Publishing Co., 1976.

Balin, Peter. *The Flight of the Feathered Serpent.* Venice, California: Wisdom Garden Books, 1978.

Beyer, Stephan. *The Cult of Tara: Magic and Ritual in Tibet.* Berkeley: University of California Press, 1973.

Blavatsky, H. P. *Isis Unveiled: A Master-Key to the Mysteries of the Ancient and Modern Science and Theology.* Pasadena, California: Theosophical University Press, 1960.

Blofeld, John. *The Tantric Mysticism of Tibet: A Practical Guide.* New York: E. P. Dutton, 1970.

_____. *Bodhisattva of Compassion: The Mystical Tradition of Kuan Yin.* Boulder, Colorado; Shambhala, 1978.

257

Boardman, John. *Greek Art* (rev. ed.). New York: Frederick A. Praeger, Inc., 1973.

_____. *Pre-Classical: From Crete to Archaic Greece.* Hammondsworth, Middlesex, England: Penguin Books, Ltd., 1967.

Brindel, June. *Ariadne.* New York: St. Martin's Press, 1981.

Boder, Patricia Janis. *Hopi Painting: The World of the Hopis.* New York: The Brandywine Press, 1979.

Brentjes, Borchard. *African Rock Art.* New York: C. N. Potter, 1970.

Broderick, Alan Houghton. *Prehistoric Painting.* London: Avalon Press Ltd., 1948.

Brownmiller, Susan. *Against Our Will: Men, Women, and Rape.* New York: Simon & Schuster, 1975.

Budapest, Z. *The Feminist Book of Lights and Shadows.* Los Angeles: Luna Publications, 1975.

_____. *The Holy Book of Women's Mysteries, parts I and II.* Los Angeles: Susan B. Anthony Coven, 1979 and 1980.

Bushnell, G. H. S. *Ancient Arts of the Americas.* New York: Frederick A. Praeger, Inc., 1965.

Butler, Bill. *Dictionary of the Tarot.* New York: Schocken Books, 1975.

Caldicott, Helen. *Nuclear Madness* New York: Autumn Press, 1979.

Case, Paul Foster. *The Tarot: A Key to the Wisdom of the Ages.* Richmond, Virginia: Macoy Publishing Co., 1947.

Cavendish, Richard. *The Tarot.* New York: Harper & Row, 1975.

Chicago, Judy. *The Dinner Party: A Symbol of Our Heritage.* Garden City, New York: Anchor Press/Doubleday, 1979.

Colegrave, Sukie. *The Spirit of the Valley: The Masculine and Feminine in Human Consciousness.* Los Angeles: J. P. Tarcher, Inc., 1979.

Crowley, Aleister (The Master Therion). *The Book of Thoth (Egyptian Tarot).* New York: Samuel Weiser, Inc., 1974.

Daly, Mary. *Beyond God the Father: Toward a Philosophy of Women's Liberation.* Boston: Beacon Press, 1973.

_____. *Gyn/Ecology: The Metaethics of Radical Feminism.* Boston: Beacon Press, 1979.

Dames, Michael. *The Silbury Treasure: The Great Goddess Rediscovered.* London: Thames and Hudson, 1976.

_____. *The Avebury Cycle.* London: Thames and Hudson, 1977.

Devambez, Pierre. *Greek Painting.* New York: The Viking Press, 1962.

Di Stasi, Lawrence. *Mal Ochio: The Underside of Vision.* Berkeley: North Point Press, 1981.

Douglas, Nik, and Penny Slinger. *Sexual Secrets: The Alchemy of Ecstasy.* New York: Destiny Books, 1979(a).

_____. *The Secret Dakini Oracle.* New York: Destiny Books, 1979(b).

Downing, Christine. *The Goddess: Mythological Images of the Feminine.* New York: The Crossroad Publishing Co., 1981.

Durdin-Robertson, Lawrence. *The Cult of the Goddess.* Huntington Castle, Clonegal, Enniscorthy, Eire: Cesara Publications, 1974.

_____. *The Goddesses of Chaldea, Syria and Egypt.* Huntington Castle, Clonegal, Enniscorthy, Eire: Cesara Publications, 1975.

Eaton, Evelyn. *Snowy Earth Comes Gliding.* Independence, California: Draco Foundation, 1974.

Edelson, Mary Beth. *Seven Cycles: Public Rituals.* New York: A.I.R., 1980.

Ehrenreich, Barbara and Dierdre English. *Witches, Midwives, and Nurses: A History of Women Healers.* Oyster Bay, New York: Glass Mountain Pamphlets, 1973.

Eliade, Mircea. *Birth and Rebirth; the religious meanings of initiation in human culture.* Translated by Willard R. Trask. New York: Harper & Row, 1958.

_____. *Shamanism: Archaic Techniques of Ecstasy.* Translated by Willard R. Trask. Princeton, New Jersey: Princeton University Press for the Bollingen Foundation, 1964.

_____. *Rites and Symbols of Initiation: The Mysteries of Birth and Rebirth.* New York: Harper & Row, 1965.

_____. *Yoga: Immortality and Freedom* (2nd ed.). Princeton, New Jersey: Princeton University Press for the Bollingen Foundation, 1969.

Emery, W. B. *Archaic Egypt.* Hammondsworth, Middlesex, England: Penguin Books, Ltd., 1963.

Emmerich, Andre. *Art Before Columbus.* New York: Simon & Schuster, 1963.

Evans-Wentz, W. Y., ed. *Tibetan Yoga and Secret Doctrine.* New York: Oxford University Press, 1958.

_____. *The Fairy-Faith in Celtic Countries.* Atlantic Highlands, New Jersey: Humanities Press, 1978.

Fairfield, Gail. *Choice Centered Tarot.* Redmond, Washington: Choice Centered Astrology and Tarot, 1981.

Faraday, Ann. *The Dream Game.* New York, Harper & Row, 1976.

Fell, Barry. *America B.C.: Ancient Settlers in the New World.* New York: Pocket Books, 1976.

Fix, Wm. R. *Star Maps.* London: Octopus Books, 1979.

Forfreedom, Ann, and Julie Ann, eds. *Book of the Goddess.* Sacramento, California: The Temple of the Goddess Within, 1980.

Fried, Martha Nemes and Morton M. Fried. *Transitions: Four Rituals in Eight Cultures.* New York: W. W. Norton, 1980.

Gardner, Richard. *Evolution Through the Tarot.* London: Rigel Press, 1970.

Garfield, Patricia. *Creative Dreaming.* New York: Random House, 1976.

Gawain, Shakti. *Creative Visualization.* Mill Valley, California: Whatever Publishing, 1978.

Gearhart, Sally, and Susan Rennie. *A Feminist Tarot* (rev. and expanded ed). Watertown, Massachusettes: Persephone Press, 1981.

Gelling, Peter, and Hilda Ellis Davidson. *The Chariot of the Sun and Other Rites and Symbols of the Northern Bronze Age.* New York: Frederick A. Praeger, Inc., 1969.

Gettings, Fred. *The Book of Tarot.* London: Triune Books, 1973.

Giedion, Sigfried. *The Eternal Present: The Beginnings of Art: A Contribution on*

Constancy and Change. New York: Bollingen Foundation (distributed by Pantheon Books), 1962.

_____. *The Beginnings of Architecture.* Princeton, New Jersey: Princeton University Press for the Bollingen Foundation, 1964.

Godwin, Jocelyn. *Mystery Religions in the Ancient World.* San Francisco: Harper & Row, 1981.

Goldberg, B. Z. *The Sacred Fire: A History of Sex in New Jersey Ritual, Religion and Human Behavior.* Secaucus, New Jersey: The Citadel Press, 1974.

Goodman, Jeffrey. *American Genesis: The American Indian and the Origins of Modern Man.* New York: Berkley Books, 1982.

Grant, Campbell. *Rock Art of the American Indian.* New York: Thomas Y. Crowell Co., 1967.

Grant, Kenneth. *Cults of the Shadow.* New York: Samuel Weiser, 1976.

Graves, Robert. *The Greek Myths,* volumes I and II. Baltimore: Penguin Books, 1955.

_____. *The White Goddess* (amended and enlarged ed.). New York: Farrar, Straus and Giroux, 1966.

Gray, Eden. *A Complete Guide to the Tarot.* New York: Bantam Books, 1972.

Griffin, Susan. *Pornography and Silence: Culture's Revenge Against Nature.* New York: Harper & Row, 1981.

_____. *Woman and Nature: The Roaring Inside Her.* New York: Harper & Row, 1979.

Griffiths, Franklyn, and John C. Polanyi, eds. *The Dangers of Nuclear War.* Toronto: University of Toronto Press, 1979.

Groenewegen-Frankfort, H. A., and Bernard Ashmole. *The Ancient World.* New York: New American Library, 1967.

Hadingham, Evan. *Secrets of the Ice Age: The World of the Cave Artists.* New York: Walker and Company, 1979.

Halifax, Joan. *Shaman Voices: A Survey of Visionary Narratives.* New York: E. P. Dutton, 1979.

Hall, Nor. *The Moon and the Virgin: Reflections on the Archetypal Feminine.* New York: Harper & Row, 1980.

Harding, M. Esther. *Woman's Mysteries, Ancient and Modern: A Psychological Interpretation of the Feminine Principle as Portrayed in Myth, Story and Dreams.* New York: Harper & Row, 1971.

Harner, Michael. *The Way of the Shaman: A Guide to Power and Healing.* San Francisco: Harper & Row, 1980.

Harrison, Jane Ellen. *Themis: A Study of the Social Origins of Greek Religion.* London: The Merlin Press, 1963.

Hawkes, Jacquetta (assisted by David Trump). *The Atlas of Early Man.* New York: St. Martin's Press, 1976.

Heresies: A Feminist Publication on Art and Politics, issue number 5, "The Great Goddess," Spring 1978.

Hutchinson, R. W. *Prehistoric Crete.* Baltimore: Penguin, 1962.

James, T. G. H. *Egyptian Sculptures.* New York: New American Library (by arrangement with UNESCO), 1966.

Jocelyn, John. *Meditations on the Signs of the Zodiac* (2d ed.). Blauvelt, New York: Multimedia Publishing Corp., 1970.

Jongeward, Dorothy and Dru Scott. *Women as Winners: Transactional Analysis for Personal Growth*. Reading, Massachusetts: Addison-Wesley, 1976.

Joy, W. Brugh. *Joy's Way: A Map for the Transformational Journey: An Introduction to the Potentials for Healing with Body Energies*. Los Angeles: J. P. Tarcher, Inc., 1979.

Jung, Carl G. *Man and His Symbols*. Garden City, New York: Doubleday & Company (a Windfall Book), 1964.

Kaplan, Stuart R. *The Encyclopedia of Tarot*. New York: U.S. Games, Inc., 1978.
_____. *Tarot Classic*. New York: Grosset & Dunlap, 1972.

Knight, Gareth. *A Practical Guide to Qabalistic Symbolism*, volumes I and II. New York: Samuel Weiser, 1978.

Kübler-Ross, Elisabeth. *On Death and Dying*. New York: Macmillan, 1969.

Lessing, Doris. *Shikasta* (Volume I in the series "Canopus in Argos: Archives"). New York: Alfred A. Knopf, 1979.

Lewis, I. M. *Ecstatic Religion*. Baltimore: Penguin Books, 1971.

Lhote, Henri. *The Search for the Tassili Frescoes*. Translated by A. H. Broderick. New York: E. P. Dutton, 1959.

Lincoln, Bruce. *Emerging From the Chrysalis*. Cambridge: Harvard University Press, 1981.

Macy, Johanna. "How to Deal with Despair." *East-West Journal*, June 1979.

Mallowan, M. E. L. *Early Mesopotamia and Iran*. New York: McGraw-Hill Book Co., 1965.

Mariechild, Diane. *Mother Wit: A Feminist Guide to Psychic Development: Exercises for Healing, Growth and Spiritual Awareness*. Trumansburg, New York: The Crossing Press, 1981.

Mees, G. H. *The Book of Signs*. Deventer: N. Kluwer, 1951.

Mellaart, James. *Earliest Civilizations of the Near East*. London: Thames & Hudson, 1978.

Metropolitan Museum of Art. *From the Lands of the Scythians: Ancient Treasures from the Museums of the U.S.S.R., 3000 B.C.–100 B.C.* Boston: New York Graphic Society, 1975.

_____. *Treasures of Tutankhamun:* exhibition catalogue, 1976.

Monaghan, Patricia. *The Book of Goddesses and Heroines*. New York: E. P. Dutton, 1981.

Monti, Franco. *Precolumbian Terracottas*. London: Paul Hamlyn, 1969.

Mookerjee, Ajit, and Madhu Khanna. *The Tantric Way: Art, Science, Ritual*. Boston: New York Graphic Society, 1977.

Moss, Richard. *The I That Is We: Awakening to Higher Energies Through Unconditional Love*. Milbrae, California: Celestial Arts, 1981.

Murray, Alexander S. *Manual of Mythology: Greek and Roman, Norse and Old German, Hindoo and Egyptian Mythology*. New York: Tudor Publishing, reprinted in 1954.

Murray, Margaret. *The God of the Witches*. Garden City, New York: Anchor Press/Doubleday, 1960.

Neumann, Erich. *The Great Mother: An Analysis of the Archetype*, (tr. Ralph Manheim). Princeton: Princeton University Press for the Bollingen Foundation, 1972.

New Larousse Encyclopedia of Mythology. London: Prometheus Press, 1968.

Nichols, Sallie. *Jung and Tarot: An Archetypal Journey*. New York: Samuel Weiser, 1980.

Patai, Raphael. *The Hebrew Goddess*. New York: Avon, 1978.

Pesek-Marous, Eduard. *Salvatore: Bull of Salvation*. Rolling Hills, California: Tau Press, 1976.

Piercy, Marge. *Woman On the Edge of Time*. New York: Alfred A. Knopf, 1976.

Piggott, Juliet. *Japanese Mythology*. London: Paul Hamlyn, 1969.

Pollitt, J. J. *Art and Experience in Classical Greece*. Cambridge: Cambridge University Press, 1972.

Potts, Billie. *A New Woman's Tarot*. Woodstock, New York: Elf and Dragon Press, 1978.

Powell, T. G. E. *Prehistoric Art*. New York: Frederick A. Praeger, 1966.

Rawson, Philip. *Tantra: The Indian Cult of Ecstasy*. New York: Bounty Books, 1974.

Reiter, Rayna R., ed. *Toward an Anthropology of Women*. New York: Monthly Review Press, 1975.

Rich, Adrienne. *Of Woman Born: Motherhood as Experience and Institution*. New York: W. W. Norton, 1976.

Roberts, Jane. *The Nature of the Psyche: Its Human Expression: A Seth Book*. Englewood Cliffs, New Jersey: Prentice-Hall, 1979.

Rosaldo, Michelle Zimbalist, and Louise Lamphere, eds. *Women, Culture and Society*. Stanford, California: Stanford University Press, 1974.

Rudhyar, Dane. *The Pulse of Life: New Dynamics in Astrology*. Berkeley: Shambhala, 1970.

————. *Astrological Timing: The Transition to the New Age*. New York: Harper & Row, 1972.

Rush, Anne Kent. *Moon Moon*. New York: Random House, and Berkeley: Moon Books, 1976.

Sandler, Donald. *Navaho Symbols of Healing*. New York: Harcourt Brace Jovanovich, Inc., 1979.

Sanford, Nevitt, and Craig Comstock. *Sanctions for Evil: Sources of Social Destructiveness*. Boston: Beacon Press, 1972.

Schell, Jonathan. *The Fate of the Earth*. New York: Alfred A. Knopf, 1982.

Segy, Ladislas. *African Sculpture*. New York: Dover Publications, 1958.

Sharkey, John. *Celtic Mysteries: The Ancient Religion*. New York: The Crossroad Publishing Co., 1975.

Shawn, Wallace, and Andre Gregory. *My Dinner With Andre: A Screenplay*. New York: Grove Press, 1981.

Sjöö, Monica, and Barbara Mor. *The Ancient Religion of the Great Cosmic Mother of All*. Trondheim, Norway: Rainbow Press, 1981.

Spretnak, Charlene. *Lost Goddesses of Early Greece: A Collection of Pre-Hellenic Mythology.* Berkeley: Moon Books, 1978.

_____, ed. *The Politics of Women's Spirituality: Essays on the Rise of Spiritual Power Within the Feminist Movement.* Garden City, New York: Anchor Press/Doubleday, 1982.

Starhawk (Miriam Simos). *The Spiral Dance: A Rebirth of the Ancient Religion of the Great Goddess: Rituals, Inovations, Exercises, Magic.* San Francisco: Harper and Row, 1979.

Stone, Merlin. *When God Was a Woman.* New York: Harcourt Brace Jovanovich, 1978.

_____, *Ancient Mirrors of Womanhood: Our Goddess and Heroine Heritage,* volumes I and II. New York: New Sibylline Books, 1979.

Strutt, Malcolm. *Wholistic Health and Living Yoga* (2d ed.). Boulder Creek, California: University of the Trees Press, 1977.

Tanner, Nancy Makepeace. *On Becoming Human.* Cambridge: Cambridge University Press, 1981.

Temple, Robert K. G. *The Sirius Mystery.* New York: St. Martin's Press, 1976.

Valiente, Doreen. *An ABC of Witchcraft, Past and Present.* New York: St. Martin's Press, 1973.

Vequard, Yves. *The Woman Painters of Mithila.* London: Thames and Hudson, 1977.

Villasenor, David. *Tapestries in Sand: The Spirit of Indian Sandpainting* (rev. ed.). Heraldsburg, California: Naturegraph Co., 1966.

von Franz, Marie-Louise. *Alchemy: An Introduction to the Symbolism and the Psychology.* Toronto: Inner City Books, 1980.

_____. *Patterns of Creativity Mirrored in Creation Myths.* Zurich: Spring Publications, 1972.

Waite, Arthur Edward. *The Pictorial Key to the Tarot.* Blauvelt, New York: Steinerbooks, 1971.

Warner, Rebecca Micca. *Tarot: An Illustrated Guide.* New York: St. Martin's Press, 1974.

Wasson, R. Gordon, Carl A. P. Ruck, and Albert Hofmann. *The Road to Eleusis: Unveiling the Secrets of the Mysteries.* New York: Harcourt Brace Jovanovich, 1978.

Whiteford, Andrew Hunter. *North American Indian Arts.* Racine, Wisconsin: Western Publishing Co., 1973.

Williams, Strephon Kaplan. *Jungian-Senoi Dreamwork Manual.* Berkeley: Journey Press, 1980.

Zain, C. C. *The Sacred Tarot.* Los Angeles: The Church of Light, 1936.

Motherpeace Images

Users of Tarot cards may find it helpful to have an index to illustrations of the new Motherpeace Tarot images. This list follows the order customary in Tarot books and shows where to find each Motherpeace image, with one column for ink drawings and a second for the full-color reproductions:

Card name	*page* number	*color plate* number
Fool (0)		backcover
Magician (I)		1
High Priestess (II)	21	1
Empress (III)		2
Emperor (IV)	48	
Hierophant (V)	54	
Lovers (VI)	61	
Chariot (VII)		2 and cover
Justice (VIII)	72	
Crone (IX)		3
Wheel of Fortune (X)		3
Strength (XI)		4
Hanged One (XII)	95	
Death (XIII)		4
Temperance (XIV)	109	
Devil (XV)		5
Tower (XVI)		5
Star (XVII)		6
Moon (XVIII)		6
Sun (XIX)		7
Judgement (XX)		7
World (XXI)	145	

Card name	*page* number	*color plate* number
SWORDS		
Ace	159	
Two	162	
Three	165	
Four	170	
Five	174	
Six		8
Seven	180	
Eight	182	
Nine	186	
Ten		10
Daughter	195	
Son	202	
Priestess		12
Shaman		12
WANDS		
Ace		16
Two	162	
Three		14
Four	170	
Five	174	
Six	13	8
Seven	180	
Eight	182	
Nine	186	
Ten		10
Daughter		cover
Son		14
Priestess		15
Shaman		15
CUPS		
Ace	159	
Two	163	
Three	165	
Four	171	
Five	175	
Six		9
Seven	180	
Eight	183	
Nine	187	
Ten		11
Daughter	195	
Son	202	
Priestess	210	
Shaman	218	

Card name	*page* number	*color plate* number
DISCS		
Ace		16
Two	163	
Three	165	
Four	171	
Five	175	
Six		9
Seven	180	
Eight	183	
Nine	187	cover
Ten		11
Daughter	195	
Son	202	
Priestess		13
Shaman		13

Index

Aces, in reading yes-no questions, 231
Achilles, 62, 203
Against Our Will: Men, Women & Rape, 49
Adept (Chariot), 69
Addiction, 116, 121, 245
Aegea, Goddess, 155
Aeon, Female, 139
Agriculture, 22, 38, 41, 45, 215, 243
Alembic, alchemical, 17
Alchemy, 17, 29, 60, 86, 107, 222
Alexander "the Great," 48
Alice in Wonderland, as shaman, 90
Alphabets, 38, 89, 156
Alternatives to Chemical Medicine, 11
Amalthea (She-goat Goddess), 86, 196, 206
Amanita muscaria (magic mushrooms), 26
Amaranth (Aztec grain), 42
Amaterasu (Japanese Sun-Goddess), 136
Amazon: 62, 67, 85, 116, 136, 154, 194, 210. *See also* Gorgon; Penthesilea
Anath (bird-Goddess), 85
Anasazi, "The Ancient Ones," 224
The Ancient Religion of the Great Cosmic Mother of All, 11
Anima, 68, 209, 213, 214
Animus, 138, 220
Animal helpers, 5, 30, 91, 93, 101, 136, 161, 189, 205, 212, 223
Animals: on cave walls, 6; slaying of, 50, 51, 56, 57; domestication of, 69, 86; goat mother and child, 196, 206; owl as form taken for flight, 211
Animal skins, 6, 30, 32, 196, 210, 215

Ankh, Egyptian symbol of life force and Isis, 139, 221
Anthony, Susan B., 143
Aphrodite, 3, 41, 42, 43, 46, 54, 85, 86, 126, 155, 180, 188, 203, 209, 214. *See also* Aegea; Britomartis; Empress; Dictyna; Rhea; Venus
Apollo (twin brother of Artemis), 207, 243
Aquarius (fixed air sign), 86, 119, 125, 168, 190
Arcana, 17–19
Archer, Artemis the Virgin, 38, 66
Archeology, 21, 29, 38, 44, 212, 242
Archetypes, 24, 32, 151, 241
Ariadne (Goddess), 129, 209. *See also* Labyrinth; Venus-Aphrodite
Aries (cardinal fire sign), 26, 30, 47, 82, 125–126, 153, 158, 190. *See also* Divine Yogini
Ark, 17
Arka (Goddess), 17
Arguelles, Jose and Miriam, 1
Arrows. *See* Bow and arrows
Artemis, 35, 38, 39, 43, 66, 68, 69, 76, 77, 85, 86, 90, 94, 126, 130, 199, 207, 210, 222, 243
Ashe, Geoffrey, on shamanism as a women's cult, 27; on Artemis and shamanism, 38
Asherim, 55, 86
Ashtoreth (Goddess), 3, 54, 55, 85
Astarte (Goddess), 3, 17, 54, 55, 85, 119, 130, 209. *See also* Venus-Aphrodite

267

Astral plane, 26, 130
Astrology, 81–88, 210
Athalme (witch's tool), 31
Athene (Goddess of wisdom), 66–70, 116, 154, 190, 196, 209–210, 245
Aurignacian period, 36
Australian Aborigines: dream-time, 36; sacred pebbles called *churinga*, 38; running women, 39; Sun Goddess, 136
Authority, 51, 53, 57, 152, 211, 217, 221
Autumn Equinox, god of, 205
Avalon, Arthur, 144, 145
Avebury, as Great Mother, 8
Axe, for carving, 30; double-headed, of Athene, 68

Bacchantes. *See* Maenads
Bacchus (early form of Pan), 113
Baez, Joan (nonviolent resistance), 140
Bailey, Alice A., on pairs of opposites, 62; on the "sin of separatism," 114; on the New Group of World Servers, 135, 240; on glamours, illusions, 141; on bad karma of gold, 154; channeling "the Tibetan," 211
Banshee, 90, 121. *See also* Calleagh
Batons of Commandment, 212
Bee-hive tombs, 101
Beltis (Goddess), 119. *See also* Venus
Bhairavi (Goddess), 31
Bird-headed drawings, 3, 4, 5, 6, 7, 30, 31, 85
Birth, 3, 6, 41, 44, 45, 47, 78, 83, 160, 161, 181, 192–193
Birth control, 37, 110
Bjornstrand, Gustav, 240
Blavatsky, Madame, 17, 36
Black rites, 36, 77
Bladelets, prehistoric, 42
Blofeld, John, on Kuan Yin, 96
Blood, menstrual, 35, 37, 44, 56, 92, 131, 169, 191, 243; African horn of, 42; of Christ as communion, 57. *See also* Mithras
Boar, 196
Boat, 17, 129. *See also* Ship
Bodhisattva (compassion and forgiveness), 140
Body, physical, 4, 7, 8, 11, 13, 17, 18, 22, 25, 30, 32, 35, 37, 43, 44, 54, 57, 64, 157
Body of light, 63, 159
Bones, carved, 7, 38, 101, 210, 243

Book of Signs, The, 44
Bondage model of social organization, 113. *See also* Devil
Boreas (the North Wind), 219
Bow and arrows, 39, 66, 130, 184
Breasts, 5, 6, 9, 30, 31, 35, 37, 38, 41, 42, 53, 83, 86, 155, 179. *See also* Artemis; High Priestess; Kuan Yin; Shamanism; Tara; Virgin Mary
Brigit (Irish Triple Goddess), 89, 90, 209
Britomartis (Cretan Goddess), 155
Broder, Patricia, on Hopi, 72, 199
Brownmiller, Susan, on rape and monogamy, 49
Budapest, Z., on ritual after rape, 123; on "building the church of the Goddess"
Buddhism, 18, 19, 63, 86, 87, 127, 135, 141, 223
Bull (Taurus), 41
Butterfly, 134, 137, 159

Caesar, Julius, 53
Caldicott, Helen, 140
Calendar, lunar, 36, 39, 101; menstrual, 7; wheels and stone circles, 82
Calleagh (Irish Banshee Goddess), 121
Calypso, sacred island of, 214
Canaanites, Moon Goddess of, 17
Cancer (cardinal water sign), 37, 83, 155, 158, 190
Candlemas (Brigit's holiday, the Feast of the Flame), 89
Capricorn (cardinal earth sign), 86, 114, 158, 190
Cardinal signs, initiating, 158, 190
Casteneda, Carlos, 70
Castration, 8
Cat as companion, 25
Cataclysm, 118, 120
Catal Hüyük (ancient matriarchal city), 38, 41, 42
Cauldron, 17, 56, 212, 222
Celibacy, 77, 80, 113
Ceres, Roman Goddess, 41, 43. *See also* Demeter
Cerridwen, magic cauldron of, 212
Chaco Canyon, New Mexico, 83, 87
Chakras (the seven energy centers of the subtle body), 26, 68, 90, 135, 156, 169
Chalice, 17
Changing Woman (Navaho Goddess), 123
Channel, energy, 26, 38, 71, 107, 119, 141, 143, 191, 199, 209–216, 229, 230, 237

Chaos, 23
Character cards, 152
Chariot, 13, 66–70
Charis (Goddess), 37
Chastity, 53–54
Chesler, Phyllis, on Amazons, 67
Chicago, Judy: *Dinner Party*, 9; *Birth Project*, 83
Child, 24, 35, 194, 199
Children, 31, 45, 47, 48, 90, 146
Christ, 53, 57, 135, 139
Churchill, Winston, 1
Circe (daughter of Hekate), sacred island of, 214
Circles, 9, 12, 36, 86, 126, 146, 156, 188, 192, 199, 237, 238
Cit, being, 144
Clairvoyance, 37
Collective unconscious (Fool's bag), 24
Communion, origins of, 56
Community, 4, 20, 41, 45, 72, 109, 135, 136, 140, 142, 156, 179, 190, 191, 192, 212, 217, 222, 239, 243
Concentration, 9, 176, 197, 207, 238
Conception, 39, 45
Consciousness, 7, 20, 22, 25, 26, 35, 36, 44, 63, 71, 91, 102, 105, 107, 116, 118, 131, 134, 135, 137, 138, 139, 141, 145, 155, 156, 185, 215
Control, 47, 52, 96, 97, 116, 118, 129, 138, 139, 148, 188, 192, 203, 217, 222
Copper (sacred to Venus-Aphrodite), 188
Corn Mother, 215. *See also* Tlazolteotl
Cornucopia, 42, 73
Cowrie shell (fertility symbol), 38
Crab (symbol for Cancer), 66
Craft, 185, 189
Craftsman god, 49
Cranes, 197, 204
Creation, 18, 20, 21, 22, 31, 129
Crone, 35, 70, 76–80, 130, 135. *See also* Hekate; Wise women
Crocodile, 25, 246
Crowley, Aleister, and his Thoth Tarot Deck, 12, 19, 55, 89, 108, 181
Crown chakra, 26, 125, 198, 217, 238
Creativity, 3, 12, 68, 70, 84, 144, 153, 160, 176, 191, 204, 205, 215, 224, 241
Crucifixion, 54
Crystal, 72
Cupid, 184

Cupules (hollows carved in rock), 30. *See also* Breasts
Cutting the cards, 230

Daly, Mary, 14, 31, 55, 57, 78
Dames, Michael, 8, 39, 147
Dance, 2, 6, 20, 30, 33, 84, 107, 136, 144, 169, 191, 197, 204, 243
Datura, 206
Daughter, 8, 12, 35, 43, 47, 67, 68, 76, 194–200
Death, 5, 8, 21–22, 35, 53, 78, 82, 100–106, 107, 118, 142, 217, 222
Delphi, 36, 90, 91
Demeter, Greek Goddess, 41, 43, 77
Demon, 36, 55, 79, 90, 186, 245. *See also* Dweller on the Threshold
Destruction, 8, 14, 31, 70, 121, 129, 142, 155. *See also* Kali
Devil, 58, 97, 113–117, 206. *See also* Pan
Diana, Moon Goddess, 86, 130. *See also* Artemis
Dictyna, Cretan Goddess, 155
Dinner Party, 9
Dionysus, 57, 84, 113, 196. *See also* Amalthea; Pan
Dis-ease, 2, 11, 75, 110, 249
Dismemberment, 5, 110
Divination, 22, 36, 80, 212, 235
Dogon (African people), 81
Dominance/submission, 8, 47, 64, 99, 115, 116, 154, 203, 244, 245. *See also* Devil; Emperor
Dots (symbols), 9, 30, 36
Douglas, Nick, and Slinger, Penny, on Tantra, 63
Dove of Aphrodite, 180, 203
Downing, Christine, 67, 68, 101
Dragonfly, 207
Dream, 36, 39, 44, 76, 80, 92, 94, 131–132, 133, 155, 176, 185, 211
Druid, 18, 82
Duality, 54, 60, 62, 69
Durdin-Robertson, Lawrence, 3, 17, 19, 37
Dweller on the Threshold, 130

Eagle, 125, 223
Eagle, Brooke Medicine, 101
Earth Mother, 4, 22, 37, 41, 44, 114, 123, 142, 157, 193, 200, 215. *See also* Tlazolteotl
Eaton, Evelyn, 156, 198

Ecclesiastes, 71
Ecology, 156
Edleson, Mary Beth, 9
Egg, 30, 35, 159, 205
Ecstasy, 4, 5, 6, 26, 33, 37, 60, 63, 97,
   110, 125, 144, 146, 155, 176, 188, 207,
   219
Ego, 8, 22, 26, 30, 32, 49, 50, 63, 64, 68,
   71, 95, 97, 98, 111, 114, 116, 134, 135,
   138, 154, 183, 190, 197, 203, 204, 228;
   death of, 5, 82, 118. *See also* Kali
Egypt, 18, 19, 32, 66, 72, 83, 205, 212.
   See also Isis, Neith, Nut
Egyptian Book of the Dead, 104
Egyptian lioness Goddess, 173
Eleusinian Mysteries, 19, 41, 42, 60, 86.
   See also Demeter
Elf, 27, 90, 146, 184
Eliade, Mircea, 20, 25, 96–97
Elixir, 17
Emotions, 26, 39, 50, 56, 70, 155, 160,
   173, 184, 194, 199, 201, 209, 213, 223
Emperor, 8, 21, 27, 89, 115, 154
Empire Strikes Back, The, 95
Empress, 12, 22, 41–46, 146, 156, 215.
   See also Demeter; Matriarchy
Equal Rights Amendment, 57
Eros, 33, 63, 131, 153, 160, 204
Esoteric, 2, 12, 18, 19, 24
Eucharist, 37
Euronome (Goddess of All Things), 87
Evolution, 20, 24; biological, 116, 152;
   cultural, 22, 152, 153; psychic, 215; as
   soul journey, 18, 25
Eyes, 12, 13, 24, 25, 32, 35, 49, 69, 104,
   117, 120, 130, 159, 199, 219, 224, 241;
   eye Goddesses, 83, 85; eye on Tara's
   hand, 215

Fairies, 71, 89, 90, 93, 146, 181, 207
Familiars (animal companions of witches),
   5, 25, 212
Faraday, Ann, 133
Fates, 71, 75, 88, 125, 196
Fatherhood, 7, 31, 32, 47, 68, 201, 204,
   221, 244
Fell, Barry, 119
Female group, the, 4, 8, 20, 29, 35, 37,
   48, 86, 110, 123, 210. *See also* Artemis;
   Shamanism
Female line, 8, 43
Fertility, 2, 3, 4, 6, 38, 41, 42, 43, 82, 90,
   113, 212, 215, 222, 243

Flight, 4, 32, 81, 92, 125, 171, 175, 206,
   217, 219. *See also* Shamanism
Fiji Islanders, 20
Findhorn (community in Scotland), 240
Fire, 3, 12, 29, 30, 48, 77 90, 92, 95, 118,
   152, 153, 158, 159, 179, 197, 217, 242.
   See also Kali; Shakti; Wands
Fish Goddesses, 86
Fix, William, 81, 94
Fixed signs, 168, 190
Fool, 20, 23–28, 52, 148, 151, 204, 228
Foremothers, 7, 9, 33
Forfreedom, Ann, 73. *See also* Maat
Fortuna, 88. *See also* Wheel
Four: directions, 168, 196, 219; elements,
   50, 152; quarters, 197
Von Franz, Marie Louise, 20, 21, 22, 26,
   49, 50, 144, 184
Freya (Goddess replaced by Odin), 94
Frog, 126
Future: 13, 22, 160, 174, 176, 191, 240,
   241; divining the, 36, 39, 54, 77, 118,
   188, 223, 231, 234; fear of, 26, 101

Gaia (Earth), 72, 139, 142
Garfield, Patricia, 133
Gearhart, Sally, 140, 221
Gemini (mutable air sign), 60, 83, 178,
   190
Giedion, Siegfried, 6, 30, 32, 43, 51, 156,
   212
Gilgamesh (hero), 49
Gimbutas Marija, 42, 43
Glandular system, 215
Gold, 154, 202, 210
Goddess, The, 67
Godwin, Jocelyn, 53, 54, 56
Goodman, Jeffrey, 119
Gorgon, 68, 85. *See also* Medusa
Grace, 37, 45, 123, 127, 160, 191
Grain, 29, 41, 42, 43
Graves, Robert, 17, 66, 85, 86, 190, 196,
   197, 207, 214, 219
Gray, Eden, 188
Great Mother, 2, 3, 25, 41, 42, 46, 47, 53,
   83, 136, 144
Great Mother, The, 17, 222
Greek vases, 61, 62
Griffin-Phoenix, 173
Griffin, Susan, 14, 219
Grounding, 93, 108, 126, 169, 189, 196,
   208, 215, 224, 228, 235, 237
Group mind, 237

Gynecology, 11, 109, 110
Gyn/Ecology, 14

Halifax, Joan, 104, 107, 108, 125
Hall, Nor, 36, 76, 92, 96, 129, 132
Hallomas (Halloween), 78. *See also* Hekate
Hanged One, 22, 25, 94–99, 205
Harpocrates (Lord of Silence), 205
Harris, Frieda, 12
Harrison, Jane Ellen, 72
Hathor (Egyptian Goddess), 38, 54, 81, 87, 212
Hawk, 219. *See also* Horus, Isis
Headstand, 96
Headless figures, 3 (drawings), 4, 6, 7, 30, 82. *See also* Kali
Healing, 2, 4, 7, 11, 13, 20, 21, 22, 32, 36, 44, 63, 67, 80, 85, 91, 92, 109, 111, 123, 124, 125, 135, 139, 155, 169, 175, 176, 187, 189, 211, 212, 217, 218, 221, 238. *See also* Blood; Gorgons; Heat; Mysteries; New Group of World Servers; Sexuality
Heart chakra, 135, 228
Hearth, 29, 56, 169
Heat that heals, 29, 92, 107, 153, 188, 212, 221. *See also* N/um; Wands
Hebrew scribes, 55
Hekate (Goddess of Dark Moon), 35, 76, 78, 80, 85, 130, 199, 221. *See also* Crone
Helena (Divine Wisdom), 140
Herbs, 11
Hercules (hero), 203
Hero, 8, 49, 56, 62, 67, 154, 186, 203, 213–214, 244. *See also* Gilgamesh; Rape
Herodotus, on Amazons, 67
Hestia (Goddess of the Hearth), 77
Heterae (prostitutes), 62
High Priestess, 12, 19 (pictures), 20, 35–40, 53, 142, 146, 155. *See also* Artemis; Cups; Isis
Hieroglyph, 18, 90
Hierophant, 43, 53–59, 60, 72, 115. *See also* Law
Hieros gamos (sacred marriage), 60
"Holy women," 3
Holy Spirit (feminine), 23, 126
Horns, 30, 38, 42, 210; horned headdress, 179, 199; Horned God, 204–208
Horus (son of Isis), 219
Hopi, 39, 72, 119, 120, 192, 199, 215
Horse, 176, 196

Hybrid figures, 30, 69, 223
Hummingbird, 169

I Ching (oracle), 39, 61, 80, 204, 222
Ice Age (Paleolithic), 4, 42, 43, 210
Illegitimacy (no such thing as), 31
Imagination, 3, 18, 46, 117, 160, 176, 179, 181, 184, 214
Imperialism, 48. *See also* Emperor
Inanna (Goddess), 3, 56. *See also* Shamanism
Incarnation, 7, 25, 54, 60, 142, 209
Indo-Aryan invaders, 47, 54, 154
Initiate, 69, 76, 77, 79, 91. *See also* Crone
Initiation, 18, 19, 22, 24, 42, 43, 60, 76, 94, 126, 129, 132, 179, 238. *See also* Mysteries; Underworld
Integration, 63, 107, 140, 148, 169, 172, 234
Intellect, 32, 51, 66, 154, 158, 203, 206, 209, 211, 219, 235
Intuition, 12, 39, 55, 115, 118, 142, 144, 159, 194, 210, 221, 235, 238, 241. *See also* Right brain
Isis (Egyptian Goddess), 3, 19, 36, 42, 54, 83, 85, 87, 126, 130, 140, 209, 219, 221. *See also* High Priestess; Mysteries; Sirius; Sothis
Ishtar (Goddess), 3, 17, 41, 46, 54, 55, 83, 85, 92, 94, 126, 209. *See also* Aphrodite; Empress; Strength; Venus
Islam, 54

Jackson, Mildred, 11
Jehovah (Yahweh), 47, 104
Jester, 24, 26
Jesus (as Hanged One), 94
Joker, 24
Journey, 4, 5, 6, 13, 18, 25, 36, 56, 63, 64, 82, 85, 90, 91, 93, 94, 100, 104, 129, 131, 223, 240. *See also* Shamanism; Trance
Judaism, 54
Judgement, 22, 58, 139–143. *See also* Gaia; Isis; Venus
Jung, C. G., 18, 113, 132, 186. *See also* Shadow; Unconscious, the
Jupiter, 50, 217
Justice, 71–75, 125. *See also* Themis

Kali (Hindu Goddess of Fire), 30, 31, 69, 82, 85, 118–122; Kali Yuga, 118. *See also* Tower

Karma, 63, 71, 72, 74, 105, 120, 154

King, 26, 47, 101, 138, 154, 155, 217, 220, 244

Kiva (Native American underground chamber), 94–95, 132

Knight, Gareth, 17

Knives, 30, 31

Kore (Maiden), 199

Krishna (Hindu flute-playing god), 205

Kuan Yin (Chinese Goddess), 86, 96, 124, 125, 140. *See also* Bodhisattva

Kübler-Ross, Elisabeth, 104, 140

Kundalini, 20, 45, 55, 90, 120, 146, 176, 191, 212, 215. *See also* Fire; Snake; Yoga

!Kung Bushpeople, 107. *See also* N/um

Labyrinth (maze), 13, 14, 79, 129, 132

Ladder spirits, 219

Lady of the Beasts, 38, 89

Lamia (Snake Goddess), 69. *See also* Neith

Language, 26, 36, 71, 92, 153, 155, 156, 242

Law, 8, 20, 47, 55, 56, 71, 72, 74, 87, 244. *See also* Justice

Laying-on of hands, 125

Leek, Sybil, on Saturn, 69

Left brain, 201

Left hand, 9, 12, 31, 36, 90, 146, 212, 213, 220, 230. *See also* High Priestess

Leo (fixed fire sign), 84, 135, 138, 153, 168, 190

Leopards, 42, 161

Lesbian-feminist women, 67. *See also* Amazon

Les Trois Freres (Sorceror of), 6, 31

Levanah (or Lebanah), 130. *See also* Blood; Moon

Lewis, I. M., 219

Libido, 77, 93, 153, 184. *See also* Wands

Libra (cardinal air sign), 74, 85, 158, 190

Light, Cassandra, 12, 232

Lightning, 31, 39, 118, 119, 121

Lilith (Moon Goddess), 55, 86, 130, 131. *See also* Demon; Moon

Lion, 176, 212

Logos, 49, 56, 204

Lord of the Beasts (Shiva), 30

Maat (Egyptian Vulture Goddess), 25, 73

Macy, Johanna, 126

Maenads, 84, 111. *See also* Dionysus

La Magdeleine (Ice Age cavern), 43

Magdalenian period (prehistoric), 6

Magic, 24, 26, 27, 31, 32, 33, 36, 76, 79, 80, 85, 90, 93, 108, 110, 126, 146, 147, 155, 156, 168, 169, 189, 203, 212, 213, 228, 240, 242. *See also* Divination; Fire; Sexuality

Magician, 29–34, 153. *See also* Wands

Maiden, 196, 198, 199, 207

Malle, Louis, 14

Mana, 243

Manas, 119

Manifestation, 18, 31, 32, 45, 88, 114, 152, 160, 181, 192, 195, 215, 240

Mantics (seers), 36

Mantra (sacred sound), 97

Marriage, 47, 49, 60

Mars, 30, 33, 50, 153, 160, 217. *See also* Creativity; Magician; Passion; Wands

Mary, Virgin, 19, 86, 126, 201. *See also* Breasts; Isis; Virgin

Masks, 12, 30, 145, 222, 223

Mastery, 33, 102, 107, 108, 110, 147, 148, 188, 189, 215, 217. *See also* Craft; Death; Fire; Shamanism

Mathematics, 38, 210

Matriarchal consciousness, 1, 7, 8, 9, 11, 12, 89, 243, 246. *See also* Strength

Matriarchal culture, 9, 22, 156. *See also* Empress

Matriarchal libraries, 48

Matrilineal descent, 43, 201, 220

Maya, 144, 145

Meditation, 18, 25, 35, 39, 60, 63, 96, 141, 144, 159, 177, 187, 189, 201, 205, 215, 235. *See also* Healing; High Priestess; Vajra

Medusa (Amazon Gorgon Queen), 69, 85, 86, 116, 211. *See also* Chariot

Menopause, 76

Menstrual cycles, 7, 35, 37, 39, 92, 101, 130, 223. *See also* Blood; *Menarche*

Medea (Greek), 222

Medicine men, 6

Medicine woman, 189, 223

Mercury, 204

Mermaid, 87, 213

Mees, G. H., 44–45

Menarche (first menstruation), 169

Microcosm, 30, 151

Midwifery, 36, 76, 109, 110

Migration, 38, 92, 119, 120, 155, 197. *See also* Tower

Mihit (Egyptian Lioness-goddess), 212

Milk, transformation into, 37
Mineral waters, 123, 125, 198. *See also* Star
Minerva (Roman Goddess of Wisdom), 67
Mithila, women painters of, 9
Mirror, 5, 44–45, 136, 199, 201. *See also* Amaterasu
Mithras, 53, 57
Moon, 7, 12, 13, 22, 35, 38, 39, 42, 66, 67, 76, 79, 92, 129–133, 221, 242. *See also* Chariot; Cups; High Priestess
Money, 156, 160, 173, 176, 193, 207, 215, 224. *See also* Discs
Morning glories, 126
Moss, Richard, 95, 96, 97, 98, 107
Mother, 2, 7, 13, 19, 35, 36, 42, 43, 46, 49, 52, 53, 56, 153, 212, 214, 242–243
Mother Goose (Aphrodite), 85
Mother Teresa, 140
Mounds, serpent (in Ohio), 95
Mount Thera (volcano), 155
Murray, Alexander, 67, 77
Murray, Margaret, 207, 221
Mutable signs, 178, 190
My Dinner with Andre, 14, 240
Mysteries, 4, 19, 26, 29, 32, 35, 37, 42, 43, 44, 53, 57, 60, 64, 90, 129, 160, 209, 215, 227, 236, 243. *See also* Empress; High Priestess; Isis; Moon

Nammu (Goddess), 87
Navaho, 21, 123, 153, 189
Negativity in Crowley, 12
Neith (Egyptian Goddess), 31, 66, 67, 68, 130. *See also* Artemis
Nemesis (Goddess of Divine Vengeance), 73
Neolithic period, 41
Neptune (Poseidon), 206
Neumann, Erich, 17, 42, 47, 49, 71, 222
New Grange (Ireland), 83, 87
Nine, 79, 185. *See also* Crone
Noah, 17
Nonattachment, 134, 169
Norns (Three Fates), 71
North Wind, 196, 219. *See also* Boreas
Nuah (predecessor of Noah), 17
Nuclear arms race, 27, 57, 58, 70, 104, 105, 115, 120, 138, 140, 141, 203, 219, 241. *See also* Dominance-submission
N/um, 107. *See also* Hanged One; !Kung
Numinous power, 9, 54, 83
Nut (Egyptian Goddess), 88. *See also* Chariot

Octopus, 184
Odin (Norse god), 94. *See also* Freya
Odysseus, 214. *See also* Calypso
Olympics, 173
Omphalos (oracular center), 91
Oracle, 36, 39, 74, 119, 155, 236, 244
Oracular centers, 212
Oracular power, 19, 54, 72, 180, 191, 241. *See also* Gaia
Original sin, 110
Orpheus, 53
Osiris, 213
Oversoul, 143, 238
Ovulation, 35, 37, 39
Owl, 209, 211. *See also* Athene; Shaman

Paleolithic period, 2, 9, 30, 41, 42, 94, 101. *See also* Ice Age
Pallas Athene, 67. *See also* Chariot
Pan (Horned Goat-god), 86, 113, 196, 206
Pandora (woman-as-evil), 55
Paradise, 25, 27, 104
Parrot, 215
Pasiphae (Cretan Goddess), 35, 130
Passion, 33, 44, 49, 64, 93, 160, 175, 176, 184, 196, 212, 219. *See also* Red
Path, 20, 50, 54, 82, 129, 185, 223
Patriarchy, 1, 8, 11, 18, 19, 47, 55, 84, 154, 221, 241, 214. *See also* Emperor
Peace, 1, 7, 8, 14, 57, 70, 125, 135, 139, 140, 146, 160, 198, 242
Peacock feather, 25, 179
Pebbles, sacred, 38
Pech-Merle cavern, 3 (pictures), 6, 30, 37
Pele (Volcano Goddess), 111
Pentagram, 172, 173, 203
Penthesilea (Amazon Queen), 62
Persephone (Daughter), 100, 197, 199. *See also* Demeter; Underworld
Perseus ("the destroyer"), 69, 203
Personality, 22, 26, 30, 32, 51, 64, 68, 75, 95, 122, 134, 135, 140, 141, 151, 159, 160, 170, 178, 185, 186, 194, 198, 204, 213, 222, 223, 238. *See also chapter on Minor Arcana*
Peyote, 147
Philosopher's stone, 107
Pilgrimage, 87
Pillar, 36, 55
Pineal gland, 25, 96
Pipe, 199, 200. *See also* Wakan-Tanka
Pisces (mutable water sign), 26, 86, 96, 155, 178, 190

Pituitary gland, 96
Planet, 14, 18, 45, 139, 141, 157, 238, 240
Play, 26, 134, 136, 138, 191, 198, 201, 204, 205, 207, 227, 228, 231, 244. *See also* Krishna; Sun; *chapter on Sons*
Pleiades, 41, 126. *See also* Empress; Star
Pluto (god of underworld), 100
Polarity, 234, 235, 243
Pneuma, 78
Pollitt, J. J., 62
Poseidon (Neptune), 70, 206
Possession, by spirits, 37, 107, 110
Prana, 92
Prayer, 14, 31, 123, 124, 153, 190, 199, 204, 236, 243
Pregnancy, 6, 39, 41, 42, 45, 109, 181, 200
Priestesses, 2, 3, 43, 53, 55, 69, 72, 82, 89, 91, 142, 155, 173, 188, 190, 194, 209–216, 222. *See also* High Priestess
Projection, 31, 55, 113, 151, 154, 185–186, 203, 217. *See also* Shadow; Shaman
Prophecy, 26, 36, 37, 72, 74, 78, 80, 91, 120, 239. *See also* Future
Prosperity-thinking, 46
Psyche, 20, 36, 63, 77, 98, 108
Pythagoras, 53, 68

Quadishtu (holy women), 3

Rainbow, 139, 192
Rainmaking 35, 39, 212, 242
Rajas, 196
Rape, 48, 49, 62, 64, 115, 123, 191, 203, 244. *See also* Emperor; Hero
Rasmussen, 95
Re (Irish Goddess), 130
Reading the cards, 22, 152, 230, 231
Rebirth, 5, 21–22, 34, 101, 126, 134, 137, 160, 173, 197. *See also* Sun
Reclining female figures, 43
Red, 9, 31, 32, 37, 42, 44, 49, 51, 63, 69, 101, 120, 153, 188, 219. *See also* Kali; Passion; Tantra; Wands
Reincarnation, 24, 25, 145
Relationship, 8, 41, 62, 70, 77, 105, 170, 184, 242
Renewal, 8, 101, 137, 141. *See also* Shedding
Restoration, 80; of the universe, 21, 227, 240
Resurrection, 94, 143, 197
Return, 7, 18, 20, 21, 25, 26, 52, 94, 101, 104, 121, 135, 139, 141, 142, 190

Reversed Tarot cards, 230, 234, 235
Rhea (Cretan Goddess), 155
Right brain, 7, 26, 36, 146, 194, 229, 241
Right hand, 9, 31, 68, 90, 145, 158, 159, 186, 220
Ritual, 2, 9, 12, 19, 42, 44, 53, 72, 84, 91, 105, 113, 123, 127, 130, 168, 169, 170, 222, 243. *See also* Witches
Roadrunner, 23
Robin, 207
Roberts, Jane, 71, 211

St. Patrick, 90
Sabbath, 92. *See also* Blood; Ishtar
Sacred caves, 7, 95, 155
Sacrifice, 37, 56, 191
Sado-masochistic pornography, 115
Sagittarius (mutable fire sign), 85, 108, 153, 178, 190. *See also* Temperance
Samadhi, 146
Salamander, 176, 212
Samsara, 87–88
Sandler, Donald, 21
Sarasvati (Indian Goddess), 89
Sarcophagi, 94
Satanism, 12
Sattva, 178
Saturn, 68, 80. *See also* Hekate
Science, 7, 38, 210
Schell, Jonathan, 116
Scorpio (fixed water sign), 85, 92, 100, 155, 168, 190. *See also chapter on Death*
Scripts, 61, 64
Seasonal cycles, 8, 71, 74, 106, 192, 210
Sekhmet (Egyptian Goddess), 212
Selene (Greek Goddess), 35, 130
Self, the, 2, 18, 27, 78–79, 116, 135, 136, 145, 151, 178, 185, 198, 222, 224, 235, 238
Separatism, 30, 49, 51, 63, 78–79, 114, 128, 134, 141, 154, 168, 179, 204, 211, 238, 244
Serapis, 53
Sex-role system, 50, 61
Sexual-creative power, 3, 9, 84, 197, 205
Sexual Secrets, 63
Sephira (emanations), 86
Sexuality, 7, 12, 31, 44, 45, 47, 48, 61, 62, 64, 82, 89, 92, 113, 115, 118, 131, 153, 160, 205, 207, 208, 209, 242. *See also* Brigit; Empress; High Priestess; Ishtar; Kali; Lilith; Magic; Pan; Tantra, Wands

Shadow, 113, 186
Shakti (Hindu Goddess), 12, 31, 34, 60, 84, 90, 146, 153, 160, 176. *See also* Kundalini; Shiva; Wands
Shaman, 6, 30, 34, 36, 77, 90, 107, 109, 110, 118, 125, 129, 153, 188, 189, 191, 194, 200, 206, 217–224, 240
Shamanism, 4, 7, 18, 29, 30, 31, 56, 81, 85, 86, 90, 94, 131, 211, 212, 244
Shedding: horns, 38; skin, 101
Ship, 17, 86, 119. *See also* Boat
Shiva (Hindu god), 30, 61, 84, 118, 146, 205
Shuffling the cards, 230
Silbury Hill (England), 8, 146
Sirius, 90, 126. *See also* Isis; Sothis
Six, 12, 63, 136
Sjöö, Monica, 10, 32–33, 36, 38, 129, 131
Sky goddess, 66. *See also* Nut
Sky-gods, 47, 154, 244
Smith, Pamela, 12
Snake, 31, 35, 43, 90, 101, 129, 155, 188, 215, 244. *See also* Bhairavi; Kundalini; Shedding
Solar: calendar, 137; consciousness, 33; eclipse, 119; plexus, 30, 49, 134
Solstices, 137, 160
Sons, 8, 47, 194, 201–208; as Talking Self, 201; as hero, 202; as Horned God, 204
Soul, 18, 20, 22, 23, 25, 60, 68, 78, 100, 101, 126, 130, 134, 135, 143, 151, 190, 213, 236. *See also* Consciousness; Flight, Journey
Sophia (Divine Wisdom), 53, 140
Sothis, 126
Space, 39, 96, 146, 147, 160
Sphinx, 246
Spider, 77, 93, 98
Spider Grandmother, 224
Spiral, 9, 87, 129, 171, 178, 188
Spiral Dance, The, 146
Spontaneity, 25, 27
Staff, 78
Star, 22, 30, 39, 78, 123–128
Starfish, 173
Starhawk, 97, 146, 194, 198, 201, 204, 205, 207
Stone Age, 154, 243
Stone inscriptions, 87, 119
Stone, Merlin, 3, 8, 14
Stonehenge, 8, 82
Strength, 12, 22, 89–93, 101
Sun, 22, 30, 63, 134–138, 159, 204

Sun Gods, 137, 138, 154, 196, 220
Sun, Patricia, 142
Surrender, 1, 62, 64, 94, 95, 160, 191, 205
Swords, 53, 154, 186
Synchronicity, 23

Taboos, 57, 197
Tamas, 168
Tanith (Phoenician Goddess), 119
Tanner, Nancy, 2
Tantra, 37, 38, 60, 63, 82, 111, 127, 144, 146. *See also* Union
Tao, 144
Tara (Tibetan Goddess), 86, 90, 91, 124, 140, 215. *See also* Bodhisattva
Tarot reading, 22, 152, 230, 231
Taurus (fixed earth sign), 41, 82, 168, 190
Telepathy, 26, 74
Television, 27, 116
Temple, Robert, 39, 92
Ten Commandments, 55
Tension, 19, 52, 61, 99, 168, 173, 191
Thoth Deck, 12
Themis (Greek Goddess), 71–75
Themis (book), 72–73
Theseus (hero), 203
Third eye, 25
Thirteen, 100, 101
Thought forms, 62, 63, 116, 158, 210, 219
Three, 50, 51
Throne, 43, 49, 220, 221
Tiamat (Goddess), 55
Tibetan Book of the Dead, 104
Tlozolteutl (Aztec Goddess), 82, 215
Tonantzin (Aztec Goddess), 214
Toolmaking, 29, 30, 32
Totem, 32
Tower, 118–122, 213, 214. *See also* Kali
Trance, 5, 9, 26, 36, 81, 90, 92, 93, 107, 191, 206, 212. *See also* Shaman
Transcendence, 148, 154
Transformation, 1, 9, 18, 26, 29, 35, 37, 38, 42, 44, 56, 83, 100, 101, 105, 108, 120, 124, 137, 141, 197, 200, 222, 223, 227, 238. *See also* Death; Mysteries
Transition, 190, 192, 240; of matriarchy to patriarchy, 7, 47, 50, 62, 67, 86, 120, 155, 220
Transmutation, 77, 84, 109, 134, 188, 222
Trapeze, 99
Tree of life, 69, 71, 72, 86, 93; Kabalistic, 136, 174

Trickster, 23, 27
Turner, Kay, 123
Turtle, 198
Twins, 60, 86, 243
Two-in-one, 65, 69

Ulysses, 214. *See also* Circe
Unclean, 55, 110
Unconscious, the 2, 25, 36, 44, 49, 69, 76, 80, 90, 100, 129, 130, 132, 160, 178, 184, 186, 194, 206, 214
Underworld, 36, 56, 76, 90, 100, 102, 129, 197, 199, 217. *See also* Artemis; Death; Hekate; Inanna; Persephone; Pluto; Shaman
Unicorn, 197
Union, 30, 60, 107, 111, 146, 215
Untamed spirit, 115, 197, 204, 212
Uranus, 119, 182, 217
Ursa Major (the Great Bear), 210. *See also* Artemis; Shamanism
Ushas (Indian Goddess), 66
Uterus, 36
Uzait (eye), 83

Vajra (diamond), 63, 141
Valkyrie, 196
Venus, 12, 44, 46, 74, 126, 139, 142, 155, 209. *See also* Aphrodite; Empress; Ishtar
Venus figures, 2, 4, 7, 9, 22, 41, 42
Vessel, 17, 124, 155, 160, 209, 213, 222, 229. *See also* Cauldron; Cups
Virgin, 17, 19, 66, 68, 77, 84, 85, 130, 197, 199, 210; Vestal, 77, 89. *See also* Arka; Artemis; Athene; Chariot; Crone; Diana; Mary
Violence, 8, 19, 57, 62, 64, 115, 204, 244
Virgo (mutable earth sign), 84, 178, 190
Visionary art, 13, 14
Visualization, 1, 11, 32, 105, 127, 146, 188, 198, 241, 242
Vogel, Karen, *vii*, *viii*, 12
Void, the, 23
Volcano, 173
Vulture, 25, 246
Vulva, 35, 36. *See also* chapter on High Priestess

Waite, Edward, 12, 19
Wakan-Tanka (White Buffalo Woman), 199
Wands, 31, 152–153
War, 8, 43, 44, 45, 50, 57
Wasp, 172
Whale, 213
Wheel, 12, 71, 73, 87, 129, 156, 176, 197
Wheel of Fortune, 81–88
When God Was a Woman, 14
Wife-battering, 47
Will, 30, 31, 68, 70, 90, 158, 219, 221. *See also* Emperor; Strength
Williams, Strephon, 133
Wine, 57
Winter Solstice, 114
Wise ones, 19, 35, 72, 76, 77, 218
Witch, 5, 26, 31, 33, 34, 38, 76, 78, 86, 89, 97, 109, 113, 115, 130, 131, 145, 153, 188, 204, 207, 211, 244. *See also* Artemis; Devil; Diana; Hekate; Horned God
Woman and Nature: The Roaring Inside Her, 14
Womb, 17, 20, 25, 35, 36, 44, 101, 132, 155, 193, 201, 205, 214. *See also* Cups; High Priestess
World, 20, 22, 26, 144–148, 151

Yab-yum (Tibetan union), 61
Yahweh (Jehovah), 47
Yin-yang, 30, 60, 68, 100
Yggdrasil (Scandinavian tree of life), 71, 94. *See also* Freya; Odin
Yoga, 12, 25, 39, 60, 63, 141, 144, 147, 156, 206, 207, 214
Yogini, divine, 32, 82, 159, 212
Yoni, 4, 85

Zero, 23
Zeus (Greek God), 47, 66, 68, 77, 196. *See also* Amalthea; Athene; Rape
Zodiac, 81–88, 210
Zulu, 20
Zoomorphic age, 51